Tolkien among the Theologians

Tolkien among the Theologians

Essays edited by Austin M. Freeman

2025

Cormarë Series No. 53

Series Editors:
Peter Buchs • Thomas Honegger • Andrew Moglestue • Johanna Schön • Doreen Triebel

Series Editors responsible for this volume:
Thomas Honegger & Doreen Triebel

Library of Congress Cataloguing-in-Publication Data

Austin M. Freeman (ed.):
Tolkien among the Theologians
ISBN 978-3-905703-53-5

Subject headings:
Tolkien, J.R.R. (John Ronald Reuel), 1892-1973
Middle-earth
Theology
The Lord of the Rings
The Hobbit

Cormarë Series No. 53

First published 2025

Set in Adobe Garamond Pro and Shannon by Walking Tree Publishers

Cover illustration 'Cuivienen' by Anke Eißmann; cover design by Stefan Honegger

Board of Advisors

Series Editors' Preface

Tolkien among the Theologians continues a tradition of addressing questions of spirituality and religion in Tolkien's work that has a long history in the Cormarë Series. At the head of this tradition stands Richard Sturch with *Four Christian Fantasists. A Study of the Fantastic Writings of George MacDonald, Charles Williams, C.S. Lewis and J.R.R. Tolkien* (CS 3, 2001), which was followed by Christopher Garbowski's *Recovery and Transcendence for the Contemporary Mythmaker. The Spiritual Dimension in the Works of J.R.R. Tolkien* (CS 7, 2004), *The Broken Scythe. Death and Immortality in the Works of J.R.R. Tolkien* (edited by Roberto Arduini and Claudio Testi, CS 26, 2013), Claudio Testi's *Pagan Saints in Middle-earth* (CS 38, 2017), and, most recently, *The Songs of the Spheres: Lewis, Tolkien and the Overlapping Realms of their Imaginations* (edited by Łukasz Neubauer and Guglielmo Spirito, CS 48, 2024).

The current volume, edited by Austin M. Freeman, not only continues this tradition, but also opens up new fields of research in bringing together scholars from widely different academic and ecumenical schools. It has been a pleasure to work with Austin and all the contributors of this volume and we hope that the readers find the final product equally enjoyable and interesting to read.

As usual, we would like to thank all those who worked on this project: our peer-reviewers who read and commented on the original manuscript, Larissa Zoller, who layouted the text, Matthias Maar, who proofread the text with great care and an eye for the details, Stefan Honegger, who was in charge of the cover design, Andrew Moglestue and Johann Schön who smoothed the wrinkles of the layout and, of course, the contributors, who invested so much time and energy into uncovering new apects of Tolkien's theology.

Walking Tree Publishers

Table of Contents

Introduction

There was a proverb in ancient Israel about seemingly unlikely people speaking the words of God: "Is Saul also among the prophets?" We hear it from the mouths of skeptics in 1 Sam 10:11-12 and again in 1 Sam 19:24. Saul had a reputation as a warrior and king, but not in any respect for what we would call religious piety. J.R.R Tolkien is not quite in the same camp as Saul here, but there is significant similarity. While Tolkien's piety is well-known (though oftentimes willfully ignored), he too made his name as a scholar of language and a storyteller, certainly not as a theologian – not even a lay public theologian like C.S. Lewis. And yet, as posthumous material continues to be produced, revealing more and more of the inner thought-processes of this multifaceted man, it becomes ever clearer that Tolkien applied the same intellectual rigor and creativity to his understanding of faith as to his professional work. As such, as I have argued in my own book (Freeman 2022), Tolkien deserves to be considered not merely as a writer of great literature – even literature with significant spiritual themes – but as an interpreter of Christian truth from a unique perspective. Thus this volume asks, in a more optimistic register, "Is Tolkien also among the theologians?"

The papers presented here were first delivered at a symposium of the same name hosted by Houston Christian University in the fall of 2022. I coordinated the symposium alongside Zak Schmoll, who also appears in these pages, and at the encouragement of Phil Tallon, our dean. The published form of these lectures consists of the keynote speeches from this multi-day event alongside a few select talks submitted to the open section of the symposium, arranged chronologically according to the theologian with whom we place Tolkien in dialogue. We were privileged in that, for those who have kept abreast of current scholarship on Tolkien's theology, few of the names contained herein require introduction.

Craig A. Boyd begins by contrasting Saruman and Gandalf according to Augustine of Hippo's writings on rhetoric, and specifically the goal of good rhetoric as opposed to sophistry. Augustine asserts that the rhetor ought to prize the good of his audience, which means their orientation toward God, rather than merely using words as a tool of domination. Boyd analyzes the two pivotal scenes between the wizards at Orthanc to demonstrate his case.

Matthew J.J. Hoskin introduces another theologian writing at the close of Antiquity, Boethius. Here, based on *The Consolation of Philosophy*, Hoskin argues that the two kings Théoden and Denethor illustrate the contrast between true and false power – one based in personal virtue and the other in external force. After commenting on Boethius's Augustinian account of love as the desire for the good of the other and its consonance with Tolkien's vision of friendship, Hoskin ends by showing how Denethor embodies the Boethian account of evil and tyranny as weakness and deprivation.

Keith Mathison takes us into the Middle Ages with a novel interpretation of Tom Bombadil as a paradigm of uniquely Franciscan spirituality. Surveying the various contested readings of Tom, Mathison opines that Tolkien saw in this pre-existing character the ability to express something important to him in *The Lord of the Rings*. Tom, as an interloper figure, brings to Middle-earth St. Francis's emphasis on renunciation of material power, joviality, and delight in the created order, among other things.

Claudio Testi, who has previously drawn many connections between Tolkien and Thomas Aquinas, here offers a few ways in which Tolkien *does not* follow a Thomistic course. Indeed, Testi argues, the idea presented in *Leaf by Niggle* in which an author may, in heaven, experience his incomplete work as perfect and fulfilled, is a new perspective in theology. Testi lays out Tolkien's hope to one day be able to live within Middle-earth in the way that the Valar dwelt within Arda, all by the grace of God the prime Creator.

My own chapter is sure to please everyone. Moving past the Middle Ages, I outline five significant ways in which Tolkien's theology coheres with that of John Calvin. First, they both emphasize the importance of original language research and humanist study of the liberal arts. Second, they highlight the metaphysical impact of promises and covenants. Third, they target idolatry as a key theological enemy. Fourth, they exalt the created order as an avenue toward divine worship. Fifth, and most surprisingly to most, Tolkien fulfills all six of Calvin's criteria for a doctrine of God's providence.

Giuseppe Pezzini continues our modern examinations by more deeply discussing Tolkien's intellectual relationship to John Henry Newman. Here Pezzini picks out their similar attitude toward history as a process of change and renewal shepherded by God. History is dynamic and cannot be arrested. The metaphor of the growing tree rules here. Second, Pezzini draws our attention to the way in which, for both Newman and Tolkien, God works through the hidden and unexpected, the humble and surprising, rather than the prominent and powerful.

Zak Schmoll introduces another Victorian, G.K. Chesterton – the theological thinker Tolkien quotes more than any other. After a section detailing Tolkien's exposure to and reception of Chesterton, Schmoll centers the famous story of the lost yachtsman in *Orthodoxy* who sets out for a foreign adventure only to unwittingly find himself at home. Schmoll argues that Chesterton's concepts of romance as the mixture of the unknown and the familiar, patriotism as love, and the importance of courage and freedom all find comfortable place in the *legendarium*.

Lisa Coutras offers a shortened form of her significant work on theological aesthetics in Tolkien and Hans Urs von Balthasar. Both thinkers emphasize the role of beauty as a transcendental alongside goodness and truth, and detail how the affective element plays a role in faith. Coutras then explores how Tolkien's two most prominent female characters, Galadriel and Éowyn, display their particular beauties. Galadriel is an echo of Mary's character, of the beauty of her soul. Likewise Éowyn, also physically beautiful, allows her physical form to be a translucent vehicle for inner beauty.

Łukasz Neubauer turns toward another prominent twentieth century Catholic theologian, Pope John Paul II. Neubauer is concerned to show that John Paul's idea of the 'civilization of death' characterized by abortion and euthanasia sets itself against the 'civilization of life' that prioritizes human flourishing before God. While Neubauer admits that Tolkien and John Paul likely never had direct intellectual contact, he draws upon Tolkien's condemnation of Denethor's suicide and the newly-published details of Elvish childbirth in *The Nature of Middle-earth* to make the case that Tolkien shares the same traditional Roman Catholic condemnation of abortion and euthanasia.

Holly Ordway's chapter expands upon her most recent work on Tolkien's spiritual autobiography. She introduces four theological contemporaries Tolkien is likely to have known: one Oratorian and three Jesuits. Ordway traces the biographical details of these now mostly unknown figures and the ways in which their lives would have intersected with Tolkien's. Ordway states that we ought not to neglect the immediate context of twentieth century English Catholicism in searching for Tolkien's theological forebears.

Finally, I invited Tim Padgett to end the symposium and this volume with a reminder that Christian unity does exist across the spectrum, and that this is demonstrated in Tolkien's own life. His ecumenical efforts have not received much attention, but Padgett offers readings of the friendships of Sam and Frodo and of Legolas and Gimli to show what it might mean for Tolkien to have genuine friendships and common cause with those who hold theological differences. He supplements this with discussion of the Protestant side of the question, namely the evangelicals and fundamentalists, during Tolkien's own lifetime.

Much more could be written to situate Tolkien within the discipline of historical theology and church history. He himself worked as translator and commentator for many Old and Middle English theological texts, and we still await scholarly examination of his theological interpretations of these documents. His emphasis on the sacrament of confession as the heart of *Sir Gawain and the Green Knight*, for instance, is highly illuminating. Other figures, such as Irenaeus, show striking similarities in areas such as the doctrine of the Fall. We encourage future researchers to continue these avenues of exploration, such that to the skeptical question "Is Tolkien also among the theologians?" we might continue to answer with a resounding "Yes!"

Austin M. Freeman, Houston Christian University

Craig A. Boyd

1

Saruman's Folly and Gandalf's Wisdom: Augustinian Rhetoric in *The Lord Of The Rings*

Abstract

This chapter contrasts Saruman and Gandalf according to Augustine of Hippo's writings on rhetoric, and specifically the goal of good rhetoric as opposed to sophistry. Augustine asserts that the rhetor ought to prize the good of his audience, which means their orientation toward God, rather than merely using words as a tool of domination. The paper analyzes the two pivotal scenes between the wizards at Orthanc to demonstrate his case

Since the early 2000s, several scholars have traced the theological and philosophical influences on Tolkien's work that range from classical and Catholic thought to the literary, cultural, and metaphysical. Alison Milbank, Peter Kreeft, and Ralph Wood have all examined such topics as the various narrative themes derived from Christianity, theistic metaphysics, and his understanding of good and evil (Milbank 2007; Kreeft 2005; Wood 2003). Others like Stratford Caldecott have explored the more sacramental elements in his works (2003). And more recently others, like Claudio A. Testi (2017), Jonathan S. McIntosh (2017), and Boyd (2019) have considered his materials with reference to Thomistic themes and the various Christian virtues exemplified in his characters.

One largely neglected domain has been the rhetorical approach Tolkien employs in the voices of his characters. Although a trio of scholars have minimally engaged Tolkien's use of rhetoric, this territory remains largely unexplored (Shippey 2003; Ruud 2010; Chisholm 2019). One could argue that the most important battles in Tolkien's *The Lord of the Rings* are often those disputed with words and arguments rather than those fought with swords and shields. Pivotal conversations tilt the narrative in profound ways: Gandalf's dialogue with Frodo concerning pity, Gollum's conversation with himself as Sméagol concerning "the Bagginses," Faramir's interrogation of Frodo about the Ring,

Gandalf's disputation with Saruman after Rohan's victory at Helm's Deep, and the extended discussion at the Council of Elrond. These are but a few of the rhetorical agons waged throughout *The Lord of the Rings* and they are every bit as important as the conflicts fought on the fields of battle.

Tolkien's vocation as a philologist – and as a sub-creator – could plausibly illuminate the ways in which he constructs not only the physical conflicts he describes but also the verbal battles. And as a Catholic, the significance of the spoken *verbum* would likely have even a greater bearing on how he conceives and weaves his narrative down to the last detail. He confesses to C.A. Furth, "The writing of *The Lord of the Rings* is laborious, because I have been doing it as well as I know how, and considering every word" (*Letters* 42). Although this reference to "every word" could easily be dismissed as hyperbolic rhetoric on Tolkien's part, it is unlikely given both the demands of his philological vocation and his fastidious nature concerning words and their meanings. A philologist of the first order would not casually construct an agon without attending to every facet of the argument and the critical role "every word" could play in an important dialogue.

This interest in the rhetorical agon is what I find especially provocative considering the importance of Ciceronian and Augustinian approaches to persuasion and argumentation. I think that Tolkien employs a kind of Augustinian rhetoric in the two critical conversations between Gandalf and Saruman at Isengard. In the first scene (recounted at the Council of Elrond), Gandalf narrates Saruman's betrayal, while the second comes after the victory at Helm's Deep. In both conversations Saruman appears as the exemplar of the wicked rhetor while Gandalf models the wisdom of the good orator. Further, I propose that the resources in Book IV of Augustine's *De Doctrina Christiana* can offer insights not found elsewhere in thinking about these rhetorical battles.

During the last two decades, two other essays on Saruman as orator have appeared, offering a rhetorical analysis as a helpful way of reading the Saruman-Gandalf disputations. The first is Jay Ruud's approach that sees the conflict in light of the classical Aristotelian account of *logos*, *ethos*, and *pathos* (2010). Ruud makes the connection between the ethos of the rhetor and his commitment to truth as well as the rhetor's ability to persuade his listeners. For Ruud,

Saruman's approach exemplifies the Sophistic tendency to win an argument at any cost, while Gandalf – in contrast – practices the approach where truth is more important than victory.

Like Ruud, Chad Chisholm (2019) also analyzes Tolkien's rhetoric with an Aristotelian lens but augments it with a Platonic gloss to contextualize the rhetorical contest. He notes, "The wizards Gandalf and Saruman, both of whom seem the most skilled and studied rhetors in Tolkien's fiction, not only represent elements of the Sophist and Classical views of rhetoric, but also embody the philosophies and values (as well as the flaws) of those systems" (Chisholm 2019: 89). But in my view, an appeal to Augustine may offer a more helpful approach, given Tolkien's Catholic orientation to the world of words. As a result, looking at two of the most important agons between the wisest of the wise can reveal how Tolkien sees rhetoric as a force for good or evil.

The Augustinian elements in the rhetoric employed by Saruman and Gandalf have had little to no attention in the secondary literature.[1] While I make no claim that there is a direct causal link between Augustine's rhetoric and Tolkien's approach to the rhetorical stylistics of Gandalf and Saruman, the careful reader might see resonances with Augustine's own ideas in these rhetorical battles. Further, we know that Tolkien possessed Augustine's works in his own personal library and would likely have studied his works in the course of his secondary and university education (Cilli 2019: 10).

The Treason of Saruman

The wizards (Istari) were Maiar who appeared in human form; and their task was to persuade rather than to dominate other creatures in Middle-earth. And since rhetoric is the method of persuasion, it follows that a rhetorical analysis of how Tolkien's wizards use persuasion is warranted. At first glance, it might seem that domination was always bad and persuasion was always good but this would be too simplistic: persuasion could be employed for opposing purposes. But first we should note that Tolkien emphasizes that the Istari were sent not

1 Matthew Fisher, for instance, rightly observes that Tolkien was an "Augustine-Catholic," but he merely offers some general comments about nature and grace and makes no reference to the critical Saruman-Gandalf agon (Fisher 2006).

to overwhelm others in terms of coercing them to do good; but "coming in shapes weak and humble were bidden to advise and persuade Men and Elves to good, and seek to unite in love and understanding all those whom Sauron, should he come again, would endeavor to dominate and corrupt" (*UT* 389). The words "persuade" and "advise" clearly indicate an appeal to rhetorical gifts and uncoercive methods. But Saruman seems to use his rhetorical skills in a manner of deceptive persuasion and manipulation. Certainly, his military campaign meant to overwhelm Théoden's forces and was a naked attempt at domination through sheer power; but his rhetorical skills were possibly even more dangerous. Gandalf appropriately warns his companions at Isengard that, "[a] wild beast cornered is not safe to approach. And Saruman has powers you do not guess. Beware his voice!" (*LotR* 577). And as Ruud notes, "[i]t is Saruman's rhetoric, rather than any magical powers, that makes him so dangerous" (2010: 143). The capacity to deceive and corrupt through the power of speech may be an even more dangerous and subtle weapon than mere magic.

The reader first learns of Saruman's wickedness at the Council of Elrond where Gandalf recounts the story of his deception by – and confrontation with – Saruman at Orthanc. By this point in the narrative, the reader has come to trust Gandalf as morally reliable as evidenced by his care for the hobbits, his rejection of Frodo's offer of the Ring, and his helpful advice all along the way. As a result, there is no doubt from his listeners at the Council (or the reader) about the veracity of his account of the encounter with Saruman.

Gandalf tells the Council that he had ridden to Orthanc because Radagast had urged him to go as swiftly as he could to Saruman to consult with the white wizard concerning the Black Riders, who were at that very moment riding north to the Shire in search of the One Ring. When Gandalf arrives, he feels something is amiss but cannot say why. A haughtiness appears in Saruman's voice which makes Gandalf even more uncomfortable. The white wizard quickly reveals that the message from Radagast to go to Orthanc was based on a lie. He derisively refers to Radagast as a "fool" and reveals that he simply manipulated Radagast in order to convince Gandalf to come to him.

As they begin their dialogue, Saruman declares himself to be "Saruman the Wise, Saruman the Ring-maker, Saruman of Many Colours" (*LotR* 259).

Gandalf responds laconically with, "I liked white better." But Saruman argues that white is merely a starting place – that the white light can be broken. Gandalf then observes that, "[h]e that breaks a thing to find out what it is has left the path of wisdom." But this breaking of the light, as Cody Jarmen writes, parallels the breaking of words: "Saruman does with light the same thing he does with language, breaking both and manipulating them for his own ends, without any concern for whether or not his behavior is on 'the path of wisdom'" (Jarmen 2016: 159). But this breaking and manipulating point to an important Augustinian theme in Tolkien, that is found much earlier in Augustine's *De Doctrina Christiana* (*DDC*).

The larger moral context here for Augustine concerns the famous distinction between enjoyment and use. He writes:

> Some things are to be enjoyed, others are to be used, and there are others which are to be enjoyed and used. Those things which are to be enjoyed make us blessed. Those things which are to be used help and, as it were, sustain us as we move toward blessedness in order that we may gain and cling to those things which make us blessed. If we who enjoy and use things, being placed in the midst of things of both kinds, wish to enjoy those things which should be used, our course will be impeded and sometimes deflected, so that we are frustrated in obtaining those things which are to be enjoyed, or even prevented altogether, shackled by an inferior love. For to enjoy a thing is to rest with satisfaction in it for its own sake. To use, on the other hand, is to employ whatever means are at one's disposal to obtain what one desires, if it is a proper object of desire; for an unlawful use ought rather to be called an abuse. (*DDC* 1.3-4)

This passage lays out three key claims. First, people are to be enjoyed for themselves – as it is only in friendship and fellowship that we can experience happiness. Later, he notes that it is primarily a person's experience of the divine Trinity who are to be enjoyed for themselves: the ultimate happiness. But this enjoyment of and fellowship with persons can be contrasted with "use," which is properly said of things.

We can use things instrumentally along the way to happiness, but those things we use are not goods in themselves. Rather, we employ these things in the service of persons and our enjoyment of them. We are never to use persons – who are to be enjoyed – for purposes other than their own good. Another way of saying this is that persons are to be enjoyed and things are to be used; conversely, we should not use persons so that we can enjoy things.

There is one third and final point Augustine makes here. Regardless of our enjoyment of persons or our use of things, our desires must always be properly oriented to appropriate ends, such as fellowship with others, the acquisition and development of the virtues, and the pursuit of truth. Any illicit desire, such as elevating ourselves through pride or giving in to perverse curiosity or acting out of a motive for lust, vitiates any particular action we might take.

When we consider the case of Saruman, we see that he never *enjoys* persons but only *uses* them. He not only uses the trees of Fangorn and the Uruk-Hai, he also uses the residents of the Shire for his own selfish and "inferior loves." In the end, he is not "blessed" but frustrated, alone, desperate, and eventually annihilated. We can see that in this way the contrast between Saruman and Gandalf becomes even more pronounced. Gandalf never uses people for bad ends; he treats them as persons and not objects for manipulation for perverse ends. In contrast, Saruman does not value persons but invariably uses them for his own illicit desire for power and domination.

Saruman's agenda is to join the "new power" (i.e., Sauron) because (1) there is hope in doing so, and (2) Gandalf will have power. Saruman says,

> We can bide our time, we can keep our thoughts in our hearts, deploring maybe evils done by the way, but approving the high and ultimate purpose: Knowledge, Rule, Order; all the things that we have so far striven in vain to accomplish, hindered rather than helped by our weak or idle friends. There need not be, there would not be, any real change in our designs, only in our means. (*LotR* 259)

What Saruman wants from Gandalf is the location of the Ring; but he fails to understand Gandalf. As one who already possesses great power, Saruman assumes that Gandalf wants the same things he does. He erroneously believes that Gandalf will be open to his arguments because he assumes that Gandalf not only desires the same things as he does, but also thinks the same way he does. Saruman is wrong on both counts.

Gandalf rejects Saruman's offer because he knows that only one person can use the Ring. Gandalf knows that not only does the Ring corrupt the one who possesses it, but that even the desire for it corrupts the one who would wield it. As Elrond tells Boromir at the Council, "the very desire of it corrupts the heart," and "its strength [...] is too great for anyone to wield at will, save only those who have already a great power of their own. But for them it holds an even deadlier peril" (*LotR* 267). Since Saruman is the greatest of the wizards, the desire for the Ring and its insidious effects make him nearly as dangerous as Sauron himself.

It is because of his illicit desire for the Ring and for the domination it would bestow upon him that Saruman imprisons Gandalf with the idea that he might change his mind; but Saruman's use of force on Gandalf only serves to further emphasize Tolkien's conviction that power and coercion are to be resisted. He writes to Naomi Mitchison:

> The supremely bad motive is (for this tale, since it is specifically about it) domination of other "free" wills. The Enemy's operations are by no means all goetic deceits, but "magic" that produces real effects in the physical world. But his magia he uses to bulldoze people and things, and his goeteia to terrify & subjugate. (*Letters* 200)

Gandalf accepts the imprisonment rather than being co-opted and betraying his friends. He stays there until his rescue and return to Rivendell. Unlike the Peter Jackson film adaptation, the agon here is not a battle between the wizards' use of their magical powers but a battle based upon trickery and deceit, where Saruman appears the initial victor.

The Return of Gandalf

The second, but more significant, scene between Gandalf and Saruman takes place after Théoden's forces win the Battle of Helm's Deep. The victors travel to Isengard where Treebeard and the other Ents have destroyed the fortress and have trapped Saruman in the tower of Orthanc. As they move towards the tower, Pippin asks Gandalf whether Saruman will use magic like pouring fire out on them or whether he would "put a spell on us at a distance" (*LotR* 577). Gandalf suggests that Saruman will not deploy magic but that a "spell" is more likely. And, then, hinting that linguistic expertise and magic might not seem all that different to the casual observed, he warns Pippin, "Saruman has powers you cannot guess. Beware of his voice!" (*LotR* 577).

The narrative here is much more vivid and evocative of Saruman's rhetorical skill than the earlier agon. Gandalf's warning to Pippin foreshadows the power Saruman's voice will exercise upon his hearers in a way that makes his oratorical expertise seem like a magical spell. The scene is a pivotal battle between the two great wizards where little outright magic plays a part and where Gandalf emerges victorious but not without a significant struggle.

When Gandalf knocks on the door, they are greeted from above by Gríma Wormtongue, who is then sent to fetch his master. And Saruman addresses the assembled crowd:

> Suddenly another voice spoke, low and melodious, its very sound an enchantment. Those who listened unwarily to that voice could seldom reports the words that they heard: and if they did, they wondered, for little power remained in them. Mostly they remembered only that it was a delight to hear the voice speaking, all that it said seemed wise and reasonable, and desire awoke in them by swift agreement to seem wise themselves. When others spoke they seemed harsh and uncouth by contrast; and if they gainsaid the voice, anger was kindled in the hearts of those under the spell [...] For many the sound of the voice alone was enough to hold them enthralled; but for those whom it conquered the spell endured when they were far away, and ever they heard that soft voice whispering and urging them. But none were unmoved; none rejected its pleas and its commands without an effort of mind and will, so long as its Master had control of it.[2] (*LotR* 578)

Saruman employs the power of his voice to persuade and lure the unwary listeners in. His appeal is not to truth but to a kind of weakness in his listeners through a perverse "sweetness" of style. He is, after all, the one who initiated the war with Rohan. But as he speaks, he skillfully turns the narrative to make it sound as if he is the aggrieved party.[3] Tolkien points out that it was only with a significant effort that any could resist the voice.

Saruman remonstrates with his listeners to leave him in peace. He claims to have done no harm. He is the victim, the wrongly accused and aggrieved. And yet, even as the injured party, he still offers his help. A seemingly gracious offer presented by an unjustly injured person. He tells Théoden: "I alone can aid you

2 There is a striking parallel here between Tolkien's description of this scene and C.S. Lewis's pivotal conversation between the Green Lady and Puddleglum in *The Silver Chair*. It could be argued that the key battles in both narratives are fought not with physical weapons but with the power of words.

3 Tolkien explains that Saruman's name in Quenya is "'Curunír', meaning 'skilled, or cunning, man'" (*Sil* 300).

now." Théoden's riders are persuaded by the argument Saruman offers. They assent to his wisdom and the apparent folly of Gandalf who had "never spoken so fair and fittingly" (*LotR* 579).

But this deviously smooth presentation is broken by Gimli when he proclaims, "The words of this wizard stand on their heads" (*LotR* 579) He sees through the "sweet rhetoric" Saruman offers and this objection angers Saruman, who almost loses his composure, but then turns to Théoden in his request for peace. Éomer also sees through the ruse and objects, telling Saruman he has "honey on his forked tongue," (*LotR* 579) noting the sweetness of style while observing the poison of the words themselves.

But Saruman continues to plead with Théoden, parlaying for peace, recalling their long "friendship" and trust in one another. But Théoden finally finds his voice, harsh and uncouth in comparison to Saruman's. And the King of Rohan displays surprisingly powerful rhetorical skills of his own. His use of anaphora plays a particularly important role in his rejoinder to the white wizard's last appeal. In response to Saruman's request for peace, Théoden says: "Yes, we will have peace [...] we will have peace, when you and all your works have perished – and the works of your dark master to whom you would deliver us [...] When you hang from a gibbet at your window for the sport of your own crows, I will have peace with you and Orthanc" (*LotR* 580). He summarily rejects Saruman's appeals by declaring, "I fear your voice has lost its charm" (*LotR* 580). And so, Théoden – like Gandalf – defeats Saruman and his rhetorical prowess with a simple but truthful response.

The colors of Saruman's cloak shift with his movement, paralleling his own ability to shift according to his need. There is no consistency to his argumentation or his loyalty. As Shippey notes, "[n]o other character in Middle-earth has Saruman's trick for balancing phrases against each other so that incompatibles are resolved" (Shippey 2003: 119). The words and their rhetorical power, like his robes, shift according to Saruman's design. It could be said that the multiple colors confuse the gaze like his words confuse the ears of his listeners. What does not change is his desire for control and domination. Gandalf's white attire stands in stark contrast, unwavering and pure. Like his white cloak, Gandalf's words are plain, unadorned, simple, and true.

Augustine's Rhetoric in Book IV of *De Doctrina Christiana*

Book IV of *De Doctrina Christiana* has provided rhetoricians, orators, preachers, and theologians with ample material for their own work as Augustine carefully engages and adapts the classical rhetorical methods of Cicero, one of the Romans he greatly admired.[4] And yet, Augustine sees the primary task of the rhetor in terms of not merely convincing the audience, but of convincing them of the truth of Christianity.

For Augustine, this fundamental difference in teleology distinguished the genuine rhetor/philosopher from the sophist. The true rhetor in the tradition of Aristotle, Cicero, and Augustine focuses upon the truth and persuading the audience of that truth, while the sophist aims primarily at winning the audience over to his own private agenda, regardless of the truth or goodness found in his perspective. It is this fundamental difference that distinguishes Gandalf from Saruman. Gandalf loves the true and the good while Saruman has an eye only to his own advantage. In this way, Gandalf represents Augustine's own views about rhetoric and Saruman shows that even if one is eloquent, it does not matter much if what he says is false.

The contrast is such that – in simplest terms – the sophist has as his end to persuade the audience to his own particular ends or goods. Those ends may be good, bad, or indifferent. The sophist focuses only on winning the audience over. Persuasion is the ultimate end to be achieved. In contrast, the genuine rhetor has as his end the good.

The virtuous orator aims not just at any end, but only the good end. This end is not just the good of the speaker but of the audience as well: the *bonum commune*, since the private good cannot (or should not) be severed from the common good. The good rhetor, for Augustine, sees the common good as always and everywhere taking precedence over the individual good of the rhetor's ego or the relative success in persuading his audience. Certainly, persuading the audience is important but it must always be subordinate to that which is higher: the *bonum commune*. This brief account, then, provides a general context for what Augustine says about how one goes about persuading the audience.

---

4 Augustine admits that it was Cicero's *Hortensius* that set him on the road to conversion (*Conf.* bk 3).

Despite the fact that he claims Book IV of *DDC* is not a treatise on rhetoric, it has all the elements of one. He claims he will not teach the rules of rhetoric but that the communicator of Christian doctrine needs to know how rhetoric functions.[5] Regardless of his stated purpose, Augustine's teaching on rhetoric orbits two main ideas: the moral goodness of the orator and his ability to persuade his audience. It is always the virtuous character of the speaker (Aristotle's and Cicero's *ethos*) and the speaker's desire for the audience to pursue the good that take precedence. The point is to move the hearers to action. Emphasizing the centrality of moving the audience both in terms of emotion and action, John C. Cavadini writes: "The art of rhetoric is useful not so much in its particular rules but precisely because it embodies a science of human motivation and therefore it helps us to learn what will make the truth not only true but moving" (Cavadini 1995: 164-65). The union of the true and the good plays a central role here.

Employing Cicero for his own purposes, Augustine accepts two general approaches concerning the orator's telos and method. First, he thinks that the role of the orator is to teach, delight, and persuade (*DDC* IV.34). Second, he thinks that the method should fall under subdued, moderate, or grand.

With regard to the purposes, the successful orator will simultaneously teach, delight, and persuade. Each of these are necessary conditions for a successful orator. And since speaking and listening are transactional, there will be an important element of audience response to the orator in terms of listening intelligently, willingly, and obediently. There is then a trifold dynamic: the orator, the words spoken, and the audience who hears the orator's words. And this is always in the context of how these various styles reflect how the orator persuades the audience of his perspective.

The orator must delight those who hear his words. Although the teaching may be true, if speakers do not hold the attention of the hearers, they will be disregarded. Augustine asks, "Who would wish to listen unless he could retain his

---

5 Much of the book focuses on the orator's ability to adapt the three main styles of speaking: the subdued, the moderate, and the grand manners. But that seems to be in the wider context of persuading the audience and leading them to truth and goodness. "We should teach the good and correct the wrong" (*DDC* IV.6). All subsequent references in the text are cited parenthetically according to paragraph.

listener with some sweet style" (*DDC* IV.25.56). In fact, the term Augustine uses here is *suitate*, which has in English cognates for "persuasion" and "suave". This "sweetness of style" is echoed in Saruman's own approach to persuading his listeners. Saruman's style aims primarily at pleasing them in such a way as to hide his wickedness. Augustine, of course, knows this is the kind of approach devious rhetors use. And he notes that any speech should make certain not "only to please" (IV.26.57) by means of its sweetness. It should, of course, move the listener to obey and act for the true and the good.

Lying behind the orator's abilities and wisdom in choosing the best method of persuasion, is the orator's character which hearkens back to Aristotle's and Cicero's *ethos*. The moral life of the orator and not his technique should determine how we weigh the words of the speaker. Augustine writes: "The life of the speaker has greater weight in determining whether he is obediently heard than any grandness of eloquent style. For the one who speaks wisely and eloquently, but lives wickedly, may benefit many students, although, as it is written, he 'is unprofitable to his own soul'" (*DDC* IV.27.59).

The key advantage Gandalf possesses over Saruman is his character. The listeners at the foot of Orthanc know that Gandalf is good and that Saruman is evil despite the differences in the rhetorical styles of each wizard. And Gandalf's resurrection is a kind of witness to his goodness while the breaking of Saruman's staff is a moral judgment on his wicked character. Wisdom and goodness, not mere style, account for genuine rhetorical success.

Although Tolkien often refers to Saruman as "one of the wise,"[6] and although he possessed eloquence, his own life was consumed with deception, duplicity, arrogance, and murderous attempts to seize power. Contrary to true wisdom, Chisholm notes that Saruman "places persuasion above all else" (Chisholm 2019: 91). This, as Augustine would say, did nothing for the benefit of his listeners or for the profit of his own soul.

The good rhetor is also the true philosopher: one who truly loves wisdom. According to Augustine, the goodness of the orator's life benefits not only himself but others who look to him. "Let him so order his life that he not only

6 The word for "wizard" has "wise" as a cognate, cf. *Letters* 202

prepares a reward for himself, but also so that he offers an example to others, and his way of living may be, as it were, an eloquent speech" (*DDC* IV.29.61). In contrast there are those who offer a "pernicious sweetness," without being the good example. This kind of persuasion works in a sweet but deceptive and wicked manner – and for Augustine this is a kind of "eloquent nonsense."

So how does Gandalf respond to this wicked but sweet style of persuasion? Saruman knows that he can appeal to both "the common good" by means of his own twisted rhetoric. Tolkien writes that the listeners felt that

> they were shut out, listening at a door to words not meant for them: ill-mannered children or stupid servants overhearing the elusive discourse of their elders, and wondering how it would affect their lot. Of loftier mould these two were made: reverend and wise. It was inevitable that they should make alliance. Gandalf would ascend into the tower, to discuss deep things beyond their comprehension in the high chambers of Orthanc. The door would be closed, and they would be left outside, dismissed to await allotted work or punishment. Even in the mind of Théoden the thought took shape, like a shadow of doubt: 'He will betray us; he will go – we shall be lost.' Then Gandalf laughed. The fantasy vanished like a puff of smoke. 'Saruman, Saruman!' said Gandalf still laughing. 'Saruman, you missed your path in life. You should have been the king's jester and earned your bread, and stripes too, by mimicking his counsellors'. (*LotR* 582)

Gandalf counters the sweet style of Saruman with mere laughter. He does not speak with eloquence because he does not need to. He does not speak with the melodious euphony that Saruman possesses, but he speaks the truth. Gandalf's response of laughter – and the pointed rebuke after – are sufficient to defeat Saruman. Instead of taking Saruman's invitation seriously, he responds with mirth, which is also a response borne of wisdom.

Augustine points out that a wise response need not be conventionally eloquent. It may be simple and to the point. He writes, "Just because it comes to fight without embellishment or armor, and apparently defenseless, this does not prevent it from crushing the enemy with the strength of its sinewy hands and disabling its opponent and destroying falsehood with its mighty limbs" (*DDC* IV.26.55).

The agon then proceeds with Gandalf moving from mirth to authority and speaking in the grand style (but still speaking the truth). In a sense, Gandalf's rhetoric picks up momentum. In a rage Saruman recognizes his defeat and turns to leave. Yet, the agon has not ended:

> 'Come back, Saruman!" said Gandalf in a commanding voice. To the amazement of the others, Saruman turned again, and as if dragged against his will, he came slowly back to the iron rail, leaning on it, breathing hard. His face was lined and shrunken. His hand clutched his heavy black staff like a claw. 'I did not give you leave to go,' said Gandalf sternly. (*LotR* 583)

Gandalf then declares Saruman cast out of the Council, he deprives Saruman's robes of their color, and he breaks Saruman's staff. Gandalf does, in fact, crush the enemy; or maybe, he merely shows how the enemy has crushed himself. But it is Gandalf's moral authority, based on his character and insight that facilitates this.

Tolkien contrasts Gandalf's pursuit of the true and the good of those in his care (the Ignatian tradition might even see Gandalf as practicing *cura personalis*) with Saruman's obsession with power at any cost. In fact, Gandalf's goodness extends even to his enemy, Saruman, offering forgiveness and an opportunity for redemption. Chisholm captures the contrast nicely when he writes: "Both a love and life of adherence to *truth* is more important than the pursuit of self-interest, empowerment, or even expediency" (Chisholm 2019: 90).

In the end, Tolkien's Gandalf demonstrates that goodness and truth – with a sufficient and maybe minimal use of style – can overcome a more powerful but morally deficient rhetorical style. It is Gandalf's *ethos* that is primary here. Tolkien's Gandalf exhibits – sans the theological commitment to the Trinity – an Augustinian approach to rhetoric with a view to the true and the good, regardless of how sweet the communication is.

About the Author

Craig A. Boyd is Professor of Philosophy & Humanities at Saint Louis University, where he also earned his PhD in philosophy in 1996. His articles on the work of J.R.R. Tolkien have appeared in such venues as *The Heythrop Journal*, *Christian Scholar's Review*, *Christianity & Literature*, *Logos: A Journal of Catholic Thought and Life* as well as in some edited volumes. Professor Boyd's most current work on Tolkien is a forthcoming volume with Cambridge University Press titled, *Tolkien on the True, the Good, and the Beautiful*. He has also written extensively on Aquinas's theory of natural law, and the virtues and vices. He (with Kevin Timpe) were the co-editors of *Virtues & their Vices* (Oxford University Press, 2014); he also co-authored with Timpe, *The Virtues: A Very Short Introduction* (Oxford University Press, 2021).

Bibliography

Augustine. 1961. *Confessions*. Translated by R.S. Pine-Coffin. New York: Penguin.

1976. *On Christian Doctrine*. Translated by D.W. Robertson. Indianapolis: Bobbs-Merrill.

Bernthal, Craig. 2014. *Tolkien's Sacramental Vision: Discerning the Holy in Middle-earth*. Kettering, OH: Angelico Press.

Boyd, Craig A. 2020. "Augustine, Aquinas, and Tolkien: Three Catholic Views on Curiositas." *The Heythrop Journal* 62.2: 222-33.

2019. "Nolo Heroizari: Tolkien and Aquinas on the Humble Journey of Master Samwise." *Christianity and Literature* 68.4: 605-22.

Caldecott, Stratford. 2012. *The Power of the Ring: The Spiritual Vision Behind The Lord of the Rings and The Hobbit*. Chestnut Ridge, PA: Crossroad.

Cavadini, John C. 1995. "The Sweetness of the Word: Salvation and Rhetoric in Augustine's *De Doctrina Christiana*." In Dwayne W.H. Arnold and Pamela Bright (eds.). *De Doctrina Christiana: A Classic of Western Culture*. Notre Dame, IN: University of Notre Dame Press, 164-81.

Chisholm, Chad. 2019. "Saruman as 'Sophist' or 'Sophist Foil?' Tolkien's Wizards and the Ethics of Persuasion." *Mythlore* 37: 89-101.

Cilli, Oronzo. 2019. *Tolkien's Library: An Annotated Checklist*. Edinburgh: Luna Press.

Fisher, Matthew A. 2006. "Working at the Crossroads: Tolkien, St. Augustine, and the Beowulf- poet." In Wayne G. Hammond and Christina Scull (eds.). *The Lord of the Rings 1954-2004: Scholarship in Honor of Richard E. Blackwelder*. Milwaukee, WI: Marquette University Press, 217-30.

Jarmen, Cody. 2016. "The Black Speech: *The Lord of the Rings* as a Modernist Linguistic Critique." *Mythlore* 32: 153-66.

Kreeft, Peter. 2005. *The Philosophy of Tolkien: The Worldview behind* The Lord of the Rings. San Francisco, CA: Ignatius Press.

Lewis, C.S. 1947. *The Silver Chair*. New York: Macmillan.

McIntosh, Jonathan A. 2017. *The Flame Imperishable: Tolkien, St. Thomas, and the Metaphysics of Faërie*. Kettering, OH: Angelico Press.

Milbank, Alison. 2007. *Chesterton and Tolkien as Theologians: The Fantasy of the Real*. London: T&T Clark.

Purtill, Richard L. 1984. *J.R.R. Tolkien: Myth, Morality, and Religion*. San Francisco, CA: Harper & Row.

Ruud, Jay. 2010. "The Voice of Saruman: Wizards and Rhetoric in The Two Towers." *Mythlore* 28.3: 141-53.

Shippey, Tom. 2003. *The Road to Middle-earth: How J.R.R. Tolkien Created a New Mythology*. New York: Houghton Mifflin.

Testi, Claudio A. 2018. *Pagan Saints in Middle-earth*. Cormarë Series 38. Zurich and Jena: Walking Tree Publishers.

Tolkien, J.R.R. 1981. *The Letters of J.R.R. Tolkien*. Edited by Humphrey Carpenter, with the assistance of Christopher Tolkien. London: George Allen & Unwin / Boston: Houghton Mifflin.

1994. *The Lord of the Rings*. New York: Houghton Mifflin.

1980. *Unfinished Tales*. Edited by Christopher Tolkien. Boston: Houghton Mifflin.

2012. *The Silmarillion*. Edited by Christopher Tolkien. New York: William Morrow.

Wood, Ralph C. 2003. *The Gospel According to Tolkien: Visions of the Kingdom in Middle-earth*. Philadelphia, PA: Westminster/John Knox.

Matthew J.J. Hoskin

Power and Weakness in Middle-earth: Boethius and Tolkien's *The Lord of the Rings*

Abstract

Boethius's *Consolation of Philosophy* is one of the great yet final works of ancient philosophy but also an enduring work of medieval philosophy, one with which Tolkien was very familiar and to which he had access in Latin, Old English, Middle English, and modern English. This chapter explores how Boethian themes of power and goodness penetrate *The Lord of the Rings*. After discussing Boethius's teaching that true power can only reside in goodness and is ultimately unshakeable and, in a sense, interior, the chapter examines the figures of Théoden and Denethor and how their own relationship to power demonstrates this fact, showing how Denethor's true weakness lay in despair and Theoden's lay in hope.

One of the most powerful scenes in *The Silmarillion* is in the very beginning, when Ilúvatar creates the world through the music of the Ainur.[1] As the Ainur make music according to the plan of Ilúvatar, one of their number, Melkor, deviates and seeks out of pride to make his own song. Yet whatever Melkor does, Ilúvatar's own music incorporates Melkor's into itself. Melkor's evil – his deviation from the good, the true, and the beautiful – is ultimately powerless. This entire opening to the *legendarium* of J.R.R. Tolkien, from the harmony of creation being expressed through music to the powerlessness of evil, is Boethian in conception.[2] Boethius's *Consolation of Philosophy*, one of the most popular and enduring works of the Middle Ages, provides a lens through which one can interpret not only

1 This paper is inevitably narrow in focus, but I would like to thank other attendees and presenters at the symposium for their helpful contributions that helped me see even more resonances between Boethius and Tolkien, not all of which were able to be incorporated into the paper. I would also like to thank Austin Freeman for organizing the symposium and the edited volume.

2 Inevitably also Platonist (*Timaeus* 47d) and Plotinian (*Enneads* 5.9.11), with resonances in the work of St. Clement of Alexandria (*Protrepticus* 9). See also, from the fourth century, Calcidius, *Commentary on Plato's Timaeus*, which was known to Boethius and was the Latin West's primary engagement with the Timaeus for centuries. Calcidius deals with the *Timaeus* passage cited above at 267, but his most interesting passages on music come earlier, for example, at 40 and 45-46. Music in these authors, including Boethius in both the *Consolation* and the *Fundamentals of Music*, was seen as representing the harmony of the cosmos and thus was at some level a participation in the nature of creation, if not in the creator himself. For the music of the Ainur and philosophical tradition, see McIntosh (2017, ch. 3).

one's own life, but much of the world's great literature as well, including that of Tolkien, who had access to the *Consolation* in four languages: Latin, Old English, Middle English, and modern English.[3]

Because Boethius is a chief transmitter of Platonism to the medieval West, a hinge figure between Late Antiquity and the Early Middle Ages, he is a fitting figure for a consideration of the impact of ancient Christian theology on the works of J.R.R. Tolkien.[4] The Greek and Latin philosophical tradition comes together at Boethius as a sort of node and passes on from him into the canon of Latin Christendom. His towering importance within that canon is evidenced by his inclusion in King Alfred the Great's translation project of essential Latin works into Old English. And this brings us to Tolkien.

Tolkien, of course, was first Professor of Anglo-Saxon at Oxford, deep in the study of the literature and language of medieval England.[5] A key feature of early medieval thought, signalled by Alfred's chosen texts, is its refashioning of late antique texts, images, and ideas, and into what one may call an "Anglo-Saxon mode."[6] The classical heritage runs through Anglo-Saxon thought, sometimes more and sometimes less consciously, refracted through Late Antiquity and appropriated by local culture. There are Anglo-Saxon influences throughout Tolkien's corpus of fictional writings,[7] and when we begin hunting for Boethian themes and echoes in the work of Tolkien, there is a sense in which we are still operating within an "Anglo-Saxon mindset." Indeed, I would venture to say that to whatever degree we may find Tolkien interacting with ancient theology in

3 For those interested in Tolkien's friend C.S. Lewis and Boethius, consult the index of Baxter 2022.

4 Besides the sort of synthesis we see in the *Consolation*, he was also a major translator of Greek philosophy for the Latin West besides his other philosophical works that transmit the ancient philosophical tradition; being a sort of encyclopedic writer is a typical approach to literature, philosophy, etc., in Late Antiquity, as argued in Bjornlie 2015. Archetypal examples are Cassiodorus' *Institutions*, Macrobius's *Saturnalia*, and Isidore of Seville's *Etymologies*; all of these texts, like Boethius's *Consolation*, were popular throughout the Middle Ages.

5 We tend to think of him as early medieval, keeping in mind his famous essay *Beowulf: The Monsters and the Critics*, as well as the dense philological book, *Finn & Hengest*, yet he also edited (and translated!) *Sir Gawain and the Green Knight* and the *Ancrene Wisse*, both important Middle English texts.

6 Medieval intellectual culture at large was a reappropriation and recasting of Late Antiquity, whether as sources for canon law in Gratian and theology in Peter Lombard, or as something against which to react in Alan of Lille's *Anticlaudianus*.

7 This is most obvious in Rohan, but even in the Shire which is a sort of microcosm of England as delightfully detailed by Day 1997. See also Tolkien's alliterative verse cast in an Old English mould, such as *The Lays of Beleriand* and *The Fall of Arthur*.

this volume, or with continental theologians of the Middle Ages, or even with moderns, his production of an imaginative synthesis drawing from disparate sources yet bodying forth a seamless whole is itself truly Anglo-Saxon – and Boethian.

Boethius and His Work

What, then, of Boethius? Anicius Manlius Severinus Boethius (c. 475-526) was a Christian aristocrat and philosopher in the reign of King Theodoric the Great, rising as high as Magister Officiorum for the Gothic king, and seeing both of his sons hold the consulship.[8] He devoted his hours of *otium* to a manifold cultivation of philosophy, culminating in his famous *Consolation of Philosophy* – written while Boethius was imprisoned by Theodoric under suspicion of treason before being executed. Boethius's *Consolation* weaves together arguments about many things, including happiness (*beatitudo*), fortune (*fortuna*), fate (*fatum*),[9] providence (*prouidentia*), and, of course, God (*Deus*).

The dramatic setting of the *Consolation* is Boethius in his room, exiled away from court to Pavia,[10] where he sits lamenting his fall from good fortune. Into Boethius's self-pity steps Lady Philosophy herself. A dialogue ensues, whereby Philosophy draws forth or explains knowledge of Fortune – herself personified in the discussion – especially what constitutes good or bad fortune, and what true happiness means. Ultimately, true happiness, argues Lady Philosophy, is something you cannot lose, and is the result of participating in and attaining to the Good (*bonum*) – and the highest Good (*summum bonum*), ultimately, is God. The degree to which we participate in God is the degree to which we are happy.

---

8 This was a powerless title since the reign of Augustus, but the day they became consuls was the happiest day of Boethius's life, as we learn in *Consolation* 2.3.

9 Interestingly, the Old English *Consolation* conflates *fortuna* and *fatum* as *wyrd* in both cases; in the Latin original, the concept of *fatum* is related to the outworking of God's will in the economy of history. God has *prouidentia* whereby he sees and plans everything that will happen. And when what God has planned occurs, that is *fatum*. *Fortuna*, at a certain level, may possibly be construed as the human experience of *fatum*. On this topic, see Hynes 2016 and Gallant 2023.

10 Although we frequently picture him in a prison, C.S. Lewis rightly points us to house arrest and exile, not a prison cell (Lewis 1967: 76-77).

None of the usual things that people pursue to make them happy – worldly power (*potentia*), pleasure (*uoluptas*), wealth (*diuitiae*) – can last. They are at the mercy of Fortune, demonstrated through the ever-turning Wheel of Fortune, as Boethius himself discovered. As a result, those who possess such worldly 'goods' are not truly happy, for they have anxiety that they shall lose those goods. And if they are *not* anxious about losing them, then they have obtained their happiness elsewhere. Therefore, the pursuit of the philosophic life and of the good is ultimately the only road to happiness, because it is the possession of the *summum bonum* that is happiness itself, and the *summum bonum* is the one true good that cannot be snatched away and is not contingent upon any external circumstance.

In this paper I will consider the specific aspects of power and love, including friendship, within the *Consolation*. Power is to be understood in two manners. First is its common usage, worldly power, as when Boethius refers to "men who wielded greater power than mine" early in the *Consolation* (1.P4). The arguments swirl concerning what a man's true nature is, and thus what his ultimate end is, and how to achieve that end, which involves attaining true happiness: that place of imperturbable calm and contentment where one is truly at peace and cannot be swayed by externals.[11] It becomes clear that true power is not the external force that a king may use over his people, whether rightly or wrongly. It is, rather, governing the *self*, living according to one's own nature,[12] and finding the resources within oneself (one's natural power) for participating in the *summum bonum*. Fortune, or *wyrd* in the Anglo-Saxon translation, can turn at any moment and take other forms of power away. But this kind of power is immune to Fortune's Wheel, immune to the shifts of fate.

Secondly, true power arises from participation in the *summum bonum* because the *summum bonum* itself is God. Part of the definition of the *summum bonum* is that it is self-sufficient, and thus the opposite of being deficient in power (3.P9). In Book 3, Prose 9, happiness itself is ultimately defined as divinity. And in Book 3, Prose 10, the corollary emerges that if true happiness is itself divinity, then our participation in divinity is our happiness. Philosophy says:

11 As opposed to being simply jolly, as many might understand happiness today.
12 Both concepts are deeply embedded in Platonism and Stoicism, not to mention in Christian tradition, as in the Desert Fathers.

"Each happy individual is therefore divine. While only God is so by nature, as many as you like may become so by participation" (trans. Watts).[13]

In Boethius, evil itself is a lack, a privation that feeds on the good, distorts, warps and ruins; such a view of evil, of course, is pervasive in Tolkien's conception of orcs, of Sauron, of the One Ring. However, since evil is not generative the way the *summum bonum* is, evil is by nature weak. Furthermore, evil cannot bring about happiness, and unwavering happiness is true power. Thirdly, evil cannot contravene the power of *wyrd*, of *fatum*, of the outworking of the *prouidentia* stored in the mind of the *summum bonum*, of God who is himself happiness. Melkor, then, in proper Boethian fashion, is powerless against the outworking of Ilúvatar's providence as fate. Evil is weakness. Let us turn now to *The Lord of the Rings*.

Power and Its Loss

In most of its treatment of power, *The Lord of the Rings* is Boethian, and particularly fruitful studies could be done on any of the main characters. I have restricted myself to Théoden, King of Rohan, and Denethor, Steward of Gondor. In Théoden we see the Boethian ideal of true power and participation in the good, the true, and the beautiful – power that lies within its bearer. In Denethor, we have a Boethian vision of worldly power and the vicissitudes of the Wheel of Fortune, leading to his demise as a loss both of the good and of power.[14] I will assess Théoden, then Denethor; but discussing Denethor and his fall into despair also requires discussing the *palantíri*.

---

13 A more straightforward, succinct Latin description of theosis, or "deification", I have yet to find – this doctrine, associated more with the Eastern church than the Western church today, is essentially the belief that participation in the divine life is part of the life of salvation, and we can grow in Godlikeness. The concept has its roots in Scripture, and then in the works of St. Irenaeus in the second century. It is summed up most famously in the phrase of Athanasius of Alexandria: "For he was incarnate that we might be made God" (*On the Incarnation* 54.3). See also Athanasius's Syriac contemporary, Ephrem the Syrian, *Hymns on the Nativity* 1.99. For more on Boethius and deification, see Wittala 2019.

14 See also Honegger (2023: 304-334), who compares Denethor's and Théoden's respective reactions to their fates and what this tells us about their ethics.

Théoden's True Power

In *The Two Towers*, the encounter between Gandalf and the bent and decrepit Théoden is a prime example of different forms of power as discussed by Boethius. Given the popularity of the Peter Jackson films, it is worth pausing here to note that the way this encounter plays out in the book is very different from its course on screen. On screen, it is very much an encounter between Gandalf and Saruman, almost directly, using literal magic to combat each other. Gandalf, being more powerful, wins. In the book, as we shall see, the real magic at hand is not in the casting of spells.

We can see Théoden as a sort of Boethius, with Gandalf as his Philosophy, while Gríma Wormtongue serves to personify Boethius's despair at his imprisonment. The true power of Gandalf here is not in the use of supernatural power as possessed by Gandalf and Saruman according to their nature as Istari.[15] Rather, keeping true to his mission not to dominate, Gandalf employs his own, embodied voice as his only 'magic.' Only the truth overcomes the mastery of Saruman. This approach to power is truly Boethian – true power basically resides 'within.' Thus Gandalf seeks the good of Théoden not through mastery or force but through eliciting the real man beneath. In doing this, Gandalf shows both his own power and that of Théoden.

Théoden, as it turns out, has all the power he needs already; no magical power is required. All he lacks is the truth, and the truth is what sets him free. The truth, given freely and for his own good, revitalizes the power locked within the man enslaved to his own fears, trapped by his own worries and weakness. Without the truth, he is weak and powerless. And yet the power he gains, and which we see increase throughout his encounter with Gandalf, is his own power. His own muscles, his own strength, his own posture, his very own self, is brought back to life by a servant of the divine.

Emblematic of this aspect of the encounter is the moment when Théoden takes up Éomer's sword: "Slowly Théoden stretched forth his hand. As his fingers took the hilt, it seemed to the watchers that firmness and strength returned

15 The wizards, or Istari, are enfleshed Maiar (like unto angels) on a mission from the Valar (like unto gods) to reassure and protect the peoples of Middle-earth at the return of Sauron (*UT* 503; see also *Sil* 361-63).

to his thin arm. Suddenly he lifted the blade and swung it shimmering and whistling in the air. Then he gave a great cry. His voice rang clear as he chanted in the tongue of Rohan a call to arms" (*LotR* 517). Théoden, grasping the power within himself, has awakened to his own true nature as the King of the Rohirrim. When the ill effects of the external pressures from Wormtongue are undone, and when Théoden turns from a certain set of external woes – such as the death of his son Théodred – he rediscovers the resources he already has. This is essentially what Lady Philosophy tells Boethius – he already has all the riches he needs to overcome his misfortune and be happy, because he has the teachings of Philosophy stored up in his mind. He simply needs to relearn what he has forgotten.

This role of Gandalf as Philosophy truly becomes apparent when Gandalf casts off his cloak and reveals his light. This visual manifestation of literal light is a bodying forth of what Gandalf is about to do as he says to Théoden: "No counsel have I to give to those that despair. Yet counsel I could give, and words I could speak to you [...] Too long have you sat in shadows and trusted to twisted tales and crooked promptings" (*LotR* 514). Having summoned Théoden forth into the light, Gandalf then begins the Platonic task of remembering, the task of Philosophy. Théoden moves from the shadows of his hall to the light of day where he can behold his kingdom and say: "It is not so dark here" (*LotR* 515). The light of the truth shines upon him, and he is no longer held by despair simply by gazing upon reality with his own eyes. Most famously, not long after this Gandalf says: "Your fingers would remember their old strength better, if they grasped a sword-hilt" (*LotR* 517). More truth is brought to Théoden's consciousness, for the sword that comes is that of Éomer, wrongfully exiled, now returned. We read: "Slowly Théoden stretched forth his hand. As his fingers took the hilt, it seemed to the watchers that firmness and strength returned to his thin arm. Suddenly he lifted the blade and swung it shimmering and whistling in the air" (*LotR* 517). Memory and truth conquer in the life of the man with true power and true happiness here in this scene. The falsehoods of Saruman are weak and powerless in comparison with simple reality. Their shadows flee.

Furthermore, Théoden, King of Rohan, whose ancestors obtained their realm from the Kings of Gondor, once he has been released from the spell of depression, finds no rival in Aragorn, son of Arathorn, the man born to be king. This is worth observing because a 'lesser' king entertaining a man who is the destined king of another, 'greater' kingdom is a moment rife with potential for fear, anxiety, or simple jealousy. But Théoden has been released from falsehood and weakness by Gandalf. His arms have grown strong. His resolve has grown deep. He will ride with his people, white though his hair may be. In sum, he knows his own power. As a result, he has nothing to fear whatsoever from Aragorn but welcomes him as a companion, as will Théoden's successor Éomer, embracing Aragorn as friend and sword-brother. The recognition of one's own position in the world, of one's power as it really is and not as one would wish, this lack of fear that someone may snatch power away – this is the true power possessed by the happy (*beatus*), in Boethius's philosophy. And that is why it is more powerful than the power of either the wicked or the fearful. Such men spend their lives attempting to bend others to their will, as Saruman attempted with Théoden, and seeking to manipulate those around them.

Indeed, Saruman makes the example of Théoden stand out all the more, for Saruman possesses both 'worldly' and 'supernatural' power. Yet this power is ultimately extrinsic to him and fails. He is reduced to his voice, and even this is not strong enough to stand up to Gandalf's truth-speaking – so he seeks his revenge by taking over the Shire as Sharky. Yet his worldly power is so feeble that he is overthrown by a few genteel Hobbits willing to stand up to him. Their own internal power and goodness have grown and been tested in the furnace of the War of the Ring and the fires of Mount Doom. This internal, true power manifests another aspect of Boethian strength. When Frodo encounters Saruman at Bag End, it is pity that he feels, rather like the pity of Bilbo that stayed his hand against Gollum in *The Hobbit.* This pity for evildoers is Boethian, as we read in Book 4, Prose 4, that the evil are to be pitied much as the sick are. Rather than staying true to his mission from the divine, rather than holding on that which neither Sauron nor Gandalf nor Fangorn nor the Hobbits can take from him, he grasps at power, twisted into the mould of the enemy, a fallen angel. From the chief of the Istari, he is murdered as a feeble, old man. His power, seemingly so great and mighty, apparent as Orthanc itself, was insecure and could be snatched away by an Ent, a disgruntled minion, and a Hobbit.

The power that is secure and that cannot be snatched away – that is the power that Théoden possesses. It is power that gives him strength to ride a horse and humility to accept the aid of someone more powerful than he. He embarks with his men from the muster of Rohan to the Pelennor Fields, to lead the ride of the Rohirrim on "a sword-day, a red day, ere the sun rises," (*LotR* 838) to Gondor – to his death. And while this death may prove the weakness and frailty of the human body, it is glorious in reality, demonstrating the true power of the King of Rohan. He chooses the good, the true, and the beautiful, seeking the highest good of the Free Peoples of Middle-earth, riding forth to the aid of Gondor not solely because it is good policy, but because it is right. Thus Théoden dies and returns to his fathers, and the Rohirrim "bemourned […] their master's fall, comrades of his hearth, crying that he was ever of the kings of earth of men most generous and to men most gracious, to his people most tender and for praise most eager."[16]

Denethor's False Power

Denethor cuts a strikingly different figure from Théoden. Both men have many of the same concerns and pressures, though. They are the political rulers of peoples whose existence is threatened by Sauron. They are old, and there is some risk of a failed succession. They are heirs to traditions going back generations, dictating to some degree what their response to danger is. They are both concerned for the welfare of their people, and they both genuinely wish to see the fall of Sauron. Yet Denethor's approach to power is abundantly different. Like Théoden before Gandalf and his companions arrived, Denethor has already given up hope. With the death of Boromir, all hope seems to rest on his younger son, Faramir, a wizard's pupil too much like himself and all-too-likely not to succeed in the test of arms that lies ahead – instead, perhaps, conspiring to supplant Denethor himself with the upstart king out of the North, Aragorn. Denethor is a man of many concerns, looking to the widespread kingdom of Gondor and its borders, especially East and South. And East and South all he sees are the seeds of the destruction of Gondor itself. If he turns North – besides

16 The closing lines of *Beowulf* as translated by Tolkien (2014, 105), but still fitting.

Rohan, whom can Men trust to rally to their aid? Ever has the world looked to Gondor for their safety.

This fear of loss of power is a necessary aspect if the power one has is the external power of this world. If one seeks mere worldly power and not the power of Boethian happiness, wherein one shares in the *summum bonum*, then it is always accompanied by fear and anxiety. Denethor fears both the loss of the realm of Gondor and his own loss of power over that realm. Because of these pressures and anxieties, which only grow after the loss of Boromir, Denethor places greater and greater pressure on his son Faramir and behaves as though Faramir were faithless and a continual failure in his duty to his lord.

This treatment of Faramir parallels Théoden's treatment of Éomer when first we meet the two, in that Théoden has cast Éomer out from his presence. However, Théoden welcomes his nephew's sword when presented at the right time. On the other hand, it is only when Faramir approaches death that Denethor shows any sort of affection. Yet, it is a fell mood that falls upon Denethor in such affection – dare we call it love? Manifestly, it is a *form* of love, but certainly not that which we find in the Latin theological tradition of which Boethius was a part. That is to say, it is an overflowing of the natural affection of a father for his son, but distorted and twisted by Denethor's despair.

Love and Friendship

To further reflect on Tolkien's use of so much of the same philosophical-theological framework as Boethius, and to demonstrate Denethor's despair, a brief excursus on love is in order. In *Consolation* 2M8, he writes that love (*amor*) binds everything together in the whole universe – all is ruled by love; love keeps the peace, both in the realm of physics and in human relations, from peoples to persons, nations to marriages to friendships. "O happy race of men / If Love who rules the sky / Could rule your hearts as well!" (lines 28-30) The sort of robust love we find in the Boethian vision is not simply natural affection, but something sturdier. It is the very force that holds the universe in order and keeps the planets on their courses, not just warm feelings on a cold night. And Denethor's feelings, as we witness in *The Return of the King*, get things quite warm.

Boethius's Sources for Love

Boethius is tapping into the tradition of Plato, who describes love as something so strong that it moves the world and brings concord and harmony among humans – not unlike music, in fact. Plato's *Symposium*, the famous dinner party where Socrates and his companions discuss what love is, sees each man offering up his ideal vision. Plato's dialogue brings the discussion from the Hollywood-esque vision of Aristophanes, the comic playwright, to higher things. What are we really pursuing through what humans today call 'romance'? Happiness? Immortality? Something bigger and better than ourselves? This desire, which is a base root of *eros*, drives the thoughtful lover to the higher things.

For Plato, love is itself driven ultimately by desire for the good or the beautiful, which is most purely found in wisdom and its pursuit of the highest good – in the Latin tradition, the *summum bonum*. Love, *eros* in the *Symposium*, maintains the root of desire and pushes the reader upwards. We are bound to what we desire. *Eros* is a substantial reality for Plato (we could even call it a *substance* in later philosophical language). The later Platonic tradition makes plain the vision of love found in the *Symposium*, as a quick survey of Plotinus would reveal.

St. Augustine, likewise, has a robust understanding of love, rooted in both Plato and the Christian Scriptures. In *De Doctrina Christiana* 1 and *De Trinitate* 7 and 9, Augustine continues this vision of love as a substantial reality that binds together lover and beloved. In the former work, he has an extended discussion of the concepts of *use* and *enjoyment*, driving ultimately towards the recognition that God is the only thing or person worthy of love above all else, and that all other loves are ordered after him. God is also the only person to be purely enjoyed. When he discusses love in *De Trin.*, Augustine writes:

> What then, after all that, is this love (*dilectio*) or charity (*caritas*) which the divine scriptures praise and proclaim so much, but love of the good (*amor boni*)? Now love means someone loving and something loved with love. There you are with three, the lover, what is being loved, and love. And what is love but a kind of life coupling or trying to couple together two things, namely lover and what is being loved? This is true even of the most external and fleshly kinds of love. But in order to quaff something purer and more limpid, let us trample on the flesh and rise to the spirit. What does spirit love in a friend but spirit? So here again there are three, love and what is being loved, and love (8.10).

Friendship (*amicitia*) is one of the abiding themes of St. Augustine's life, from the friends of his youth that we meet in the *Confessions* to the long-distance friends of his letters to the discussions of friendship in his magnum opus, *De Civitate Dei*.

For Augustine, as for the ancients at large, friendship was a substantial love, something deeper than just people one can tolerate at times and with whom one can share some laughs. It is a deep relationship with its own duties, with give and take, as well as with affection and shared interests that bind the friends together. Friendship, as a substantial love itself, involves taking delight in one's friend. Such friendship is also part of the vision of Boethius in the *Consolation*, embraced within *amor* in the verse passage already cited: "Love promulgates the laws / For friendship's faithful bond" (*Consolation* 2M8.26-27). Both Augustine and Boethius are aware of the possibility of false friends, as well, which makes a true friend all the more precious, rare, and precarious.

Tolkien's Vision of Friendship

As in Augustine and Boethius, so in *The Lord of the Rings* – friendship is substantial. Indeed, it is one of the major themes running through the entire book, beginning with Frodo and his conspirators. Along the way, friendships are made and strengthened, including between those who would naturally mistrust each other, Legolas and Gimli. The hobbits provide us the most ample examples of friendship. Frodo's friends make sacrifices for him out of a sense of friendly duty, helping move him out of Hobbiton and even conspiring to run away with him to help keep him safe on the journey. And the journey takes them far and changes them, but the four hobbits who return to scour the Shire in *The Return of the King* are still friends, still bound by affection and the delight in one another as before, even if now they are also an effective fighting force and allies in arms. It is their love for Frodo and one another that propels much of the plot of *The Lord of the Rings*. It is love that holds it all together – love rooted in affection and delight in the other, rooted in self-sacrifice, rooted in a desire to see the beloved friend succeed. It is strong. It is powerful. Love saves the world.

Despair as Deprivation

And now we return to Denethor. The fell mood that descends darkly when Denethor remembers his love for his son is a mood of complete and utter weakness. He has an enormous amount of power as Steward of Gondor. Denethor still holds the rulership of the City. He still commands the guard of Minas Tirith. He still holds sway over those within the walls and without. He still has the power of leadership and even the duty to preserve the lives of the people of Gondor. He even has the ability and authority to bring his poisoned, dying son to a place where he can be healed. Yet Denethor lacks that inner power of strength that comes from seeking first the highest good, the truest happiness, whereby participation in divine reality results in a true, unwavering strength. This is the strength that enables another leader of men to ride to his death in order to save others, resolved and contented even as an undead Witch-king slays the steed from beneath him. Denethor, unlike Théoden, has no real power – the evil of despair has fallen upon him.

This is certainly a Boethian theme, for the whole point of the *Consolation* is raising Boethius out of despair and placing him on a firm footing to rediscover true happiness. Even if there is no moral fault in one who is overcome by depression or despair, the mood itself is, in patristic terms, an evil mood, distorting and transforming good things so that they appear dry and lifeless to the victim. Boethius's *Consolation*, in fact, begins with an expression of Boethius's despair, which Philosophy, in her first speech, promptly upbraids as a manifestation of Boethius's *affectus*, which can rightly be rendered by 'passions' in English – passions, those deadly movements of the soul that draw the victim from virtue toward vice. Theologically, Denethor has been struck by dejection, one of the eight deadly thoughts of Evagrius Ponticus who writes: "Sadness is the maw of a lion and readily devours one afflicted by it."[17]

17 Evagrius Ponticus, *On the Eight Thoughts* 5.2 (trans. Sinkewicz 2003, 81).

Evil as *Privatio Boni*

In the theology of Boethius and the majority tradition of the ancient church, evil is non-being.[18] It is a lack or a deprivation. At most, it is a twisting or distortion of being. Boethius sets forth this teaching in the *Consolation* when he dialogues with Philosophy about the goodness and power and happiness of God, and how, if anything tries to go against God in his goodness and power, it is utterly weak and powerless. Boethius and Philosophy say that God is happiness itself, which includes his utter self-sufficiency. God lacks nothing. Moreover, he "controls all things by the helm of goodness, and all things [...] have a natural inclination toward the good" (*Cons.* 3P12). As a result, anything that goes against God cannot preserve its own nature, let alone its happiness. Given God's perfect self-sufficiency and immoveable happiness, a movement against God would be utterly powerless. Ultimately, Philosophy declares that since God can do all things, and God cannot do evil, evil is nothing. This, in sum, is the view of the Platonic tradition and the ancient church. Another way of casting it is to say that since God is being itself (as per Gen 3:14, "I am that I am"), and God himself is good, then anything that moves away from God and goodness moves towards non-being. Evil, by definition, has turned from God and goodness. Therefore, it is a lack, a privation.

Shippey has argued that this Boethian understanding of evil as privation and nothingness, essentially internal, is at odds with the stronger 'heroic' vision of evil of Alfred, and that Alfred's translation of the *Consolation* betrays the heroic understanding.[19] In Alfred's understanding and recasting of evil, evil has some measure of reality to it, a perspective that carries weight for someone who has lived through the Viking raids of the ninth century. Boethius's perspective, on the other hand, is characterized as an internalization that may be philosophically coherent but lacks real world power. Whether this is a fair characterization of Alfred's translation or not, it is a misunderstanding of Boethius and the Platonic-Augustinian understanding of evil that he represents and which Anselm of Canterbury and Thomas Aquinas would later refine. Evil is a privation or distortion of the good, a movement away from self-sufficiency and being

18 Or a thoroughgoing treatment of the question of Boethian/Platonist evil in Tolkien, see Houghton and Keesee 2005.

19 Shippey (2003: ch. 5).

to weakness and non-being, from happiness to despair. To say that because Viking raids have tangible destructive force, and that evil is therefore real, is perhaps to make a psychological point, but to entirely miss the theological point, which is that everything they do that qualifies as evil is precisely destruction, devastation, and distortion. Furthermore, such an argument loses sight of the evils witnessed by Boethius, not to mention those witnessed by the tradition from which he writes – let us not forget that the sack of Rome in 410 is what triggered Augustine's *City of God*, itself a source for much Boethian thought. In fact, I would argue that to defend his people against such privations a monarch need not abandon the Platonic-Augustinian tradition that underlies Boethius on this point.

Shippey makes use of his characterization to argue that the Ring is both a real force of external power in and of itself and simultaneously amplifies the power of the one who wears it. It is elastic, manifesting both the 'heroic' vision of evil from Alfred and the 'classical' from Boethius. To move further into the territory of the Ring, however, it is worth taking account of what has already been said to note that if God is being and God is good, then anything that has being is, to some measure, good. Inasmuch as the Ring exists, the Ring is good. It is a substantial reality, just as love is. And as a substantial reality, it also is possessed of power, and that power is not always going to manifest itself in a purely evil manner, because power is linked to being which is linked to God, who is good, and whose purposes cannot be thwarted. Hopefully this foregoing discussion has helped clarify our understanding of evil in Boethius and Tolkien in order to apply these concepts to the figure of Denethor and his despair.

Despair, as witnessed in the behaviour of Denethor in *The Return of the King*, is manifestly a lack, a privation, a movement towards non-being. Despair is a kind of besetting sadness that drains away all hope, energy, strength, and happiness. Most particularly, it is a rejection of hope, and we see that this is the case with Denethor. He has no hope for Faramir. He has no hope for Gondor. He had already given up the meager hope of clinging to power with the approach of Aragorn. Denethor has abandoned all hope and headed for the houses of the dead on purpose. His despair, like all despair, is clearly and obviously evil, leading him to perform deeds that are themselves evil, such as seeking to burn himself and his remaining son alive. Being and life are bound together in ancient Christianity – and Denethor plans to rob both himself and his son of both. Unlike the case of Théoden, there is nothing Gandalf can do for Denethor in the evil of his despair. As Gandalf had said to Théoden: "No counsel have I to give to those that despair" (*LotR* 514).

And so Denethor's descent into powerless madness is also a descent into hell, but not the Underworld of the shades of the departed in Dante and Virgil, but the abode of Milton's devils.[20] It is a spiritual descent,[21] signalled by his declaration, "We will burn like heathen kings before ever a ship sailed hither from the West. The West has failed. Go back and burn!" (*LotR* 825). Happiness and power are found in participation in the highest good, in God. And here we see that Denethor has abandoned God.

The word 'heathen,' as defined by the first edition of the *Oxford English Dictionary*, is a Germanic word that refers to those who are not Christians or Jews, who worship multiple gods – false gods, not the one, true, living God who is possessed of real power, not the God of Boethius or the opening of *Sil*, not even the One of Plato or Plotinus.[22] Furthermore, he speaks of returning to a time *before* anyone came from the West – not only that, Denethor declares that the West has failed. The West in *The Lord of the Rings* refers not merely to a point on the compass, but to Valinor, and more closely, sunken Númenor. That is to say, Denethor's own words reveal that he is not participating in the *summum bonum*, the divine life. To the degree that Denethor is not participating in the divine life and has rejected the true, the good, and the beautiful in submitting to despair, he is enshrouded in evil. And evil, as seen from the beginning of creation with Melkor, is powerless.

The Weakness of Tyranny

Yet from our perspective, as readers of this story, it seems that evil is powerful, and its power is demonstrated in this very episode. When Denethor dies, we discover that he has in his possession a *palantír*. Denethor has sat in the White Tower gazing at the *palantír* and seeking what knowledge he may gain from it in order to aid him in his defense of Gondor. However, Sauron is also in possession of a

20 That said, for the Virgilian influence here, see Freeman 2020a.
21 For the hopelessness of those who abandon Eru as typified by Denethor, see Freeman (2022: 320-23).
22 See also Shippey (2003: ch. 6).

palantír, and he warps and twists what Denethor sees, directing the show (as it were) that is presented to him. As a result of Sauron's greater external power in the *palantír*, Denethor is filled with a despair that goes beyond the natural response to his sons' deaths to true, deep desolation. His own mental power and will are not enough to stand up against Sauron, and down he falls.

How is it, then, that Sauron and his evil are not powerful? How, on a smaller stage, is the evil of Sauron orchestrated into Ilúvatar's good, true, and beautiful symphony as had been done with his master Melkor's? As Boethius tells us, the tyrant's power is limited to the physical. A tyrant cannot force someone to do anything. He can threaten and indeed follow through with taking away someone's life or freedom or good fortune. In other words, he can take away those things that Boethius has already established are not the source of either true happiness or real power. A tyrant cannot take away the sort of inner power possessed by a man like Théoden or Aragorn. He writes: "You cannot impose anything on a free mind, and you cannot move from its state of inner tranquillity a mind at peace with itself and firmly founded on reason" (*Cons.* 2P6). In the face of the leaders of the Free Peoples of Middle-earth who choose not to move from inner tranquillity, Sauron is weak and powerless. Moreover, his ability to help bring Denethor to despair through the manipulation of the *palantír* points more to Denethor's weakness than any strength on Sauron's part.

Boethius has more to say, though. Not only does the tyrant lack power over others where it really counts, his power over others is precisely the kind of power that is itself a source of weakness, not a source of true happiness. Monarchs, tyrannical and otherwise, are themselves subject to various fears and insecurities. We read: "What sort of power is it, then, that strikes fear into those who possess it, confers no safety on you if you want it, and which cannot be avoided when you want to renounce it?" (3P5). Boethius also reminds us of the passions that rule tyrants, enslaving them: "Here in one heart so many tyrants rule, / The king's own will's deposed, the enslaver slaved" (4M2). Not only is the tyrant's power over others illusory, he himself is a slave to his passions. This matches Denethor very well when he is overcome by the passion of despair and Sauron with his will to power over others. And thus we see Denethor and his false power. Pressed by all the anxieties and fears natural to his position, struck by the death of one son and the looming death of the other, concerned about losing his power to some nobody Ranger, and then filled with a twisted and distorted view of the world by unwise use of a *palantír*, Denethor has no power. His descent into an evil, heathenish death is simultaneously a loss of all true power.

A final word about the *palantír* is in order. The *palantíri* show themselves to be particularly dangerous objects. Both Denethor and Saruman use them with disastrous results. Their knowledge is warped, their vision is obscured, their power is diminished. Both of them are deceived and tricked by Sauron. Not even Saruman has enough power to properly use the *palantír* to his own advantage. However, Aragorn does. Aragorn is a Man who lives according to his own nature. He pursues the good above power itself. He knows who he is, as Isildur's heir. And therefore, secure in who he is, he can wisely and cautiously use the *palantír* to his own advantage, and draw the attention of Sauron, showing him that a King from the North is on the move to confront him. He shows him Andúril, the reforged sword formerly known as Narsil that had cut the One Ring from Sauron's finger. Aragorn has within himself the resources necessary to use the *palantír*, facing the Eye of Sauron and demonstrating himself to possess true power in a Boethian sense.

Conclusion

In closing, we have seen throughout this paper the ways in which the characters and drama of *The Lord of the Rings* unfold according to Boethian archetypes through analysis of Théoden and Denethor. Théoden, through the grace given to him by Gandalf, finds true power in himself to be able to shake off the shackles of falsehood and remember, like Boethius, who he is and what his nature is. This then drives the rest of the Théoden narrative until his death on the Pelennor Fields. Denethor, on the other hand, with a warped and twisted (and, therefore, evil) view of reality, finds himself sunk in despair, leading to his own death on a pyre of his own creation, joining the heathen kings of old, separated from the *summum bonum*. The test of true power lies in the *palantíri*, and we see that neither Saruman nor Denethor has the power necessary to use them rightly – nor even Sauron, but only Aragorn, a Man who knows who he is and what he must do; a Man, therefore, who is truly powerful. And so Sauron, distracted and disturbed by King Aragorn II Elessar, Sauron in his evil, falls, for evil is weakness.

About the Author

MATTHEW J.J. HOSKIN, PhD, is Professor of Christian History at Davenant Hall and a specialist in the history of Christianity in Late Antiquity, especially the world of the Latin-speaking Church Fathers and their letters. The result of almost ten years of research, his book *The Manuscripts of the Letters of Pope Leo the Great* came out in 2022, surveying a vast array of medieval manuscripts and placing them in their contexts within the history of European intellectual culture. He seeks to broaden contact with classical Christian thought and practice through blogging, podcasts, and tweeting @mjjhoskin. He lives in Thunder Bay, Ontario, with his wife and two sons as well as a full set of Playmobil Vikings and a large but still growing library of Arthurian literature.

Bibliography

ATHANASIUS. 2011. *On the Incarnation*. Edited and translated by John Behr. Crestwood, NY: SVS Press.

AUGUSTINE of Hippo. 1991. *On the Trinity*. Translated by Edmund Hill. Hyde Park, NY: New City Press.

BAXTER, Jason M. 2022. *The Medieval Mind of C.S. Lewis: How Great Books Shaped a Great Mind*. Downers Grove, IL: IVP.

BJORNLIE, Shane. 2015. "The Rhetoric of Varietas and Epistolary Enyclopedism in the Variae of Cassiodorus." In Geoffrey Greatrex and Hugh Elton (eds.). *Shifting Genres in Late Antiquity*. Farnham, Surrey: Ashgate, 289-304.

BOETHIUS. 1969. *The Consolation of Philosophy*. Translated by V. E. Watts. Harmondsworth: Penguin.

1973. *Tractates, The Consolation of Philosophy*. Edited and translated by H. F. Stewart, E.K. Rand, and S.J. Tester. Cambridge, MA: Harvard University Press.

1989. *Fundamentals of Music*. Translated by Calvin M. Bower. New Haven & London: Yale University Press.

CALCIDIUS. 2016. *On Plato's Timaeus*. Edited and translated by John Magee. Cambridge, MA: Harvard University Press.

CLEMENT of Alexandria. 1929. "The Exhortation to the Greeks." In *Clement of Alexandria*. Edited and translated by G.W. Butterworth. Loeb Classical Library 92. Cambridge, MA: Harvard University Press, 3-263.

DAY, David. 1997. *The Hobbit Companion*. New York: MetroBooks.

Dubs, K.E. 1981. "Providence, Fate, and Chance: Boethian Philosophy in *The Lord of the Rings*." *Twentieth Century Literature* 27.1: 34-42.

Ephrem the Syrian. 1989. *Hymns on the Nativity*. In *Ephrem the Syrian: Hymns*. Translated by Kathleen E. McVey. New York: Paulist, 61-217.

Freeman, Austin. 2020a. "Pietas and the Fall of the City: A Neglected Virgilian Influence on Middle-earth's Chief Virtue." In Hamish Williams (ed.). *Tolkien and the Classical World*. Cormarë Series 45. Zurich and Jena: Walking Tree Publishers, 131-63.

2020b. "Flesh, World, Devil: The Nature of Evil in J.R.R. Tolkien." *Journal of Inklings Studies* 10.2: 139-71.

2022. *Tolkien Dogmatics: Theology through Mythology with the Maker of Middle-earth*. Bellingham, WA: Lexham Press.

Gallant, Richard Z. 2019. "The Dance of Authority in Arda: Wyrd and Providence in the Elder Days of Middle-earth." *Hither Shore* 16: 124-44.

Honegger, Thomas. 2023. *Tweaking Things a Little. Essays on the Epic Fantasy of J.R.R. Tolkien and George R.R. Martin*. Cormarë Series 50. Zurich and Jena: Walking Tree Publishers.

Houghton, John William, and Neal K. Keesee. 2005. "Tolkien, King Alfred, and Boethius: Platonist Views of Evil in *The Lord Of The Rings*." *Tolkien Studies* 2: 131-59.

Hynes, Gerard. 2016. "Tolkien's Boethius, Alfred's Boethius." In Lynn Forest-Hill (ed.). 2016. *The Return of the Ring. Proceedings of the Tolkien Society Conference 2012*. Volume I. Edinburgh: Luna Press, 131-40.

Irvine, Susan and Malcolm R. Godden. 2012. *The Old English Boethius with Verse Prologues and Epilogues Associated with King Alfred*. Cambridge, MA: Harvard University Press.

Lewis, C.S. 1967. *The Discarded Image*. Cambridge: Cambridge University Press.

McIntosh, Jonathan. 2017. *The Flame Imperishable: Tolkien, St. Thomas, and the Metaphysics of Faerie*. Kettering, OH: Angelico Press.

Plato. 1977. *Timaeus and Critias*. Translated by Desmond Lee. Harmondsworth: Penguin.

Plotinus. 1991. *The Enneads*. Translated by Stephen MacKenna, abridged by John Dillon. Harmondsworth: Penguin.

Shippey, Tom. 2003. *The Road to Middle-earth*. Third edition. First edition 1982. Boston, MA: Houghton Mifflin.

SINKEWICZ, Robert E. (trans.). 2003. *Evagrius of Pontus: The Greek Ascetic Corpus.* Oxford: Oxford University Press.

TOLKIEN, J.R.R. 1979. *The Silmarillion*. London: George Allen & Unwin.

2004. *The Lord of the Rings.* 50th Anniversary One-Volume Edition. Boston, MA and New York: Houghton Mifflin Company.

2014. *Beowulf: A Translation and Commentary Together with Sellic Spell.* Edited by Christopher Tolkien. London: HarperCollins.

WICHER, A. 2021. "Some Boethian Themes in JRR Tolkien's *Lord of the Rings*." *Romanica Silesiana* 20(2): 1-24.

WITTALA, Michael. 2019. "Every Happy Man Is a God: Deification in Boethius." In Jared Ortiz (ed.). *Deification in the Latin Patristic Tradition*. Washington, DC: Catholic University of America Press, 231-52.

Keith A. Mathison

Franciscan Spirituality in the House of Tom Bombadil

Abstract

Tom Bombadil has long been one of the most enigmatic characters in *The Lord of the Rings*. This chapter argues that Tom came into Middle-earth from a different sub-created world with a different system and a different history. He is a character from a different tale who was drawn in to Middle-earth in order to provide an adventure for the hobbits. This chapter also argues that Tolkien uses the mysterious character of Tom Bombadil to absorb Roman Catholic religious elements into the story of *The Lord of the Rings*. Tom specifically represents a particular aspect of Roman Catholic spirituality exemplified by Francis of Assisi: renunciation of power and possessions, pacifism, love for and communion with nature, devotion to Mary, and an almost childlike penchant for joyful song.

Those who are familiar with *The Lord of the Rings* know that when Frodo, Sam, Merry, and Pippin leave the Shire they enter the Old Forest. In this Forest, the trees are thick, and the four hobbits soon find themselves wandering and growing more anxious by the moment. The heat is stifling. The trees seem to be closing in around them. Just as they are about to lose hope, they see the path before them, and at the end of the path they see a "green hill-top, treeless, rising like a bald head out of the encircling wood" (*LotR* 113). The hobbits hurry down the path and arrive at the foot of the hill. Here we read that the "wood stood all round the hill like thick hair that ended sharply in a circle round a shaven crown" (*LotR* 113).

One cannot help but be struck by this unusual imagery. Here in the middle of the Old Forest, the hobbits see a hill that looks like a tonsured head. The tonsure hair cut was part of a rite in the Roman Catholic Church connected with a man's ordination. It was worn by those in monastic orders as well. The tonsure signified a man's dedication to God (Parente et al. 1951: 284). But why would J.R.R. Tolkien, himself a devout Roman Catholic, introduce such imagery at this point in the story? Why would he describe a hill in the middle of the Old Forest in such terms? Is it merely a description of the physical features of the hill, or does it have a deeper significance?

In this chapter, I will argue that Tolkien's introduction of such religious imagery at this point in the story is significant in that it provides an important clue about the nature of a character that the hobbits will soon encounter in the Old Forest. There is sufficient evidence to indicate that Tolkien uses the enigmatic character of Tom Bombadil to absorb Roman Catholic religious elements – and specifically Franciscan spirituality – into the story of *The Lord of the Rings*.

Tom Bom, Jolly Tom, Tom Bombadillo!

Tom Bombadil first appears in *The Lord of the Rings* after Merry and Pippin have been swallowed up by Old Man Willow. Frodo cries out for help, and then he and Sam encounter Tom Bombadil. To be more precise, they first hear a deep voice happily singing a strange song, and then Tom comes into view along the path (*LotR* 119). To say that Tom looks unusual is an understatement. He is taller than a Hobbit but shorter than a Man. He has a red face covered with wrinkles from his habitual laughter, blue eyes, a long beard, and an old tall hat with a long blue feather in the band. He wears a blue coat and big yellow boots and is using a large leaf to carry a pile of white water-lilies back to his bride (*LotR* 119). He is not the kind of person one would expect to meet while journeying through an old forest – even an old forest in Middle-earth.

At the Council of Elrond, the hobbits learn that he has many names. He is known by the Elves, for example, as Iarwain Ben-adar, meaning "oldest and fatherless" (*LotR* 265). After the council, Tom is rarely mentioned until late in the story. When Frodo and Sam discover that they are in imminent danger in Shelob's lair, Sam says that he wishes Tom were near them (*LotR* 719). On the journey home after the destruction of the Ring, Gandalf says he is going to speak with Tom (*LotR* 996). Finally, at the very end of the story, as Frodo passes into the West, he is reminded of a dream he had when he was in Tom's house (*LotR* 1030).

The Bombadil Enigma

Tolkien's sub-creation is filled with all manner of beings: an omnipotent Creator (Eru Ilúvatar), the Valar, the Maiar (including the Istari, or wizards), Elves, Men, Hobbits, Dwarves, giant Eagles, Ents, Huorns, skin-changers, *Mearas*, fire-drakes, dragons, wights, wargs, the Watcher in the Water, Orcs, trolls, Balrogs, the Nazgûl, fell beasts, large spiders, stone-giants, Mûmakil, Bill the pony, and more. The origin and nature of many of these beings are fairly well understood within Tolkien's world. There are some beings, such as Ungoliant, a giant spider-like creature in the *Silmarillion*, whose exact origin is mysterious, but by far the most enigmatic character in *The Lord of the Rings* is Tom Bombadil. His unusual comments and characteristics rise above the level of these other figures, and readers have been trying for decades to figure out exactly who or what he is.

One of the first unusual things we notice about Tom in the story is that he is frequently singing. The first time we meet Tom, he is happily singing a strange, seemingly nonsensical, song.[1] After freeing Merry and Pippin from Old Man Willow, he invites the hobbits to his house and sings along the way. When the hobbits catch up with Tom at his house, he welcomes them with a song. Almost every time we encounter Tom, there is some reference to music and song, and even when he is merely talking, his speech has a musical, rhythmic pattern (Shippey 2003: 107).

We also learn that Tom's memory goes back to ancient days. He tells the hobbits tales of the forest and its creatures, particularly Old Man Willow who, as they have already discovered, is very dangerous. They learn that Old Man Willow's heart is rotten but that he remains strong. Tom's tales and songs then continue to go farther and farther back into history, "into ancient starlight" (*LotR* 131). His knowledge and memory are vast.

The most unusual thing about Tom is that the One Ring seems to have no effect on him. When Frodo gives the ring to Tom, Tom puts it to his eye and laughs. He then puts it on his finger, and he doesn't vanish from sight. He makes the ring disappear and then reappear. When Tom returns the ring, Frodo looks at it suspiciously "like

---

1 His singing style is reminiscent of the way the Elves sing in *The Hobbit*.

one who has lent a trinket to a juggler" (*LotR* 133).[2] When Frodo puts the ring on again, the hobbits cannot see him, but Tom can (*LotR* 131-32).

Goldberry's words about Tom add to the mystery. When Frodo initially asks Goldberry, "Who is Tom Bombadil?" she answers, "He is" (*LotR* 124). She goes on to say: "He is as you have seen him." She then adds: "He is the Master of wood, water, and hill." She explains that the land doesn't belong to him, but he is the master. No one has ever caught him. He has no fear. He is master. Three times, in quick succession, she refers to him as "master" (*LotR* 124). What is the meaning of this?

Tom also talks about himself, but his words only draw us deeper into the enigma. When Frodo asks Tom, "Who are you, Master?" Tom says,

> Don't you know my name yet? That's the only answer. Tell me, who are you, alone, yourself and nameless? But you are young and I am old. Eldest, that's what I am. Mark my words, my friends: Tom was here before the river and the trees; Tom remembers the first raindrop and the first acorn. He made paths before the Big People, and saw the little People arriving. He was here before the Kings and the graves and the Barrow-wights. When the Elves passed westward, Tom was here already, before the seas were bent. He knew the dark under the stars when it was fearless – before the Dark Lord came from Outside. (*LotR* 131)

Tom also indicates some limits to his knowledge and power. He says, for example, that he is not a master of the weather. He says that his knowledge fails out east and that his country has borders that he will not pass (*LotR* 147-48).

Tom and Goldberry are not the only ones who reveal information about him. Several of those who attend the Council of Elrond in Rivendell talk about Tom as they attempt to determine what to do with the One Ring. Gandalf indicates that Tom does not have power over the Ring, but neither does the Ring have power over Tom. Tom is his own master. Gandalf continues by explaining that Tom cannot alter the Ring, and he cannot break the power it has over others. Gandalf then adds: "And now he is withdrawn into a little land, within bounds that he has set, though none can see them, waiting perhaps for a change of days, and he will not step beyond them" (*LotR* 265).[3]

---

2 The significance of the comparison of Tom to a juggler will become clearer as we proceed.

3 Observe that both Tom and Gandalf explicitly mention the borders of Tom's country, and both indicate that Tom will not step outside of these borders. The significance of this observation will be explained below.

The Elf Erestor asks whether Tom could keep the Ring in his own lands. Gandalf responds that he would not do it willingly. If the whole free world begged him, he might, "but he would not understand the need." Further, if given the Ring, "he would soon forget it, or most likely throw it away. Such things have no hold on his mind. He would be a most unsafe guardian" (*LotR* 265). Glorfindel says taking the Ring to Tom would only postpone the inevitable. Eventually, Sauron would learn of its location and would direct all his power towards it. Glorfindel does not think Bombadil's power alone could defy Sauron's. He concludes: "I think that in the end, if all else is conquered, Bombadil will fall, Last as he was First; and then Night will come" (*LotR* 266). Galdor agrees with Glorfindel, saying of Tom: "Power to defy our Enemy is not in him, unless such power is in the earth itself. And yet we see that Sauron can torture and destroy the very hills" (*LotR* 266).

When we consider everything said by Tom and about Tom in *The Lord of the Rings*, it is not difficult to understand why there has been so much debate about his nature and identity. There are many theories about who or what he is and what he might represent. Among the many theories are the suggestions that Tom is Eru Ilúvatar (Head 2008), one of the Valar (Hargrove 1986: 20-24), one of the Maiar (Foster 1978: 492), a nature spirit (Flieger 2017: 191; Fuller 1968: 23; Petty 2003: 144; Noel 1977: 127, 129), the incarnation of Arda (Noad 1991: 83; Jensen 2002), the incarnation of the music of the Ainur (Secord 2013), a type of unfallen Adam (Pearce 2015: 47), or an unsolvable mystery (Hammond and Scull 2005: 139).[4]

Tom Bombadil in the History of Tolkien's Work

If we are to have any hope of resolving the nature of Tom Bombadil as he appears in *The Lord of the Rings*, it is important first to grasp where he fits in the history of Tolkien's literary output. The earliest versions of the stories that would develop into the *legendarium* (the works concerning Arda and Middle-earth) were written around 1916 or 1917 (See *BLT1*). Tolkien continued working on and developing these tales until the end of his life. However, not all of Tolkien's stories were part

4 Readers interested in the full case for any or all of these views are encouraged to read the sources cited. I have offered my own brief explanation and evaluation of these theories elsewhere (Mathison 2020).

of this *legendarium*. Many originated as stories he told his children. *Roverandom*, for example, was a story he told after one of his sons lost his toy dog on a beach (Carpenter 2000a: 164). *The Hobbit* also began life as a story he told his young children in the late 1920s. Tolkien began to put this story in writing in the early 1930s. It was published in 1937 (Scull & Hammond 2017b: 513). The difference between *Roverandom* and *The Hobbit* is that although neither was originally part of the *legendarium*, "*The Hobbit* was *drawn into* Middle-earth [...]" (*RS* 7).

Like *Roverandom* and *The Hobbit*, Tom Bombadil also began as a story Tolkien told his children. Tom's visible features and his clothing were based on those of a doll that belonged to his son Michael. The story eventually evolved into a poem, "The Adventures of Tom Bombadil" published in 1934. In addition to Tom, this poem includes the characters of Goldberry, Old Man Willow, and the Barrow-wight (Scull and Hammond 2017b: 27-29). Like *The Hobbit*, Tom Bombadil was 'drawn into' Middle-earth. Tom was drawn in because of the writing of *The Lord of the Rings*. After the success of *The Hobbit*, the publishers desired a sequel. Tolkien wanted to publish *The Silmarillion*, but that collection of tales did not quite work as a sequel to *The Hobbit*. By the end of 1937, however, he had written the first draft of the first chapter of what would become *The Lord of the Rings*. At this early stage in the writing, he did not yet know exactly where the new story was going. He continued writing, but for a long time, he remained unsure of the direction the tale would take. He was creating it as he went along (see *RS* 5).

Because he was creating the story as he wrote, Tolkien thought he needed "an 'adventure' on the way" for the hobbits. To fill this need, he put Tom Bombadil, a character he had already invented for another purpose, into the story (*Letters* 192). In his notes to himself at this stage in the writing, he speaks of Tom Bombadil as an "aborigine." He says that Tom "knew the land before men, before hobbits, before barrow-wights, yes before the necromancer – before the elves came to this quarter of the world" (*RS* 117). Tom is no longer merely the funny looking doll Tolkien brought to life in his children's stories.

In 1962, Tolkien reworked and republished the original poem about Tom and wrote a new one about him. In the 1962 collection, containing these and other poems, these works are portrayed as being taken from the margins of the *Red Book of Westmarch*, the Hobbit collection that also included *The Lord of the Rings*

(Scull and Hammond 2017b: 30-33). To summarize, Tom Bombadil was not originally a part of the Middle-earth *legendarium*. He was 'drawn in' because the story needed an adventure.

What Does Tom Bombadil Represent?

The very fact that there are so many theories concerning what Tom is and what he represents should give us pause. It may indicate that those who believe the enigma is unsolvable are, in fact, correct. It may also indicate that we are still missing important information. I would like to suggest, however, that there is sufficient evidence to allow us to state *with some reservation* what Tom most likely represents and to state *with certainty* what Tom is and is not.

First, what does Tom Bombadil represent? According to Tolkien, Tom "represents something that I feel important" (*Letters* 178). Tolkien also mentions several of these things that Tom represents. But do the things Tolkien explicitly mentions point to something deeper? Several letters provide important clues that, when considered together and compared with what is said about Tom and Goldberry in the narrative, shed significant light on this aspect of the enigma. First, consider what Tolkien writes in Letter 142. Here Tolkien says:

> *The Lord of the Rings* is of course a fundamentally religious and Catholic work; unconsciously so at first, but consciously in the revision. That is why I have not put in, or have cut out, practically all references to anything like 'religion', to cults or practices, in the imaginary world. For the religious element is absorbed into the story and the symbols. (*Letters* 172)

The religious element could not be explicit because, as Tolkien explains in another letter, the Third Age "was not a Christian world" (*Letters* 220).

Most readers of Tolkien know that he was devoutly Roman Catholic. But most do not consider the potential ramifications this has for the Bombadil enigma. Many readers are even surprised that Tolkien says *The Lord of the Rings* is "a fundamentally religious and Catholic work." There are no churches in the story, no priests, no formal worship, and nothing that looks explicitly religious, much less Roman Catholic. But Tolkien explains this here (and elsewhere). He says the religious element, which for Tolkien is a Roman Catholic religious element, "is absorbed into the story and symbolism." Christian elements cannot be explicit in a fictional world that exists thousands of years before Christianity.

I suggest that certain elements of Tolkien's Roman Catholicism were 'absorbed into' the character of Tom Bombadil. These were specific emphases that Tolkien believed were important enough to have represented in Middle-earth even though they could not be mentioned explicitly. Tolkien elaborates on these specific emphases in his letters. In Letter 144 (April 25, 1954), for example, Tolkien says, "even in a mythical Age there must be some enigmas, as there always are. Tom Bombadil is one (intentionally)" (*Letters* 174).

This comment is significant. Here Tolkien says that Tom is an *intentionally* enigmatic part of the story. In other words, Tolkien meant Tom to be mysterious. Later in the same letter, Tolkien makes a lengthier comment about Tom. He says:

> Tom Bombadil [...] represents something that I feel important, though I would not be prepared to analyze the feeling precisely. I would not, however, have left him in, if he did not have some kind of function. I might put it this way. The story is cast in terms of a good side, and a bad side, beauty against ruthless ugliness, tyranny against kingship, moderated freedom with consent against compulsion that has long lost any object save mere power, and so on; but both sides in some degree, conservative or destructive, want a measure of control. But if you have, as it were taken 'a vow of poverty', renounced control, and take your delight in things for themselves without reference to yourself, watching, observing, and to some extent knowing, then the question of the rights and wrongs of power and control might become utterly meaningless to you, and the means of power quite valueless. It is a natural pacifist view, which always arises in the mind when there is a war. (*Letters* 178-79)

Tolkien describes Tom here as "representing something" that Tolkien believes to be important. He mentions a vow of poverty, renunciation of control, delighting in things for themselves, and pacifism.

In Letter 153 (September, 1954), Tolkien explains that Tom "is *master* in a peculiar way: he has no fear, and no desire of possession or domination at all. He merely knows and understands about such things as concern him in his natural little realm" (*Letters* 192). He is not "master" in the sense of being an owner or having dominion. He is "master" in a different sense. Again, we see the lack of desire for possession, and again we see a delighting in his own natural realm. Tolkien then explains that Tom represents something important, namely rational knowledge of the external world (*Letters* 192).

Francis of Assisi: The Little Poor Man

In order to understand what Tolkien is doing with Tom Bombadil, we must first know something about the founder of the Franciscan order. Francis of Assisi was born in late September in the year 1182 (House 2001: 14). His life story has been told and retold in hundreds of works ranging from adulatory hagiography to scholarly biography. Many elements of Franciscan thought and practice are similar to those found in all monastic orders: contemplation, prayer, participation in the life of the church, among others. However, there are certain characteristics that are distinctive to Francis and his order.

One of the first things many authors mention is that Francis belonged to the tradition of "holy fools" (Bodo 1995: 1-3; House 2001: xv; Rohr 2014: xxi, 34). Francis, so the story goes, said to his followers: "The Lord has told me that he wanted to make a new fool of me" (Rohr 2014: xxi). He saw himself as a troubadour for God and told his first followers: "We are the jongleurs of God" (Brother Ramon 1994: 19). In the twelfth and thirteenth centuries, troubadours wrote and sang lyric poems about love. The jongleurs were more like minstrels or court jesters, singing, *juggling*, and performing acrobatic feats (Chesterton 1957: 59-74). Francis, as a jongleur, was a "holy fool." As a jongleur of God, Francis was often engaged in cheerful singing and almost child-like behavior (Bodo 1995: 35, 67, 124; Brother Ramon 1994: 21, 51; Chesterton 1957: 48, 70, 116; House 2001: 74).

As a troubadour, Francis wrote songs such as the "Canticle of the Sun." This famous song reflects another well-known characteristic of Francis, his love for all of God's creatures. His encounters with animals are the stuff of legend, and, as Chesterton observes, they take on the form of fairy-stories (Chesterton 1957: 132).[5] He speaks and preaches to the animals, rocks, trees, and considers himself the brother of all God's creatures (Bodo 1995: 37; Brother Ramon 1994: 134; House 2001: 108, 147, 177). Some Franciscan authors have described Francis's ability to communicate with animals as something like a reversal of the Fall (Bodo 1995: 26; Brother Ramon 1994: 113). Francis becomes like pre-fallen Adam in the Garden of Eden.

---

5 According to Oronzo Cilli (2019, 54), Tolkien had a copy of Chesterton's biography of Francis in his personal library. This does not prove that Tolkien read the biography, but if Tolkien did read it and if he noticed Chesterton's remark about fairy stories, it may have sparked ideas in his mind.

Another thing that sets Francis apart is his radical vow of poverty. Francis renounced all personal possessions, and his followers were to do the same (Bodo 1995: 1-3; House 2001: 103; Thoman 2020: 56, 195). Richard Rohr (2014: 93) observes that "power, prestige, and possessions were of no interest" to Francis. This view of poverty goes beyond mere monetary factors. It is also directly tied to his view of violence. Francis argued that if a person owns possessions, he will need weapons to defend them (Bodo 1995: 7). Francis rejected the use of physical weapons. His view of violence is illustrated well in the way he thought of the Crusades, which were ongoing during his lifetime. He believed "that crusades should be fought with words not swords" (House 2001: 143). Or, as Chesterton (1957: 114) put it, Francis believed it was "better to create Christians than to destroy Moslems."

All of these things, and especially the vow of poverty, remind us of Tom Bombadil. Of course, these similarities between Francis and Tom do not by themselves serve as definitive proof, but is there anything more concrete that might lend weight to the idea that Tom Bombadil represents certain elements of Franciscan spirituality? Yes, there is. Many Christian readers of *The Lord of the Rings* have observed the correspondence between significant dates in the Fellowship's journey and dates in the traditional Christian calendar. For example, the Fellowship departs from Rivendell on December 25, the traditional date of the birth of Christ, and the Ring is destroyed on March 25, the traditional date of the crucifixion (Pearce 2015: 136).

If Tolkien is using dates as part of the way he absorbs the religious element into the story, might there be any significance to the dates associated with Tom Bombadil? According to the timeline of events in Appendix B of *The Lord of the Rings*, the hobbits meet Tom Bombadil on September 26 (*LotR* 1091). This is significant because many works (especially older ones) mention September 26 as Francis of Assisi's birthday (Little 1897: 82; O'Reilly 1926: 3). Of course, this may be a coincidence, but when considered together with what Tolkien says about Tom representing a vow of poverty, pacifism, and a love of nature, and the way he is described as always singing and behaving in an almost child-like manner, the case appears stronger. And it matters little whether September 26 actually was Francis's birthday. What matters is that it was celebrated as his date of birth by enough people to become a traditional date and make it into books that would have been available to Tolkien.

Additional evidence is available when we turn to Goldberry. Tom is utterly devoted to Goldberry. The first time we encounter Tom, he is using a large leaf to carry white water-lilies to her (*LotR* 119). When we first see her, she is seated with pots containing white lilies at her feet (*LotR* 123). From the early medieval period onward, white lilies were used as symbols of the Virgin Mary. Mary is often depicted in medieval paintings of the Annunciation with white lilies in pots at her feet. In some of these paintings, Gabriel is holding a white lily in the presence of Mary (Steffler 2002: 22). If Tom represents a Franciscan element in the story and if Goldberry represents Mary to some degree, this would explain Tom's utter devotion to her. Why? Because in addition to poverty, pacifism, singing, and a love of nature, Francis is known for his maximalist Mariology and extreme Marian devotion (Fehlner 2008: 63).

Another interesting thing we observe in Tolkien's story is Goldberry's song as the hobbits approach Tom's house. She sings:

> *Now let the song begin! Let us sing together*
> *Of sun, stars, moon and mist, rain and cloudy weather,*
> *Light on the budding leaf, dew on the feather,*
> *Wind on the open hill, bells on the heather,*
> *Reeds by the shady pool, lilies on the water:*
> *Old Tom Bombadil and the River-daughter!* (*LotR* 122)

By itself, this might not mean much, but when considered in light of the previous observations, it potentially provides some corroborating evidence. One of the most famous works of Francis of Assisi is his song "The Canticle of the Sun." In this song, he sings of the sun, moon, stars, weather, and wind. Of course, there is not a one-to-one correspondence between Goldberry's song and Francis's song, and we should not expect one, but there is substantial overlap in terms of the content and theme. Both celebrate these parts of nature. Given the other similarities, the song becomes a stronger clue.

Finally, consider Tom's often comical behavior. Chesterton describes Francis as a "jester," explaining that the freedom Francis found in being a servant was a "freedom almost amounting to frivolity" (1957: 78). The dramatic nature of Francis's conversion resulted in his decision "to become more and more of a fool; he would be the court fool of the King of Paradise" (Chesterton 1957: 83). Tom's jester-like manner also belies a deeper dignity.

I am not suggesting that Tom Bombadil *is* Francis of Assisi, or even a Franciscan. Nor am I suggesting that Goldberry *is* the Virgin Mary (or Clare of Assisi or Lady Poverty). What I am suggesting is the possibility that, as Tolkien made *The Lord of the Rings* a more religious work in his revisions by 'absorbing' specifically Roman Catholic religious elements into the story and its symbolism, he may have deliberately absorbed some elements of a specifically Franciscan spirituality into the character of Tom Bombadil. Tom, then, might be the embodiment or representative of something Tolkien believed was needed in the story: a particular aspect of Roman Catholic spirituality exemplified by Francis, specifically a renunciation of power and possessions, a pacifistic attitude, a love of nature, a devotion to Mary, and an almost childlike penchant for joyful song. It is a form of spirituality that is a unique way of responding to the Creator and his creation.

Objections immediately occur. For example, Tom Bombadil and Goldberry are married. Some will protest that Franciscans are not married. Regardless of the fact that the Third Order of Franciscans does permit marriage (House 2001: 194), this objection is only relevant if I were suggesting that Tom *is* Francis or *is* a Franciscan. He is neither. Tom is not the kind of symbol that has a one-to-one correspondence with some other thing. Tom is a strange creature who *represents* certain elements of something Tolkien believed to be important but could not explicitly include in the story. There is no one-to-one correspondence between Tom and that which he represents. There couldn't be. This is why it also does not matter that Tolkien never changed Tom's physical description or his oddly-colored clothing. He always looked like the little toy that belonged to his son. He always wore the clothes that the doll wore. Tolkien did not describe Tom wearing a friar's robe. That would have been to include the religious element too explicitly and anachronistically.[6]

6 It is worth noting that Tolkien visited Assisi while on vacation with his daughter Priscilla. Scull and Hammond (2017a: 493-98; 2017b: 582) describe this visit in some detail.

What is Tom Bombadil?

If my suggestion about what Tom *represents* is accurate to any degree, it still does not answer the question concerning exactly what kind of being Tom *is* within the cosmology of Arda. On this point, the evidence definitively indicates that Tom is not a Middle-earth being at all. In order to explain what I mean, it is necessary to examine one more Tolkien letter, tucked away in Wayne Hammond and Christina Scull's *The Lord of the Rings: A Reader's Companion*, and therefore rarely mentioned in debates over Tom's nature. In this letter, Tolkien says the following in response to a question about Tom Bombadil:

> I think there are two answers: (i) External (ii) Internal; according to (i) Bombadil just came into my mind independently and got swept into the growing stream of *The Lord of the Rings*. The original poem about him, in the curious rhythm which characterizes him, appeared in the Oxford Magazine at some time not long before the war. According to (ii), I have left him where he is and not attempted to clarify his position, first of all because I like him and he has at any rate a satisfying geographical home in the lands of *The Lord of the Rings*; but more seriously because in any world or universe devised imaginatively (or imposed simply upon the actual world) there is always some element that does not fit and opens as it were a window into some other system. You will notice that though the Ring is a serious matter and has great power for all the inhabitants of the world of *The Lord of the Rings* even the best and the most holy, it does not touch Tom Bombadil at all. So Bombadil is 'fatherless', he has no historical origin in the world described in *The Lord of the Rings*. (Hammond and Scull 2005: 133-34)

This is enormously important for understanding what we are to think of Tom Bombadil. The attempt to discover Tom's origin within Middle-earth has been such a difficult puzzle because *he has no origin within Middle-earth*.[7]

Based on what Tolkien himself wrote in this letter, it appears that he intentionally left an element in the story that he *knew* was inconsistent within the sub-created world of Middle-earth. This is probably why there are so many plausible theories about what Tom Bombadil is. He has certain attributes that are similar to a variety of beings within Middle-earth – Valar, Maiar, Elves, etc. But no one

7 The same basic idea is communicated in an unpublished 1964 letter to Przemysław Mroczkowski (Mathison 2023). In that letter, Tolkien explains that Tom comes from "a different world." He has a different history and walked into the world of Middle-earth. Tolkien explains that Tom "was therefore wholly outside the closed circle of power and domination and hostilities in which all the other creatures are enmeshed." This is why the Ring did not affect him as it affected every other being who did have their origin in Middle-earth.

can nail down with absolute certainty which of these he is because he isn't *any* of them. He came into that world *from the outside*, from a different world with a different system and a different history. He is a character from a different tale who was drawn in to Middle-earth.[8] This is the element of truth in the theories about Tom that suggest he breaks the fourth wall. Only in this case, Tom breaks not only the fourth wall but the boundaries between fictional worlds.

Tom Bombadil had his origins in a story Tolkien began telling his children in the 1920s. The world this character inhabited was not Middle-earth. Tolkien created other characters who existed in other worlds (for example, Mr. Bliss, Roverandom, and Farmer Giles of Ham), and he created stories about these characters. Tom Bombadil and his little realm began their existence as a separate sub-creation in the mind of J.R.R. Tolkien. That entire little realm, along with all of its characters (including Goldberry and Old Man Willow), was dropped into the middle of the Old Forest because, as Tolkien was writing *The Lord of the Rings*, he felt that the four hobbits needed an adventure along the way (*Letters* 192). This helps us understand why both Tom and Gandalf make a point of observing that Tom will not step beyond the boundaries of his land. That little realm retains its own boundaries and characteristics even though it now co-exists with Middle-earth in the Old Forest.

Tolkien knew that Tom had no origin within Middle-earth, but keeping Tom allowed him a means to do something he felt was necessary. It enabled him to open a window into another world and another system. In the character of Tom Bombadil, he could absorb into the story of *The Lord of the Rings* certain Franciscan religious elements such as a lack of concern for possessions and a pacifistic perspective on war.

8 The difficulty we have in understanding who or what Tom Bombadil is would be the same kind of difficulty we would face if the hobbits had run across Roverandom the dog or Mr. Bliss in the middle of the Old Forest. To use a contemporary film example, it would be as if the Avengers encountered Darth Vader in one of their adventures. It's the intersection of two different fictional worlds.

Conclusion

Every serious fan of Tolkien knows that he was obsessive about achieving internal consistency within his sub-created world. It is why he was not able to publish the *Silmarillion* within his own lifetime. I believe that the widespread knowledge of Tolkien's obsession for internal consistency is one reason debates about Tom Bombadil have continued for as long as they have. Readers who know about Tolkien's personality naturally assume that he made Tom completely consistent within the sub-created world of Arda and Middle-earth. However, in this one case, that assumption is incorrect. Tom Bombadil is a non-Middle-earth being who walked into Middle-earth. Tolkien knew this, but keeping Tom in Middle-earth provided Tolkien a means by which he might absorb into the story of *The Lord of the Rings* the Roman Catholic religious element that was so important to him personally.

Tom Bombadil has always been and will likely always remain something of an enigma. Barring the discovery of more letters or documents containing previously lost evidence, we may never have absolute certainty about everything Tolkien was doing with this character. We do know that he represented something Tolkien believed was important to include in the story. As Tolkien indicated, in a world threatened by total destruction, a world in which both sides are striving for control, it is important to include the viewpoint of a character who has no interest in power or possessions. It was important for Tolkien to include a character with proto-Franciscan sensibilities.

Tolkien's own opinion of this Franciscan sensibility appears to be that of Rivendell, and

> the view of Rivendell seems to be that it is an excellent thing to have represented, but that there are in fact things with which it cannot cope; and upon which its existence nonetheless depends. Ultimately, only the victory of the West will allow Bombadil to continue, or even to survive. Nothing would be left for him in the world of Sauron. (*Letters* 179)

In short, it appears that Tolkien believes that the kind of spirituality represented by Tom Bombadil is a good thing in itself, but it cannot cope with a malicious tyrant intent on taking over the world and destroying everything in his path. In such cases, the free peoples of all nations must come together and fight if anything good, including the House of Tom Bombadil, is to survive.

About the Author

Keith A. Mathison is professor of systematic theology at Reformation Bible College in Sanford, Florida. He earned his BA from Houston Baptist University (now Houston Christian University), his MA from Reformed Theological Seminary and his PhD from Whitefield Theological Seminary. He is the author of several books including *Toward a Reformed Apologetics* and *The Lord's Supper*. He has also contributed chapters to several books including *Theology and Tolkien: Practical Theology*. He enjoys bad puns, the sound of the ocean, and all things J.R.R. Tolkien. He lives in Florida with his wife and a Yorkie named Bella.

Bibliography

Beier, Barb. n.d. "Bombadil Discovered." <http://tolkien.cro.net/else/bbeier.html> (accessed 3 April, 2023).

Bodo, Murray. 1995. *The Way of St. Francis: The Challenge of Franciscan Spirituality for Everyone*. Cincinnati, OH: St. Anthony Messenger Press.

Brother Ramon. 1994. *Franciscan Spirituality*. London: SPCK.

Carpenter, Humphrey. 2000a. *J.R.R. Tolkien: A Biography*. Boston, MA: Houghton Mifflin.

(ed.). 2000b. *The Letters of J.R.R. Tolkien*. Boston, MA: Houghton Mifflin.

Chesterton, G.K. 1957. *Saint Francis of Assisi*. New York: Image.

Cilli, Oronzo. 2019. *Tolkien's Library: An Annotated Checklist*. Edinburgh: Luna Press Publishing.

Fehlner, Peter. 2008. "The Franciscan Mariological School and the Coredemptive Movement." *Marian Studies* 59, Art. 8: 59-88.

Flieger, Verlyn. 2017. *There Would Always Be a Fairy Tale*. Kent, OH: The Kent State University Press.

Foster, Robert. 1978. *The Complete Guide to Middle-earth*. New York: Ballantine Books.

Fuller, Edmund. 1968. "The Lord of the Hobbits. J.R.R. Tolkien." In Neil D. Isaacs and Rose A. Zimbardo (eds.). *Tolkien and the Critics: Essays on J.R.R. Tolkien's The Lord of the Rings*. Notre Dame, IN: University of Notre Dame Press, 17-39.

Hammond, Wayne and Christina Scull. 2005. *The Lord of the Rings: A Reader's Companion*. Boston, MA: Houghton Mifflin.

Hargrove, Gene. 1986. "Who is Tom Bombadil?" *Mythlore* 13.1: 20-24.

HEAD, Ronan J. 2008. “Tolkien: Tom Bombadil as God.” *By Common Consent.* 8 May 2003. <https://bycommonconsent.com/2013/05/08/tolkien-tom-bombadil-as-god/> (accessed 3 April, 2023).

HOUSE, Adrian. 2001. *Francis of Assisi.* New Jersey: Hidden Spring.

JENSEN, Steuard. 2002. “What is Tom Bombadil?” 27 October 2002. <http://tolkien.slimy.com/essays/Bombadil.html> (accessed 3 April, 2023).

LITTLE, W. J. Knox. 1897. *St. Francis of Assisi: His Times Life and Work.* London: Isbister and Company Limited.

MATHISON, Keith A. 2020. “The Bombadil Enigma” 16 June 2020. <https://www.keithmathison.org/post/the-bombadil-enigma> (accessed 9 September, 2023).

2023. “The Bombadil Enigma, Part Two: The Mroczkowski Letter” 31 March 2023. <https://www.keithmathison.org/post/the-bombadil-enigma-part-two-the-mroczkowski-letter> (accessed 3 April, 2023).

NOAD, Charles E. 1991. “The Natures of Tom Bombadil: A Summary.” In T.A. Shippey et al. *Leaves From the Tree: J.R.R. Tolkien's Shorter Fiction.* London: The Tolkien Society.

NOEL, Ruth S. 1977. *The Mythology of Middle-earth.* Boston, MA: Houghton Mifflin.

O'REILLY, W. 1926. *St. Francis at Assisi.* Dublin: Catholic Truth Society of Ireland.

PARENTE, Pietro, Antonio PIOLANTE, and Salvatore GAROFALO. 1951. *Dictionary of Dogmatic Theology.* Trans. Emmanuel Doronzo. Milwaukee, WI: The Bruce Publishing Company.

PEARCE, Joseph. 2015. *Frodo's Journey.* Charlotte, NC: Saint Benedict Press.

PETTY, Anne C. 2003. *Tolkien in the Land of Heroes.* Cold Spring Harbor, NY: Cold Spring Press.

ROHR, Richard. 2014. *Eager to Love: The Alternative Way of Francis of Assisi.* Cincinnati, OH: Franciscan Media.

SCULL, Christina and Wayne G. HAMMOND. 2017a. *The J.R.R. Tolkien Companion and Guide. Volume 1: Chronology.* Revised and expanded edition. First edition 2005. Boston and New York: Houghton Mifflin.

2017b. *The J.R.R. Tolkien Companion and Guide. Volume 2: Reader's Guide Part One: A–M.* Revised and expanded edition. First edition 2005. Boston and New York: Houghton Mifflin.

SECORD, Levi. 2013. “Who is Tom Bombadil?” 15 January 2013. <http://whoistombombadil.blogspot.com> (accessed 3 April, 2023).

Seth, Priya. 2018. “Tom Bombadil: Cracking the ‘Enigma’ Code.” 10 January 2018. <https://priyasethtolkienfan.wordpress.com> (accessed 3 April, 2023).

Shippey, Tom. 2003. *The Road to Middle-earth*. Boston, MA: Houghton Mifflin.

Steffler, Alva William. 2002. *Symbols of the Christian Faith*. Grand Rapids, MI: William B. Eerdmans Publishing.

Theories About Tom Bombadil. 2022. *Fandom*. 9 June 2022. <https://lotr.fandom.com/wiki/Theories_about_Tom_Bombadil> (accessed 3 April, 2023).

Thoman, Bret. 2020. *A Knight and a Lady: A Journey into the Spirituality of Saints Francis and Clare*. Kansas City, MO: Pax Publishing.

Zimbardo, Rose A. 1968. “Moral Vision in *The Lord of the Rings*.” In Neil D. Isaacs and Rose A. Zimbardo (eds.). *Tolkien and the Critics: Essays on J.R.R. Tolkien's The Lord of the Rings*. Notre Dame, IN: University of Notre Dame Press, 100-08.

Claudio A. Testi

Aquinas, Tolkien, and the Music of Niggle

Abstract

In this article I would like to explain the relationship between Tolkien and Aquinas (and theology in general), and then examine in detail a Tolkienian theological question that I believe has received little study. In particular, I will try to demonstrate that:

- Tolkien's writings do not express a completely Thomistic perspective.
- Tolkien, instead, was fundamentally a narrator because, for him, theology lies in the function of the stories, therefore he wrote theological passages above all to give coherence to his stories.
- Nevertheless, in Tolkien's work, there is profound theological content, as I will show by analysing "Leaf by Niggle", his letters, and his *legendarium*.

I Introduction

J.R.R. Tolkien and Thomas Aquinas are my two main 'intellectual loves' and the center of my scientific production. No one in the world would be happier than I if Tolkien's works could be said to be Thomistic in the strictest sense; but this is not the case, as I have already shown analytically in other essays.[1] Here, I would like to briefly explain my position on the relationship between Tolkien and Aquinas (and theology in general), and then examine in detail a Tolkienian theological question that I believe has received little study.

In particular, I will first try to demonstrate that Tolkien's writings do not express a completely Thomistic perspective, as can be clearly seen in the Music of the Ainur and in the Elvish philosophy with regards to fate. Instead, Tolkien was fundamentally a narrator because, for him, theology lies in the function of the stories. Therefore, he wrote theological passages above all to 'explain' and to give coherence to his stories.

1 See: Testi 2007; Testi 2012 ; Testi 2016; Testi 2019; Testi 2020; Testi "Tolkien and Aquinas on Death" (forthcoming).

Nevertheless, in Tolkien's work, there is profound theological content, as I will show by analyzing "Leaf by Niggle", which thematizes in an original way how sub-creation can flow into creation. I will then show that this theological idea is present not only in this story but also in his essays, his letters, and his *legendarium*. Finally, I will conclude by saying that, based on what I know, this is a truly original philosophical-theological idea of Tolkien's.

II The Music of the Ainur: Tolkien and Aquinas

II.1 The Music of the Ainur

The "Ainulindalë," or Music of the Ainur, is an Elvish tradition that is essentially about the creation of the world. In the draft that Tolkien wrote in 1951,[2] which was later also merged into *The Silmarillion* of 1977, many phases are distinguished, among which I recall here the five fundamental ones:

1. Eru creates the Ainur.
2. The Ainur develop the themes proposed by Eru and, during the perfomance, Melkor introduces a dissonance.
3. Eru shows the Ainur an image of their Music.
4. Eru sends the Secret Fire by saying the word *Eä*, causing this image to become real.
5. Some of the Ainur (Valar or Maiar) physically enter Eä.

Some scholars have seen a re-narration of the Christian idea of the creation of our world by God in this process. If this were the case, however, it should be said that the Elves were not good Christian theologians! As Tolkien himself admits, in this mythology the created world is already affected by evil, the dissonance of Melkor is already present in phase 2, while, in Genesis, evil enters the world after the original sin.[3]

In the passing from phase 3 to 4, some authors have noted a strong similarity to the metaphysics of Thomas Aquinas, who distinguished two fundamental 'principles' in all created entities. First, there is the essence (*essentia*), or *what*

2 Christopher Tolkien labels this "Ainulindalë D" (see *MR* 29-39).
3 Cf. *Letters* 286 and Testi (2018: 25ff.).

entities are. For example, the essence of a man is his humanity. Second, there is the act of existing (*actus essendi*). The idea of 'humanity' does not necessarily imply that a man actually exists in the world; a unicorn has an essence but not an existence. The act of existence must then be distinguished from the essence of the entity because the essence only 'explains' *what* a thing is (in this case, it is a man), not *whether* a thing is.

In fact, the image that Eru shows to the Ainur (phase 3) could be seen as the essence of the world, which alone is not enough to make the world exist: for this, we need the subsequent act of existence, which Eru confers by saying the word *Eä* (phase 4). But if this is true, then it is also true that Elvish mythology differs from Thomistic metaphysics because, for Thomas, we find this distinction in every creature (even in the angels, and therefore also in the Ainur), while in the creation of the Ainur (phase 1) there is no mention of their passing from essence to existence.

II.2 Fate and Free Will

The themes of fate and free will are intimately linked to the Music of the Ainur, as shown by "Fate and Free Will," a treatise on Elvish philosophy written by Tolkien after 1968. It begins with some philological considerations for defining two Quenya words. *Umbar* (*amarth* in Sindarin) is "the order and conditions of the physical world (or of Eä in general) as far as established and pre-ordained at Creation" (*NME* 227). *Ambar* (*amar* in Sindarin) are, by contrast, "processes of the Earth (as established at its Creation directly or mediately by Eru), which was part of Eä, the Universe; and so approached in some uses the sense 'Fate'" (*NME* 227).

The Elvish philosophy of fate outlined here can be summarized by three fundamental principles:

1. Eru fixes physical events in *umbar*, and *ambar* is the 'historical' process that will bring them about.
2. The intentional free will of an individual is not included in *umbar-ambar*.
3. Eru does not immediately know how a free individual will react to an event fixed in *umbar*.

Point 3, therefore, paints Eru as *not omniscient* because, at first, he does not know how free creatures will react in the face of certain events, similar to the author of a story who does not immediately know how his characters will behave:

> The author is not in the tale in one sense, yet it all proceeds from him (and what was in him), so that he is present all the time. Now while composing the tale he may have certain general designs (the plot for instance), and he may have a clear conception of the character (independent of the particular tale) of each feigned actor. But *those are the limits of his "foreknowledge"*. Many authors have recorded the feeling that one of their actors "comes alive" as it were, and does things that were not foreseen at all [...] so, some of the Eldarin philosophers ventured to say, it was with Eru. (*NME* 230, emphasis added)

These considerations are sufficient for understanding the weakness of Elvish theology, which basically considers God (Eru) in an anthropomorphic way. He is seen 'only' as a very powerful entity, but somehow immersed in time, because He knows something (free choices) only 'after' these have occurred. If this were the case, Eru, as well as not being omniscient, would not even be omnipotent (in fact, He *cannot* know free choices in advance) nor would he be Thomas's *ipsum esse subsistens.*

For Aquinas, in fact, God is the Being subsisting per se, a pure act without potentiality, whose essence is precisely identical to His existence; God's essence is His act of being, and His act of being is His essence. This also means that *the act with which God creates is God's being, and the act of understanding is God's being.* If this were not so, God's being and activity could be separated, and He would no longer be pure and simple act. Because of this simplicity and actuality outside of any temporal flow, He is omniscient because He is His act of understanding and His act of creating:

> God knows all things whatsoever that in any way are. Some of them may not be in act now, still they were, or they will be; and God is said to know all these with the knowledge of vision: *for since God's act of understanding, which is His being,* is measured by eternity; and since eternity is without succession, *comprehending all time, the present glance of God extends over all time, and to all things which exist in any time, as to objects present to Him.* (Aquinas, *ST* I.14.9, emphasis added)

We could thus say that God is the creating and knowing act that 'now' (in the timeless sense) creates and knows everything in the same act. He creates Abraham Lincoln 'now,' just as he creates Tolkien, *The Lord of the Rings*, or this paper 'now.' In this way, He also knows 'now' the free choices of every person – which, being something and not nothing, are created by Him. This is why divine providence, unlike *umbar-ambar*, includes free will: "*The very act of free will* is traced to God as to a cause, it necessarily follows that everything happening from the exercise of free will *must be subject to divine providence*" (Aquinas, *ST* I.22.2 ad 4, emphasis added).

That is why the most appropriate image to express the relationship between creatures and God is that of a circle whose center (God) is equally distant from the points of the circumference (creatures) who are therefore known/wanted/created by God 'now,' in a single act that is His very essence:

> We must observe that God knows things differently from man. Man is subject to time and therefore knows things temporally, seeing some things as present, recalling others as past, and foreseeing others as future. But God is above the passage of time, and his existence is eternal. *So his knowledge is not temporal, but eternal.* [...] Eternity is *totally at once*, just as a point lacks parts that are distinct in location. For a point can be compared to a line in two ways: first as included in the line, whether at the beginning, middle or end, second as existing outside a line. A point within a line cannot be present to all the parts of the line, but in different parts of the line different points must be designated. But *a point outside the line can view all parts of the line equally, as in a circle, whose central point is indivisible and faces all the parts of the circumference and all of them are somehow present to it*, although not to one another. (Aquinas, *De Rationibus Fidei* c.10, emphasis added)

II.3 Tolkien: Theology in Function of Narration

This brief analysis is not aimed at denigrating Elvish philosophy, but at understanding the purpose of Tolkien's writing pages of theology within his *legendarium*. In fact, even here, he did not seek to write as a philosopher-theologian, but basically to endow his secondary world with a speculative *substratum* that made it coherent and credible. From this perspective, "The Music of the Ainur" and "Fate and Free Will" are mainly written in order to coherently 'explain' the origin of the conflict between light and darkness and some phrases contained in *The Lord of the Rings*, such as "a chance-meeting [between Gandalf and Thorin in Bree] as we say in Middle-earth" (1080; cf. *NME* 229) or that Bilbo "was meant to find the Ring" (*LotR* 56; cf. *NME* 228n3).

In summary, therefore, it is one thing to say that Tolkien knew Thomas and that he may have been influenced by him (cf. Testi 2019), but it is quite another to say that the philosophy of the *legendarium* is Thomistic. In fact, Elvish philosophy does not reflect some fundamental contents of Aquinas's perspective, such as the real distinction between essence and existence or the idea of God as pure act.

For this reason, in my opinion, the greatness of Tolkien lies in his being an unmatched narrator – one who wrote theological passages above all to give greater coherence to his stories and secondary world, and whose catholicity (shared also by Aquinas) is reflected in having sub-created a pagan world in harmony with Christian revelation (cf. Testi 2018).

III "Leaf by Niggle"

However, even with these clarifications, it remains true that within Tolkien's works there are deep spiritual, philosophical, and theological insights, as demonstrated in "Leaf by Niggle".

III.1 Premise

"Leaf by Niggle" was published in 1945, but was written between 1938-39 (*Letters* 320) and 1944 (*Letters* 112-13),[4] during which time Tolkien was working on *The Lord of the Rings* and his theory of sub-creation set out in "On Fairy-stories". The story is completely detached from the *legendarium* and remains unique in Tolkien's works, both for its genesis (conceived in a dream, *Letters* 113) and its writing (very fast and effortless, *Letters* 257).

The apparently light and banal story in fact contains an enormous wealth of content, so much so that critics have given divergent interpretations of it. However, I am convinced that the philosophical and theological content of the story has not yet been adequately disclosed: in order to try to do this, I will concentrate on some crucial moments of the narrative.

4 On the evolution and the composition of "Leaf by Niggle" see Testi, "Tree".

III.2 The Tree and the Forest

"Leaf by Niggle" tells of a sad painter who lives in the countryside and is unable to finish a painting (started with a leaf that later became a tree in a forest that reaches the mountains) because he is continually interrupted by unexpected visits (12). One day he has to ride his bicycle to the City downstream (17) and call a doctor for the wife of his neighbor, Parish, who is lame. As a consequence of his ride in bad weather, Niggle falls ill. As soon as he recovers, however, he has to leave for an already-planned trip and is led by a Driver to a Workhouse where he is cared for. Here, he works so hard that, after having understood his mistakes, he becomes a master at managing his time (24). Following a period of rest in the dark (25), two Voices decide to let him proceed to the next stage (29). So, on a sunny day (28), Niggle catches a train to a station where an uphill staircase (31) leads him to a bicycle that looks just like his own. He thus arrives in front of his Tree, which is now alive and perfectly realized. "'It's a gift!' he said. He was referring to his art, and also to the result; but he was using the word quite literally" (31).

The tree is identifiably his own, but different: "All the leaves he had ever laboured at were there, as he had imagined them rather than as he had made them; and there were others that had only budded in his mind, and many that might have budded, if only he had had time" (32). Moreover, the Tree's surroundings are still incomplete. To finish them, he understands that he needs Parish, who arrives and admires the beauty of the place (35). Back in the City, there is gossip about Niggle, and his painting disappears from the memory of its inhabitants, but the painter, helped by the Spring Tonic, completes *Niggle's Picture.* He then decides to depart to the next stage – the distant Mountains (33), of which it is said that "what lies beyond them, only those can say who have climbed them" (39).

The story ends with the two Voices appreciating the work that Niggle and Parish have done in that region, now renamed Niggle's Parish, which causes the two protagonists to laugh out loud (43).

III.3 The Central Theme of "Leaf by Niggle"

So what is "Leaf by Niggle" about? On different levels, it describes how something good, even if left unfinished (the painting in the countryside) and forgotten on a certain level (in the City), can be discovered (the Tree) on a subsequent one (Niggle's Parish) in a previously unimagined context (the Leaves that Niggle could imagine) of health, appreciation, joy, and completeness that go beyond imagination (what lies beyond the Mountains). The heart of the story is therefore the relationship between sub-creation and creation and how the former can, in a certain place, converge and exist at the same level as the latter: in other words, how the imagined picture in the countryside also concretely exists in Niggle's Parish.

From this point of view, "Leaf by Niggle" is a perfect commentary on these lines from "On Fairy-stories": "It is not difficult to imagine the peculiar excitement and joy that one would feel, if any specially beautiful fairy-story [the painting done by Niggle] *were found to be 'primarily' true* [the Tree within Niggle's Picture], its narrative to be history, without thereby necessarily losing the mythical or allegorical significance that it had possessed," (*TOFS* 78, italics and notes added). Or take this statement: "Probably every writer making a secondary world, a fantasy, every *sub-creator*, wishes in some measure to be a *real maker*, or hopes that he is *drawing on reality*: hopes that the peculiar quality of this secondary world [the painted Tree] (if not all the details) [the whole picture] are derived from Reality, or *are flowing into it* [the realized Tree and Niggle's Parish all the way to the Mountains]" (*TOFS* 77, italics and notes added).

Tolkien himself, who published "On Fairy-stories" together with "Leaf by Niggle" in 1964,[5] states that this is precisely the theme of "Leaf by Niggle". "Though one ["On Fairy-stories"] is an 'essay' and the other ["Leaf by Niggle"] is a 'story', they are related: by the symbol of the Tree and Leaf, and *by both touching in different ways on what is called in the essay 'sub-creation'*" (*TL* 5, emphasis added; see also Letter 195 quoted below).

5 The first edition of *TL* in fact contains only these two contributions, as well as a brief introductory note by Tolkien.

During the period in which he composed "Leaf by Niggle", "On Fairy-stories" and *The Lord of the Rings*, Tolkien truly believed that certain sub-creations (paintings, tales or others), even if abandoned or forgotten in this world, could in another place be found to be truly completed and appreciated. For him, this place was Heaven, as he explicitly said to his sons. "There is a place called 'heaven' where the *good here unfinished is completed* [Niggle's Parish concluded]; and where the *stories unwritten, and the hopes unfulfilled, are continued* [cf. the work done by Niggle with Parish]. We may laugh together yet… [see the finale of "Leaf by Niggle"]," he writes to his son Michael in 1941 (*Letters* 55, emphasis and notes added). And in 1945 he remarks to his son Christopher: "I think you are moved by *Celebrimbor* because it conveys a sudden sense of endless *untold* stories: mountains seen far away, never to be climbed, distant trees (*like Niggle's*) never to be approached – or if so only to become 'near trees' (unless in Paradise or *N's Parish*)" (*Letters* 110-11, emphasis added).

IV Niggle's Music

This theological intuition, although 'narrated' and not systematically argued as professional theologians do, is not restricted to the confines of "Leaf by Niggle", but is also found within the *legendarium*, as I will try to show below.

IV.1 Niggle and "Ainulindalë": A False Analogy

It is Tolkien himself who compares his mythology to "Leaf by Niggle":

> In my myth I have used 'subcreation' in a special way (not the same as 'sub-creation' as a term in criticism of art, though *I tried to show allegorically how that might come to be taken up into Creation* in some plane in my 'purgatorial' story Leaf by Niggle (Dublin Review 1945)) […] So in this myth, it is 'feigned' (legitimately whether that is a feature of the real world or not) that He gave special 'sub-creative' powers to certain of His highest created beings: that is a guarantee that what they devised and made should be given the reality of Creation. Of course within limits, and of course subject to certain commands or prohibitions. (*Letters* 195, emphasis added)

Now, within Tolkien's mythology, the text which thematizes these problems more than any other is certainly "The Music of the Ainur," as Tolkien himself states:

> The Valar or 'powers, rulers' were the first 'creation': rational spirits or minds without incarnation, created *before* the physical world. [...] The Ainur took part in the *making of the world as 'sub-creators'*: in various degrees, after this fashion. They interpreted according to their powers, and *completed in detail*, the Design propounded to them by the One. This was propounded first in musical or abstract form, and then in an 'historical vision'. In the first interpretation, the vast Music of the Ainur, Melkor introduced alterations, not interpretations of the mind of the One, and great discord arose. The One then presented this 'Music', including the apparent discords, as a visible 'history'. At this stage it had still only a validity, to which the validity of a 'story' among ourselves may be compared: it 'exists' *in* the mind of the teller, and derivatively in the minds of hearers, but *not on the same plane as teller or hearers. When the One (the Teller) said 'Let it Be', then the Tale became History, on the same plane as the hearers; and these could, if they desired, enter into it.* (*Letters* 284, emphasis added)

Returning to the parallels between the "Ainulindalë" and "Leaf by Niggle", one could therefore easily think that, just as Niggle enters his picture when it becomes real, so the Ainur enter their music [cf. phase 5 above] when its representation is caused to exist by Eru on their own plane [cf. phases 3-4]. But let us look at the reaction of the Valar to their entry into Eä:

> But behold! When the Valar entered into the World they were *at first astounded and at a loss*, for it was as if *naught was yet made which they had seen in vision*, and all was but on point to begin, and yet unshapen; and *it was dark*. For the Great Music had been but the growth and flowering of thought in the Timeless Halls, and the Vision only a foreshowing; but now they had entered in at the beginning of Time, and the Valar perceived that the World had been but foreshadowed and foresung, and they must achieve it. *So began their great labours* in wastes unmeasured and unexplored, and in ages uncounted and forgotten, until in the Deeps of Time and in the midst of the vast halls of the World there came to be that hour and that place where was made the habitation of the Children of Ilúvatar. And in this work the chief part was taken by Manwë and Aulë and Ulmo. But *Melkor*, too, was there from the first, and *he meddled in all that was done*, turning it, if he might, to his own desires and purposes; and he kindled great fires. When therefore Earth was young and full of flame Melkor coveted it, and he said to the Valar: 'This shall be my own kingdom! And I name it unto myself!' (*MR* 14, emphasis added; cf. 40)[6]

Clearly, the entry of the Valar into their realized sub-creation is extremely different from that of Niggle. When they enter, they first feel astounded and at

6 I'm citing this text from "Ainulindalë," written in 1946-48, because it is only in this version that the Valar's reaction to their entry into Eä and the work they subsequently carry out are described in greater detail. This passage is substantially preserved in the subsequent edition of 1951 (*MR* 31), while it is absent both in the "Ainulindalë" of 1917-18 (*BLT1* 57-58) and in that of the 1930s (*LR* 161).

a loss, while Niggle feels wonder and joy for the Tree received as a gift. The atmosphere is dark, while in Niggle's Picture the sun shines. Their surroundings are unshapen; there is nothing finished and perfect, while Niggle's Tree is perfectly finished. The Valar must then complete their work, like Niggle must finish with the surroundings of the Tree; but in Niggle's Picture this work will be carried out in an atmosphere of great serenity with no one to hinder it, while the Valar will continually have to face and repair the destruction wrought by Melkor.

It must therefore be concluded that the analogy between "Leaf by Niggle" and the entry of the Valar into their sub-creation is wrong and, moreover, a careful re-reading of the aforementioned Letter 153 shows that Tolkien himself mentioned these differences between the two narratives. Nevertheless, the theme of "Leaf by Niggle" can be found in the *legendarium*, still always within a musical horizon, and to this we now turn.

IV.2 Niggle and the Final Music: A Fitting Analogy

For the idea of a sub-creative vision taking real form, we must look not at the first but at the Final Music (or Second Music) that will be sung at the Great End, an element attested in *all* versions of the "Ainulindalë":

> [1917-18:] Never was there before, nor has there been since, such a *music* of immeasurable vastness of splendour; though it is said that *a mightier far shall be woven* before the seat of Ilúvatar by the *choirs of both Ainur and the sons of Men*[7] after the Great End. Then shall Ilúvatar's *mightiest themes be played aright*; for then Ainur and Men will know his mind and heart as well as may be, and all his intent. (*BLT1* 53, emphasis added)

> [1930s:] Never was there before, nor has there since been, a music so immeasurable, though it has been said that a greater still shall be made before Ilúvatar by the choirs of the Ainur and the *Children of Ilúvatar* after the end of days. *Then shall the themes of Ilúvatar be played aright, and take being in the moment of their playing, for all shall then understand his intent in their part, and shall know the comprehension each of each, and Ilúvatar shall give to their thoughts the secret Fire*, being well pleased. (*LR* 157, emphasis added)

---

7 Christopher Tolkien notes that, in later editions, "sons of Men" will be replaced with "Children of Ilúvatar", and considers this an unintended change on the part of his father, which is then strangely maintained to the end (*BLT1* 63). In this regard, however, it should be remembered that the *Athrabeth* (composed 1958-60) seems to confirm the presence of both Children of Ilúvatar in the performance of the second Music (*MR* 318-19, 333).

> [1948-51:] Never since have the Ainur made any music like to this music, though it has been said that a greater still shall be made before Ilúvatar by the choirs of the Ainur and the Children of Ilúvatar after the end of days. Then shall the themes of Ilúvatar *be played aright, and take Being in the moment of their utterance, for all shall then understand his intent in their part, and shall know the comprehension of each, and Ilúvatar shall give to their thoughts the secret fire*, being well pleased. (*MR* 9, emphasis added)

> [Published *Silmarillion*] Never since have the Ainur made any music like to this music, though it has been said that a greater still shall be made before Ilúvatar by the choirs of the Ainur and the Children of Ilúvatar after the end of days. *Then the themes of Ilúvatar shall be played aright, and take Being in the moment of their utterance, for all shall then understand fully his intent in their part, and each shall know the comprehension of each, and Ilúvatar shall give to their thoughts the secret fire*, being well pleased. (*Sil* 15-16, emphasis added)

This idea of a great final music has been present since the very first draft of "Ainulindalë" in 1917-18 (*BLT1*) and is preserved in the subsequent versions from the 1930s (*LR*), 1948-50 (*MR*) and 1951 (incorporated into the 1977 *Sil*). However, it was only from the 1930s (*LR*) that it was said that the themes sung by Men could be *taken to be* at the very moment in which they were uttered or thought, thanks to the Secret Fire conferred by Ilúvatar. This data is of great importance and, for this reason, it is necessary to try to understand these mysterious words. For this, "Leaf by Niggle" can be useful to us.

In fact, there are very important similarities between the Final Music and Niggle's work on Niggle's Picture. First, this Final Music isn't just the Ainur's business because Men will also take part. Likewise, Niggle needs Parish's cooperation to get his job done. It is therefore a "polyphonic" work in which everyone will know exactly what to do ("all shall then understand fully his intent in their part") and will understand the role of the others ("each shall know the comprehension of each"). This is exactly what happens with Niggle, who knows perfectly well what he has to do to complete the job ("but it needed continuing up to a definite point. Niggle saw the point precisely"; LN 33-34), in perfect agreement with Parish ("Niggle and Parish agreed exactly where to make the small house and garden"; LN 34-35).

Second, just as the Final Music is "at the end of the days" and not at the beginning, so Niggle's work takes place after his departure from the country and at the end of a long journey (which will continue beyond the Mountains). The settings are therefore both eschatological.

Third, as with the first Music, here too it will be a question of completing the themes proposed by Ilúvatar. Only this time, the themes "shall be played aright;" therefore, there will be no discordant notes or obstacles that will prevent the performance from being perfectly completed. The same thing happens with Niggle's work after his stay at the Workhouse, where he took care of himself and understood his limitations. This allowed him to reach the *definite point.*

Fourth, unlike ordinary sub-creation, in which the product is a secondary world placed on a different plane of existence compared to the primary one (so much so that, in the first Music, the *Eä* of Eru is necessary to give primary reality to the sub-creation of the Ainur), here, what is said and thought immediately becomes a reality placed on the same level of existence as the sub-creator ("take Being in the moment of their utterance [...] and Ilùvatar shall give to their thoughts the secret fire," *MR* 9). This is also thanks to the mysterious Secret Fire ("Ilúvatar shall give to their thoughts the secret fire"). The exact same thing happens with Niggle who, especially after drinking the Spring Tonic ("After drinking," LN 36), simply thinks of new flowers and plants ("Niggle would think of wonderful new flowers and plants," LN 36) and Parish 'physically' sets in place what Niggle thinks ("Parish also always knew exactly how to set them," LN 36).

IV.3 Other Confirmations

This final perspective is not only present in "Leaf by Niggle" and "Ainulindalë" but is also hinted at in "Mythopoeia," written between 1931 and 1935 (Scull and Hammond 620-22):

> In *Paradise* perchance the eye may stray
> from gazing upon everlasting Day
> [...]
> Salvation changes not, nor yet destroys,
> *garden nor gardener*, children nor their toys.
> Evil it will not see, for evil lies
> not in God's *picture* but in crooked eyes,
> not in the source but in malicious choice,
> and not in sound but in the tuneless voice.

> *In Paradise* they look no more awry;
> and though they make anew, they make no lie.
> Be sure they still will make, not being dead,
> and poets shall have *flames* upon their head,
> and harps whereon their faultless fingers fall:
> there each shall choose for ever from the All.
> (*TL* 90, emphasis added)

Here too, as in "Leaf by Niggle" and in the Music, Tolkien envisages an activity that will occur in a time and place different from the present ("Paradise"). Evil will be absent and what the sub-creator ("gardener") has sub-created ("garden") will be saved in a "picture" where the poets will be crowned with "flames" (a symbol of creative inspiration similar to the Secret Fire in the "Ainulindalë" or the Tonic in "Leaf by Niggle"). Thanks to this, they will continue to be sub-creators in a new way ("make anew"), and always in reference to the complete Whole ("the All").

An intuition along this same line can perhaps also be found in a dialogue between Gimli and Legolas in *The Lord of the Rings*, written by Tolkien in 1946-47 (Scull and Hammond 539):

> 'It is ever so with the things that Men begin: there is a frost in Spring, or a blight in Summer, and they fail of their promise,' [said Gimli]. 'Yet seldom do they fail of their seed,' said Legolas. 'And that will *lie in the dust and rot to spring up again in times and places unlooked-for. The deeds of Men will outlast us*, Gimli,' [Just as Niggle's picture, even though it is completely annihilated in the City, will survive on an even greater level of existence than the actual picture]. 'And yet come to naught in the end but might-have-beens, I guess,' said the Dwarf. 'To that the Elves know not the answer,' said Legolas. (*LotR* 873, emphasis and notes added)

Men are inconstant (just like Niggle) and yet their unfinished works, even if apparently forgotten (as will happen in the City with Niggle and his painting) will survive beyond the existence of the Dwarves and the immortal Elves. This means that what is unfinished will be found beyond the story of Eä (to which the Elves are linked), albeit in a mysterious way, so much so that Legolas admits that he does not have all the answers.

V Conclusion

In light of what is written above, we can affirm that, from the 1930s-50s, Tolkien deeply reflected on the existence of a time and a place where an *unfinished good (for example, an unfinished story or an unfinished painting) can be preserved and completed at the same level of existence as the artificer.* This horizon is sketched in "Mythopoeia" and in the "Ainulindalë" of the early 1930s, theorized in "On Fairy-stories" (1937-43), narrated in "Leaf by Niggle" (1942, published in 1945), shared with his children, mentioned in *The Lord of the Rings* (late 1940s), and confirmed in *Morgoth's Ring* (1951).

Furthermore, to my knowledge, this perspective is a truly original philosophical-theological idea, which I have not found written about by any other author (narrator, philosopher, or theologian).

Of course, the idea that true happiness somehow involves satisfying all our authentic desires is not new. Take three premodern definitions of happiness, the first of which is Aquinas's own:

> The name of beatitude is understood the ultimate perfection of rational or of intellectual nature; and hence it is that it is naturally desired, since everything naturally desires its ultimate perfection. (Aquinas, *ST* 1.62.1)
>
> Happiness is a state which is made perfect by the union of all good things. (Boethius, *De Consolatione Philosophiae*, 3.pr2)
>
> Happiness [...] includes a sufficiency of suitable benefits and excludes all need. (Anselm, *De Concordia Praescientiae et Praedestinationis* 3.13)

Thomas Aquinas even goes so far as to affirm that the well-being of the same body is required for perfect bliss: "For since it is natural to the soul to be united to the body; it is not possible for the perfection of the soul to exclude its natural perfection. Consequently, we must say that perfect disposition of the body is necessary, both antecedently and consequently, for that happiness which is in all ways perfect" (*ST* I-II.4.a6).

This thesis is obviously linked to the dogma of the resurrection of bodies. For Catholic theology, in fact, the human being will be resurrected with their physical body and thus live in a physical world, albeit a completely transformed one where there will be new heavens and a new earth. Thomas Aquinas tried to explore this mystery in various works (*SCG* 4.79-88; *Comm. Sent.* D.43-44, *ST* Suppl. 75-86). Without going into the merits of a very complex issue, it should be briefly recalled that for Aquinas, after the resurrection every human being will truly have their own body and all that pertains to it, such as limbs, hair and nails (*ST* Suppl. 80.a1-2), sex (*ST* Suppl. 81.a3; *SCG* 4.88), and the exercise of the senses (*ST* Suppl. 82.a3). This prospect is astonishing to us today, since the resurrection of the flesh is rarely discussed (even in religious circles). However, even considering this physical and bodily dimension to Christian eschatology, I have found no explicit reference to the fact that at the end of time man complete in body and soul will find his sub-creations fully realized on an unimaginable physical level as it happens in Tolkien's perspective.

In Tolkien, in fact, we find something more specific, because it is linked to the connection between sub-creation and creation. This astounding horizon is therefore, in my opinion, Tolkien's most original theological idea. Not being a systematic theologian, however, he explored and developed it as a great storyteller by writing profound and wonderful stories, novels and poems.

About the Author

Claudio A. Testi graduated with a degree in philosophy from the University of Bologna and obtained his PhD in Philosophy from the Pontifical Lateran University of Rome. He is President of the Philosophical Institute of Thomistical Studies of Modena and Co-Founder of the Italian Association for Tolkien Studies. He teaches Formal Logic at the Dominican Philosophical Seminary in Bologna and his publications range from exegetical studies on Aquinas's Metaphysics to essays in logic and epistemology. As Tolkien scholar, he has edited more than ten books on Tolkien and has written several articles on Tolkien (his "Tolkien's Work: Is it Christian or Pagan?" has been published on *Tolkien Studies* 10 (2010)). His book *Santi Pagani nella Terra di mezzo di Tolkien* (2015, ESD) has been issued in English in 2018 (*Pagan Saints in Tolkien's Middle-earth*, Walking Tree Publishers).

Bibliography

Anselm of Canterbury. 2000 [c. AD 1108]. *De Concordia Praescientiae et Praedestinationis et Gratiae Dei cum Libero Arbitrio*. In *Complete Philosophical and Theological Treatises of Anselm's of Canterbury*. Translated by Jasper Hopkins and Herbert Richardson. The Arthur J. Banning Press, Minneapolis, MN. <https://jasper-hopkins.info/DeConcordia.pdf> (accessed Jan 20 2023).

Aquinas, Thomas. [c. AD 1265]. *Summa Theologiae*. Translated by Aquinas Institute. Version 21.1210.1123 <https://www.aquinas.cc/la/en/~ST.I> (accessed Jan 20 2023).

[c. AD 1265b]. *De Rationibus Fidei*. Translated by the Aquinas Institute, <https://aquinas.cc/la/en/~DeRatio> (accessed Sept 21 2024)

Boethius, Anicius Manlius. 2009 [c. AD 524]. *De Consolatione Philosophiae*. Translated by W.V. Cooper. The Ex-classics Project. <https://www.exclassics.com/ consol/consol.pdf> (accessed Jan 20 2023).

Garth, John. 2022. "The Chronology of Creation." In Richard Ovenden and Catherine McIlwaine (eds.). *The Great Tales Never End*. Oxford: Bodleian Library Publishing, 70-87.

Scull, Christina and Wayne G. Hammond. 2006. *The J.R.R. Tolkien Companion and Guide. Reader's Guide*. First edition. London: HarperCollins.

Testi, Claudio A. 2007. "Tolkien, l'analogia e la verità delle fiabe." *Endóre* 9.10: 17-26.

2012. "Terra-di-mezzo tra paganesimo e rivelazione." *Realitas* 1: 27-48.

2015. "Analogy, Sub-Creation and Surrealism." *Hither Shore* 12: 178-93.

2018. *Pagan Saints in Middle-earth*. Cormarë Series 38. Zurich and Jena: Walking Tree Publishers.

2019. "Tolkien and Aquinas." In Roberto Arduini, Giampaolo Canzonieri, and Claudio A. Testi (eds). *Tolkien and the Classics*. Cormarë Series 42. Zurich and Jena: Walking Tree Publishers, 57-72.

2020. "Review of J. McIntosh, *The Flame Imperishable*." *Hither Shore* 17: 169-75.

forthcoming. "Tolkien and Aquinas on Death." In William Sherwood (ed.). *Tolkien 2019 – Proceedings of the 2019 Tolkien Conference*. Edinburgh: Luna Press Publishing. .

forthcoming. "From 'The Tree' to the 'Leaf by Niggle' up to the Mountains and Beyond."

Tolkien, J.R.R. 1977. *The Silmarillion*. Edited by Christopher Tolkien. London: George Allen & Unwin.

1981. *The Letters of J.R.R. Tolkien*. Edited by Humphrey Carpenter, with the assistance of Christopher Tolkien. London: George Allen & Unwin / Boston: Houghton Mifflin.

1983. *The Book of Lost Tales, Part One*. (The History of Middle-earth 1). Edited by Christopher Tolkien. London: George Allen & Unwin.

1987. *The Lost Road and Other Writings*. (The History of Middle-earth 5). Edited by Christopher Tolkien. London: Unwin Hyman.

1988. *Tree and Leaf*. First edition 1964. Second edition. London: Unwin Hyman

1993. *Morgoth's Ring*. (The History of Middle-earth 10). Edited by Christopher Tolkien. London: HarperCollins.

2004. *The Lord of the Rings*. 50th anniversary edition. First edition 1954-55. Boston, MA: Houghton Mifflin.

2008. *Tolkien On Fairy-Stories*. Edited by Verlyn Flieger and Douglas A. Anderson. London: HarperCollins.

2022. *The Nature of Middle-earth*. Edited by Carl F. Hostetter. London: HarperCollins.

Austin M. Freeman

Tolkien and Calvin: Five Convergences

Abstract

This chapter investigates five significant ways in which Tolkien's theology coheres with that of John Calvin. First, they both emphasize the importance of original language research and humanist study of the liberal arts. Second, they highlight the metaphysical impact of promises and covenants. Third, they target idolatry as a key theological enemy. Fourth, they exalt the created order as an avenue toward divine worship. Fifth, and most surprisingly to most, Tolkien fulfills all six of Calvin's criteria for a doctrine of God's providence.

"Why did it come to me? Why was I chosen?" a mournful Frodo asks about his being fated to bear the Ring of Power. "Such questions cannot be answered," Gandalf replies. "You may be sure that it was not for any merit that others do not possess: not for power or wisdom, at any rate. But you have been chosen" (*LotR* 61). Tolkien articulates a doctrine of unconditional election by God, and so we find the impetus to examine Tolkien's relationship to a hero more unlikely than a hobbit: John Calvin. What does the severe predestinarian Protestant have to do with jocular, comfortable, Catholic Tolkien? And he's French, to boot!

Aside from the fact that Calvin's image as cold, joyless, and dusty is a false one – and by the way, predestination is not the heart of his or of any other Reformed theologian's system – there are indeed several parallels between Tolkien and Calvin worth exploring. Nor are these mere surface-level parallels – such as the fact that both men were raised Roman Catholic and lost their mothers during childhood. Here I will dwell upon ideas that are central to both men: the importance of linguistic study, the beauty of the natural world, the metaphysical power of promises, and the nature of human freedom. In each of these, we shall find that Tolkien, completely unknowingly, aligns himself with the Genevan Reformer.[1]

Philology and Humanism

We begin broadly by noting that Tolkien and Calvin shared an interest in – and indeed a scholarly method rooted in – the discipline of philology and textual criticism. It is likely not necessary to expatiate on the importance of philology for Tolkien. By the Edwardian period, philology as a discipline had found success as a method by which scholars could reconstruct the lost history of humanity through the history of words and sound changes. This tied directly into the burgeoning field of comparative mythology and sparked the young Tolkien's imagination and his drive to explore the forgotten past.

From a young age, Tolkien had been fascinated with the epics and myths of the ancient world, but derived much of his pleasure from the sounds of the language itself. In danger of losing his scholarship at Oxford because he was busy reading Gothic rather than Greek and Latin, Tolkien soon changed course from the study of classics to the study of language directly. He saw in the histories of individual words a window into the human experience in different times and places.

By the time he was hired by the New English Dictionary (later Oxford English Dictionary) to produce etymologies and definitions, he was already acknowledged as an expert. While now of course widely known for his fantasy work, Tolkien was then globally renowned for his mastery of Old and Middle English philology. Nor did Tolkien keep his academic pursuits siloed from his faith. He frequently used his insights into Anglo-Saxon word-forms and their histories to illuminate theological points in the texts upon which he worked. His commentary on *Beowulf* shows how a single word like *féond* (158-159) or *slíðe* (175-176) may cast light on the dark recesses of pre-Christian Germanic religion.

1 A brief methodological note: I confine myself mostly to quotations from the 1559 edition of the *Institutes*, translated by Henry Beveridge. This is not because Calvin has no other important works, but because this is the work most familiar to a wide audience and because the *Institutes* are, after all, what Calvin intended them to be: a summary in one place of his key thoughts on Reformed doctrine and practice.

His own constructed languages, like Quenya, are inextricably connected to the Elvish contact with God (Eru) and his angels (the Valar).

Calvin, too, was trained in the same fields as Tolkien, though to a lesser degree of expertise. His first published work, a commentary on Seneca's *De Clementia*, demonstrates a combination of philological expertise, rhetorical skill, and comfort with the classics. Furthermore, Calvin drew upon the riches of the Middle Ages much as Tolkien did. Premier Reformation scholar Richard Muller notes that Calvin's works display a "blending of humanistic methods in rhetoric and philology with nominally scholastic materials" (2000: 15). Muller and others also deny that Calvin rejected medieval scholasticism or medieval thought wholesale, despite his protestations against the "*scholastici*," here most likely certain professors at the University of Paris. This means that Calvin, to a limited extent, shares with Tolkien an appreciation for the Middle Ages. In particular, Calvin seems to have enjoyed the work of Bernard of Clairvaux.

It must be said, however, that it was Luther rather than Calvin who stood in strict continuity with late medieval theology. Calvin's own thought, like Tolkien's, comes not from the technical and systematic realm but from the humanist one. The Swiss Reformation relied on the insights of humanism rather than the debates of the universities. Alister McGrath, in *The Intellectual Origins of the European Reformation* (2004: 125), explains how the turn *ad fontes* (to the original sources) was first made as a way of benefitting from the eloquence of the classical Latin writers. Much like the British Romanticism out of which Tolkien's own early thought arose (and indeed Romanticism lies in direct descent from it),[2] Christian humanism sought to emphasize the holistic beautification of all of life: art, music, poetry, law, and community. But humanism's renewed interest in philology and the classical languages inevitably turned toward a concern for accuracy in translations, and then toward accuracy in *biblical* translations.

The advances in philology soon revealed the inadequacies in Jerome's *Vulgate* and spurred new discoveries in the Hebrew and Greek texts of scripture that would have radical implications for theology. Picking up on the path laid out by Erasmus, Melanchthon, and Luther, Calvin developed his philological skill

2 On Tolkien and Romanticism, see Eilmann 2017 and Sherwood & Eilmann 2024.

predominantly in the service of rhetorical eloquence, but soon as a method of expounding the true meaning of scripture to the populace in commentaries and sermons. Ironically, then, Calvin's training in humanism, classics, and philology – the same training Tolkien underwent – resulted in his leaving the Roman Church, whereas Tolkien himself used these skills in its service.

Keeping the Covenant

In what follows I will offer four specific thematic parallels, organized in roughly ascending order of prominence, beginning with the idea of the metaphysical importance of promises. Calvin deploys the concept of *covenant* throughout his writings, though not to the degree that his theological descendants will eventually ascend. He takes his audience's familiarity with the idea more or less for granted. If Calvin were to offer a single concise definition, he would state that a covenant is a contractual obligation between two parties which includes blessings for obedience and curses for disobedience, administered by a mediator and solemnized by a "seal" or symbol. The two most prominent covenants in Christian theology perhaps loom so large that they become invisible again, like the giant's letters in C.S. Lewis's *Silver Chair*. These are of course the Old and New Testaments, and Calvin is right to point out that the Latin *testamentum* or testament is most properly equivalent to the Greek *diatheke* or covenant.

In brief, the Reformed use of covenant as a structuring principle in theology constitutes a trademark of the movement. In later developments after Calvin, we find God initially instituting a covenant of good works with Adam in the Garden, with the tree acting as the sign. With the invasion of sin, God introduces the covenant of grace, in which he binds himself to rescue humanity, manifesting ultimately in Christ's death and resurrection and the signs of baptism and the eucharist. In between are older administrations of the covenant of grace, most especially the Abrahamic and Mosaic covenant with Israel, under the sign of circumcision.

Tolkien speaks many times, directly and indirectly, of "the necessity of keeping promises (even those with intolerable consequences) that, together with observing prohibitions, runs through all Fairyland. This is one of the notes of the horns of Elfland, and not a dim note" (*TOFS* 74). As Tolkien's predecessor and influence G.K. Chesterton explains in "Ethics of Elfland," all fairy tales involve a prohibition. 'Live in the fairy king's castle for a year and a day, but tell nobody who you are.' 'You and I will share the results of our day's hunting, but you must not keep anything back from me.' In other words, we know that Tolkien views promising as a weighty and even mystical activity, such that his thought is consonant with the Reformed picture of covenant.[3]

We think here of the special blessing that Ilúvatar bestows on the Númenóreans after their faithful service in the First Age. Using Eärendil's star as a covenant sign that the island was prepared (and indeed the name of the island, Elenna, 'Starwards,' makes reference to this star) the Valar bring the Edain to this island of blessing and grant them a greatly increased lifespan. But the covenant is conditional, for the Númenóreans may not sail so far west of the island that they lose sight of its shore. This is known as the Ban of the Valar, and its breaking brings a great curse that destroys the island and the kingdom.

We might also point out the two most solemn oaths recorded: the terrible oath of the sons of Fëanor, and the compact of Cirion and Eorl, and the way they correspond to Calvin's definition of covenant. Each has blessings and curses, binding duties, a seal, and a mediator. Cirion and Eorl, the two rulers of Gondor and Rohan, meet at a holy place watched over by the Valar so that their oaths may be of deepest solemnity. They bring only essential servants, and go unarmed as witnesses to their "words and deeds in the high place" (*UT* 316). Everyone stands in silence with bowed heads (*UT* 317-18). Then each makes a solemn oath of alliance with the other:

> 'I will now declare what I have resolved, with the authority of the Stewards of the Kings, to offer to Eorl son of Léod, Lord of the Éothéod, in recognition of the valour of his people and of the help beyond hope that he brought to Gondor in time of dire need. To Eorl I will give in free gift all the great land of Calenardhon from Anduin to Isen. There, if he will, he shall be king, and his heirs after him, and his people shall dwell in freedom while the authority of the Stewards endures, until the Great King returns. No bond shall be laid upon them other than their own laws and will, save in this only: they shall live in perpetual friendship with Gondor and its enemies shall be their enemies

3 Indeed, Calvin's exposition of the third commandment focuses on the fact that an oath is a form of worship and by necessity calls God to witness to the truth of the promise (*Inst.* II.8.22-27). See also IV.13.

> while both realms endure. But the same bond shall be laid also on the people of Gondor.' (*UT* 316)

Note the explicit condition that they should live as allies. Eorl in response highlights the graciousness of the covenant and the gift of kingship and calls down an explicit curse on his own disobedience.

> At last, when Eorl had swiftly passed all these things through his thought, he spoke, saying: 'Lord Steward of the Great King, the gift that you offer I accept for myself and for my people. It far exceeds any reward that our deeds could have earned, if they had not themselves been a free gift of friendship. But now I will seal that friendship with an oath that shall not be forgotten. [...] Hear now all peoples who bow not to the Shadow in the East, by the gift of the Lord of the Mundburg we will come to dwell in the land that he names Calenardhon, and therefore I vow in my own name and on behalf of the Éothéod of the North that between us and the Great People of the West there shall be friendship for ever: their enemies shall be our enemies, their need shall be our need, and whatsoever evil, or threat, or assault may come upon them we will aid them to the utmost end of our strength. This vow shall descend to my heirs, all such as may come after me in our new land, and let them keep it in faith unbroken, lest the Shadow fall upon them and they become accursed.' (*UT* 318)

Cirion responds in Quenya, the Elf-Latin, to further solemnize the occasion and in fact, in an unprecedented move, invokes the holy name of the One, God Himself:

> 'This oath shall stand in memory of the glory of the Land of the Star, and of the faith of Elendil the Faithful, in the keeping of those who sit upon the thrones of the West and of the One who is above all thrones for ever.' Such an oath had not been heard in Middle-earth since Elendil himself had sworn alliance with Gil-galad King of the Eldar. (*UT* 319)

The solemnity of the ceremony is indisputable, but this is not in itself what reveals Tolkien's tendency to elevate covenant-keeping. It is rather the direct involvement of the supernatural in the making of the oath. Eorl, who had not initially invoked God or the Valar, afterward states: "May those whom we called in witness of our oaths have us in their keeping. Let us part now in hope!" (*UT* 321). He means God and the Valar, to whom Cirion had given the oath's 'keeping.' Cirion answers: "I believe that the words of my oath, which I had not fore-thought ere I spoke them, were not put into my mouth in vain. We will part then in hope" (321). In other words, his eruption into Quenya was a form of divine inspiration, and the oath itself bestowed and sealed by the very gods who thus *name themselves* as witnesses.

The other prominent oath in Middle-earth is the terrible promise of the sons of Fëanor, which also invokes the name of God, but calls hell down upon themselves if they allow anyone, even one of the Valar, to keep a Silmaril from them. They name Manwë and Varda in witness (*LR* 234; *Sil* 83; *SME* 97). Note that in both instances the holy powers and even God Himself are directly involved with the establishment of a covenant. And these are not mere words. Tolkien's covenants and promises have metaphysical heft. We read that "many quailed to hear the dread words. For so sworn, good or evil, an oath may not be broken, and it shall pursue oathkeeper and oathbreaker to the world's end" (*Sil* 83; *MR* 112). And indeed it does, for all of Fëanor's sons. Their final destinies are written by the oath they take here. The same can be said of the Oathbreakers of Dunharrow, bound even beyond death to fulfill the promise they made with Isildur upon the black stone of Erech, their covenant seal (what Tolkien explicitly calls a "covenant-stone," *Letters* 541).[4]

War against the Idols

It is here, in the establishment of a sacred covenant, that we see another surprising link between Tolkien and Calvin. Idolatry, the worship of another god, is a violation of the covenant that the Old Testament consistently equates to spiritual adultery.[5] As Calvin writes in his exposition of the first commandment, God is "provoked to jealousy whenever we substitute our fictions in his stead; just as an unfaithful wife stings her husband's heart more deeply when her adultery is committed openly before his eyes" (*Inst.* II.8.16). Idolatry is the

4 "But the oath that they broke was to fight against Sauron, and they must fight therefore, if they are to fulfil it. For at Erech there stands yet a black stone that was brought, it was said, from Númenor by Isildur; and it was set upon a hill, and upon it the King of the Mountains swore allegiance to him in the beginning of the realm of Gondor. But when Sauron returned and grew in might again, Isildur summoned the Men of the Mountains to fulfil their oath, and they would not: for they had worshipped Sauron in the Dark Years. Then Isildur said to their king: 'Thou shalt be the last king. And if the West prove mightier than thy Black Master, this curse I lay upon thee and thy folk: to rest never until your oath is fulfilled. For this war will last through years uncounted, and you shall be summoned once again ere the end'" (*LotR* 782).

5 I take the title of this section as a play on the influential book of the same name (Eire 1989).

corruption of our natural impulse to worship God, directing it instead toward an improper object, which is always ultimately ourselves.[6]

For Calvin, all are without excuse for their idolatrous urges, based on his reading of passages such as Romans 1. Here all human beings are born with a *sensus divinitatis*, an inborn awareness of God's existence which is then universally suppressed in sin as a result of the fall.[7] Tolkien also affirms such a sense. Eru states: "Each *fëa* [soul] must of nature remember Me (from whom it came), yet that memory is veiled, being overlaid by the impress of things new and strange that it perceives through the body" (*NME* 258). Souls know God by nature, but sin and the world occlude this knowledge. It is not likely that Tolkien derived this idea from Calvin, but from the seemingly standard Anglo-Saxon view we find in *Beowulf*, Aelfric of Eynsham's *De falsis diis*, or Wulfstan's adaptation of Aelfric, *De falsis deis*. The noble pagans could acknowledge the God of natural revelation as the source of all good gifts, but turn instead to the idols and the demons lurking behind them.[8] And given the theological preeminence of the fall in Tolkien's own theology, it seems assured that he would subscribe to Calvin's famous dictum that the human mind is a perpetual idol factory (*Inst.* I.11.8).[9]

In fact, Tolkien locates idolatry as the driving force behind his whole story. "In *The Lord of the Rings* the conflict is not basically about 'freedom', though that is naturally involved. It is about God, and His sole right to divine honour. The Eldar and the Númenóreans believed in The One, the true God, and held worship of any other person an abomination" (*Letters* 243).[10] For the Men of the West, "the refusal to worship any 'creature', and above all no 'dark lord' or satanic demon, Sauron, or any other," constitute almost the entirety of their religion (*Letters* 206). By the time of *The Lord of the Rings* in the Third Age,

6 This Tolkien too affirms (*MR* 334, 397). See, for instance, Tolkien's equation of the modern State with idol-worship (*Letters* 244).

7 See for example Helm 1998.

8 For Tolkien's discussion of this, see *Beowulf* 170-71.

9 *Unde colligere licet, hominis ingenium perpetuam, ut ita loquar, esse idolorum fabricam.*

10 Tolkien comments elsewhere: "They thus escaped from 'religion' in a pagan sense, into a pure monotheist world, in which all things and beings and powers that might seem worshipful were not to be worshiped, not even the gods (the Valar), being only creatures of the One" (*Letters* 204). Here, despite a clear denial of latria to the Valar, Tolkien must nevertheless leave space for *doulia*, since he depicts the Valar as being invoked and answering prayers, much as the saints and angels of Roman Catholicism would do. Calvin flatly and derisively denies this distinction (e.g. *Inst.* I.12.2-3).

Eru has no organized worship and no sacred site, though he can be worshiped personally (as Faramir does).

Tolkien further asserts that when mortals *do* worship the One, their worship is characterized by a restrained aniconicity. This brings us to the final point of consonance between Calvin's and Tolkien's views on idolatry. Idolatry lies not only in the worship of false gods but in worshiping the true God falsely. When painting a picture of the purest form of worship in Middle-earth, on the island of Númenor, Tolkien rather strangely describes a faith without priests, without ecclesiastical hierarchy, without ritual or sacrifice, without images.[11]

Now, obviously, Tolkien himself has no issue with the use of religious images in worship, and the practices Calvin labels as superstitious and blasphemous (Mary and the Mass) are, for Tolkien, at the core of his devotional life. But his writings show a decided lack of emphasis on physical depictions of God. His *Letters* make no mention of the use of images outside of artistic appreciation or private devotion.[12] More significantly, Eru is nowhere described, embodied, or even particularly anthropomorphized aside from the biblically-warranted mention of hand and face in the "Ainulindalë". Indeed, the use of images in the worship of Eru is actually denied outright (*LR* 66).

This is all in keeping with Calvin's own "war against idols," which included a characteristic emphasis that served to distinguish the purity of Reformed worship not only from the false gods and "superstition" of late medieval Roman Catholicism, but also from the improper worship of the non-iconoclastic Lutherans (Eire 1989: 1-2). Calvin and the Reformed steadfastly refused to adorn their churches with any images or religious art, seeing all such expressions as violations of the second commandment.

---

11 Cf. *Letters* 193: "There are thus no temples or 'churches' or fanes in this 'world' among 'good' peoples. They had little or no 'religion' in the sense of worship […] I do not think Hobbits practised any form of worship or prayer (unless through exceptional contact with Elves). The Númenóreans […] were pure monotheists. But there was no temple in Númenor (until Sauron introduced the cult of Morgoth). The top of the Mountain, the Meneltarma or Pillar of Heaven, was dedicated to Eru, the One, and there at any time privately, and at certain times publicly, God was invoked, praised, and adored: an imitation of the Valar and the Mountain of Aman." Interestingly, Calvin names invocation, praise, and adoration as three of the four duties we owe to God, alongside that trust which Tolkien will elsewhere call *estel* (*Inst.* II.8.16).

12 Calvin, it should be noted, also supported the use of religious art outside of public worship.

Having received no word from Eru as to how he wishes to be worshipped, and knowing instinctively that no image can circumscribe him, it seems as if the people of Middle-earth therefore more or less refrain from organized religion. The only ecclesiastical official of which we ever hear is the Númenórean king (*Letters* 206).[13] Do we find here an echo of what later Reformed writers will come to call the regulative principle of worship?[14]

The Theater of God's Glory

"If ever there was a theologian who saw the universe sacramentally it was Calvin," writes philosopher Nicholas Wolterstorff (1983: 160). Our fourth point of contact will be here, in a sacramental ontology that celebrates the natural world as a mode of God's presence. Here I subdivide the discussion of Tolkien's and Calvin's theology of nature into two pieces: first, the importance of creation and artistry, of the world as God's masterpiece; and second, in the beauty of nature itself, in a theological aesthetics that produces divine praise.

Now, I will not spend much time demonstrating Tolkien's concern for the doctrine of creation or his affinity for the natural world. I want instead to point out the way in which Tolkien sees the world as what he calls "Primary Art," the archetype for the derivative works of human artists (*TOFS* 78). In his justly famous poem "Mythopoeia," Tolkien defiantly asserts against mechanistic materialism that the world requires an artistic as well as a scientific reading. Our sensitivity to the artistry of the cosmos arises directly from our creation in the image of God. When we do, therefore, read creation correctly, we see it shot through with signs of God's presence. Tolkien admires the poetry of Francis Thompson for its astronomical and geological images, which he believes portray "Catholic ritual writ large across the universe." He also praises the mixture of awe and familiarity which he sees as a hallmark of Catholic thought (Hammond & Scull 2017: 1294). He does not use the later term 'sacramental theology,' but that is what he means.

---

13 I point out that for Calvin, also, our only mediator to God is Jesus Christ the priest-king.

14 See here Calvin's comment on Deut 12:32 (*Harm.*): "By forbidding the addition, or diminishing of anything, he plainly condemns as illegitimate whatever men invent of their own imagination; whence it follows that they, who in worshipping God are guided by any rule save that which He Himself has prescribed, make to themselves false gods."

Tolkien repeatedly refers to creation as a cosmogonical drama, with the earth as center stage and the main action as the war of God's children against the Devil.[15] God's providence in creation is therefore "God's management of the Drama" (*MR* 329). God, as Author, is therefore infinitely greater than the drama itself, and remains 'outside' of it, even though, as Tolkien says, "that Drama depends on His design and His will for its beginning and continuance, in every detail and moment" (*MR* 335).

Calvin appeals to this same metaphor, though in an even more expansive way than Tolkien. "Wherever you turn your eyes, there is no portion of the world, however minute, that does not exhibit at least some sparks of beauty; while it is impossible to contemplate the vast and beautiful fabric as it extends around, without being overwhelmed by the immense weight of glory" (*Inst.* I.5.1). Nature acts as a mirror in which we can behold the otherwise invisible God through his works (*Inst.* I.5.1). Belden Lane (2011) observes that Calvin's emphasis on nature as a theater of God's glory manifests in Calvin's emphasis on liturgy and corporate worship, in human beings joining the chorus of praise lifted up by nature. As Calvin says, "This is, indeed, the proper business of the whole life, in which men should daily exercise themselves, to consider the infinite goodness, justice, power, and wisdom of God, in this magnificent theater of heaven and earth" (*Comm. Gen.* 2.3). Such is the vast canvas on which God's drama of redemption is set.

Lane argues that when Calvin deploys the image of theater, he draws upon a long tradition of drama used for religious purposes to please and instruct audiences. This tradition is itself indebted to Aristotle's *Poetics*.

> He viewed the sudden Aristotelian reversal found at the heart of great tragedy and comedy alike as corresponding to the drama of the gospel. Aristotle had spoken of the unexpected 'reversal' [...] found at the hinge of every good plot. This sudden change of fortune occasions a telling encounter for the principal character(s) of the play, effecting a change of heart and mind on the part of the audience as well. (Lane 2011: 60)

This all sounds very much like Tolkien's *eucatastrophe*:

15 *Letters* 146-47, 149; *MR* 330, 333, 337-38, 349, 375; *NME* 230-31.

> [T]he sudden happy turn in a story which pierces you with a joy that brings tears (which I argued it is the highest function of fairy-stories to produce) [...] the Resurrection was the greatest 'eucatastrophe' possible in the greatest Fairy Story – and produces that essential emotion: Christian joy which produces tears [...] because it comes from those places where Joy and Sorrow are at one, reconciled, as selfishness and altruism are lost in Love. (*Letters* 100; cf. *TOFS* 75)

This confluence should be unsurprising since Calvin and Tolkien are working from a common literary tradition, as we pointed out above.

What is somewhat more surprising is that Calvin and Tolkien agree on the linchpin of this reversal, the point at which this creation drama finds its climax. Tolkien writes that the true myth "has entered History and the primary world; the desire and aspiration of sub-creation has been raised to the fulfillment of Creation. The Birth of Christ [the Incarnation] is the eucatastrophe of Man's history. The Resurrection is the eucatastrophe of the story of the Incarnation" (*TOFS* 78). Here, Calvin differs slightly in emphasis but agrees in substance, locating our eucatastrophe in Christ's death:

> In the cross of Christ, as in a splendid theater, the incomparable goodness of God is set before the whole world. The glory of God shines, indeed, in all creatures on high and below, but never more brightly than in the cross, in which there was a wonderful change of things [*in qua admirabilis facta est rerum conversio*] – the condemnation of all men was manifested, sin blotted out, salvation restored to men; in short, the whole world was renewed and all things restored to order. (*Comm. John* 13:31)

And yet, Calvin bemoans, "the greater part of mankind, enslaved by error, walk blindfold in this glorious theatre," so that "the brightest manifestation of divine glory finds not one genuine spectator among a hundred" (*Inst.* I.5.8). Our world of sin has corrupted and begrimed our sight. We have lost that sense of wonder which we ought to feel at the natural world, and so God mercifully adds his written word to the book of nature. Calvin writes: "The knowledge of God, which, in other respects, is not obscurely exhibited in the frame of the world, and in all the creatures, is more clearly and familiarly explained by the word" (*Inst.* I.10.1). Both word and world are designed for the same purpose: to show us how to worship God with "perfect integrity of heart and unfeigned obedience" while depending on his infinite goodness (*Inst.* I.10.2).

Tolkien makes the same conceptual moves, locating knowledge of God within nature and expecting that this knowledge will result in praise:

> Those who believe in a personal God, Creator, do not think the Universe is in itself worshipful, though devoted study of it may be one of the ways of honouring Him. And while as living creatures we are (in part) within it and part of it, our ideas of God and ways of expressing them will be largely derived from contemplating the world about us. (*Letters* 400)

This is also the subject of one of Tolkien's most theological passages, written to a young girl investigating the meaning of life for a school paper:

> The chief purpose of life, for any one of us, is to increase according to our capacity our knowledge of God by all the means we have, and to be moved by it to praise and thanks. To do as we say in the *Gloria in Excelsis*: [...] We praise you, we call you holy, we worship you, we proclaim your glory, we thank you for the greatness of your splendour. And in moments of exaltation we may call on all created things to join in our chorus, speaking on their behalf, as is done in Psalm 148, and in The Song of the Three Children in Daniel II. PRAISE THE LORD [...] all mountains and hills, all orchards and forests, all things that creep and birds on the wing. (*Letters* 400)

But, just like Calvin, Tolkien accepts that the Fall has had a profound effect on our ability to absorb the available natural knowledge of God the Creator.

We need what he calls Recovery, and what he further describes as a return, renewal of health, and regaining of a clear view of this cosmic theater and the drama taking place within it:

> I do not say 'seeing things as they are' and involve myself with the philosophers, though I might venture to say 'seeing things as we are (or were) meant to see them' – as things apart from ourselves. We need, in any case, to clean our windows; so that the things seen clearly may be freed from the drab blur of triteness or familiarity – from possessiveness. (*TOFS* 67)

The optical metaphor of seeing through a dirty window or in a mirror is also quite Calvinist. Calvin deploys famous images such as mirrors and spectacles.

After this point Tolkien and Calvin begin to diverge, as Calvin will place much more emphasis upon scripture in granting knowledge, specifically of God the Redeemer, while Tolkien broadens the scope to include myth and fantasy literature. This is likely due to their further differences on the effects of the fall, and there is more to be said on this issue, but we must move on to our final point.

The Secret Providence of God

Tolkien has a strong view of divine providence; this much is indisputable. Consider Eru's declaration in the creation narrative: "No theme may be played that hath not its uttermost source in me, nor can any alter the music in my despite. For he that attempteth this shall prove but mine instrument in the devising of things more wonderful, which he himself hath not imagined" (*Sil* 17).[16] But whether for Tolkien God's (or Eru's) foresight is determinative, and to what extent God responds to his creatures' free decisions, is a more complex question.[17] Here, I will pick out one of possibly several strands that Tolkien weaves, and which I believe best synthesizes all of his comments on the nature of fate, free will, and providence. In all of this, we shall see that Tolkien is largely in alignment with Calvin. Nor is this entirely surprising, since the views of Calvin are very close to those of Augustine and Thomas Aquinas.[18]

In comparing Tolkien's position on providence to Calvin's, I note two things. First, despite common stereotypes, predestination is not the centerpiece of Calvin's theology. Second, as stated at the outset, Tolkien is not a Calvinist. There will obviously be divergences as well as convergences on this score, but that is not the purpose of this paper.

Calvin treats of providence and predestination several times throughout his corpus. Aside from the *Institutes* (e.g. I.16-17), his most extensive account is *Concerning the Eternal Predestination of God* (1552).[19] I shall condense his doctrine down to six major points. Henry Beveridge, in his translation of the *Institutes*, summarizes Calvin's doctrine of providence by noting (1) it encompasses both past and future; (2) it can use but does not require secondary causes; (3) God cares for the Church in a special way; (4) its unfolding is usually secret but always just.[20] Calvin specially addresses the common objections against his

16 Cf. Calvin, *Inst.* I.17.5. Note also the remarkable confluence in I.14.17, where Satan does God's will despite his rebellion.

17 Tolkien's views on providence receive more extended treatment in my *Tolkien Dogmatics* (2022: 69-75). The primary source here is a document titled "Fate and Free Will," appearing first in *Tolkien Studies* and then in *NME*.

18 For Thomas, see, e.g., *SCG* III, esp. 75-76.

19 In this latter work, however, Calvin writes: "What my mind on this momentous subject is, my 'Institute' furnishes a full and abundant testimony, even if I should now add nothing more" (11).

20 Beveridge further picks out fifteen points that Calvin articulates in *Inst.* I.17.6-10, and if we had more space we might walk through each in turn, showing how Tolkien and Calvin align in all of them.

theology of providence in a short treatise devoted specially to the purpose, *The Secret Providence of God* (1558). Here we can see, for example, that (5) Calvin nowhere denies the existence of human freedom as a secondary cause beneath the plane of God's causation, despite directly affirming that (6) no event, down to the smallest breath of wind, occurs by chance. Can Tolkien affirm all six of these distinctive points in Calvin's doctrine of providence? Indeed he can! Let us analyze each of these six points as they occur in Tolkien's works.

The first four theses are uncontroversial. Does Tolkien believe that (1) God's providence extends to future truths? Yes, clearly. God is the Author of the Great Tale, and has plans for its ending (e.g. *Sil* 18).

Does Tolkien believe that (2) God's providence operates through means and also miraculously? Again, yes. Tolkien affirms miracle, both in Middle-earth and the real world (*Letters* 100; *TOFS* 252-4). But he also notes how the free decisions of creatures (secondary causes) actually operate to accomplish God's purposes, as we noted above in the Ainulindalë.

Does Tolkien believe that (3) God cares specially for the Church? Yes, since the Roman Catholic Church is "the True Church, the temple of the Spirit dying but living, corrupt but holy, self-reforming and rearising" (*Letters* 339). Fictionally, he can write:

> If we are indeed the Eruhin, the Children of the One, then He will not suffer Himself to be deprived of His own, not by any Enemy, not even by ourselves. This is the last foundation of Estel [hope], which we keep even when we contemplate the End: of all His designs the issue must be for His Children's joy. (*MR* 320)[21]

Does Tolkien believe that (4) God keeps his providence secret? Yes. Discussing the difference between our enjoyment of the journey to Mordor as readers in contrast to the misery experienced by the characters themselves, Tolkien writes "we have in us an eternal element, free from care and fear, which can survey the things that in 'life' we call evil with serenity [...] Not in the same way, but in some such way, we shall all doubtless survey our own story when we know

21 Here in the fictional world, Elves and Men act as the stand-ins for the Church, over against Orcs and other servants of the enemy, including evil Men. Were we to equate the Children with humanity as a whole in the primary world, we would end in universalism, which Tolkien does not hold.

it (and a great deal more of the Whole Story)" (*Letters* 106-7). Here Tolkien explains that when we have access to the whole sweep of our creation narrative, we will experience pleasure in the way God has governed it. We might reapply the words of Gandalf here: "Many folk like to know beforehand what is to be set on the table; but those who have laboured to prepare the feast like to keep their secret; for wonder makes the words of praise louder" (*LotR* 970).

Turning now to (5) the role of secondary causes and (6) the extent of God's control, we note the following. Tolkien writes, "in every world on every plane all must ultimately be under the Will of God" (*Letters* 191). Within Middle-earth, "the will of Eru [...] may not be gainsaid," (*SD* 382). Despite Tolkien's prioritization of freedom, he also avers: "Free Will is derivative, and is only operative within provided circumstances; but in order that it may exist, it is necessary that the Author should guarantee it, whatever betides : sc. when it is 'against His Will', as we say, at any rate as it appears on a finite view" (*Letters* 195).[22] In other words, all free decisions fall under the permissive will of God (*Letters* 110). Rather than a world of libertarian freedom in which God occasionally intervenes, for Tolkien, God's sovereignty is absolute, and freedom is a *gift* that God must bestow and continually uphold (e.g. *Sil* 41-42). It is not a natural right, and could logically be curtailed whenever God wishes.[23]

But we can go further. Tolkien also implies that our free decisions operate on a different 'plane' than God's own sovereign rule. One of his characters illustrates this when he ponders: "Fatherhood is a choice, and yet it is not wholly by a man's will. Perhaps this peril is my choice, and yet also outside my will. I don't know" (*LR* 51). Tolkien offers the analogy of an Author and his story, in which the Author exercises a peculiar form of providence over all elements of his world. Here is the crucial passage:

> Many authors have recorded the feeling that one of their actors 'comes alive' as it were, and does things that were not foreseen at all at the outset and may

22 This final phrase ("on a finite view") is important, since it implies that things which *appear* to be against God's will are not, and such an appearance is in fact simply the result of our limited perspective.

23 Here we should distinguish between God's *potentia ordinata* and *potentia absoluta*. God covenants to uphold free will such that due to his faithfulness he will never truly violate it, though he has the abstract power to do so if he had not so covenanted.

> modify in a small or even large way the process of the tale thereafter. All such unforeseen actions or events are, however, taken up to become integral parts of the tale when finally concluded. Now when that has been done, then the author's 'foreknowledge' is complete, and nothing can happen, be said, or done, that he does not know of and will or allow to be. (*NME* 230)

Here we should not let the analogy escape us, nor should we assume a greater scope to the freedom of the characters than is merited. An author's character, after all, no matter how much he or she 'comes alive,' can never actually do anything, however small, apart from the author's decision. Any deviations from the original 'plot' are also themselves assented to by the author.

Conclusion

Here we have discovered five convergences between Tolkien and Calvin, established despite Tolkien's nowhere relying on or being influenced by Calvin whatsoever. They emphasize covenant-keeping, condemn idolatry, see the world as a theatre of God's glory, and affirm the secret providence of God. Are these, then, mere coincidences? Hardly. Instead, they illustrate the way in which two markedly disparate minds, separated by both time and tenor of thought, can find in the great theological tradition – what C.S. Lewis calls that "great level viaduct" – ample resources for appreciation and appropriation.[24] The stream extending through Augustine and the early Christian humanists finds outlet in both Calvin and Tolkien. It contains within itself enough richness and complexity to serve both Frenchmen and Faerie.

---

24 "We are all rightly distressed, and ashamed also, at the divisions of Christendom. But those who have always lived within the Christian fold may be too easily dispirited by them. They are bad, but such people do not know what it looks like from without. Seen from there, what is left intact despite all the divisions, still appears (as it truly is) an immensely formidable unity. I know, for I saw it; and well our enemies know it. That unity any of us can find by going out of his own age. It is not enough, but it is more than you had thought till then. Once you are well soaked in it, if you then venture to speak, you will have an amusing experience. You will be thought a Papist when you are actually reproducing Bunyan, a Pantheist when you are quoting Aquinas, and so forth. For you have now got on to the great level viaduct which crosses the ages and which looks so high from the valleys, so low from the mountains, so narrow compared with the swamps, and so broad compared with the sheep-tracks" (Lewis 2014: 12-13).

About the Author

Austin M. Freeman (PhD Trinity Evangelical Divinity School) is chair of the department of apologetics at Houston Christian University. He is the author of *Tolkien Dogmatics*, a systematic theological exploration of Tolkien's beliefs. He has edited and contributed essays and articles to many other works in the field of Tolkien studies and the theology of fantasy literature in general.

Bibliography

Aquinas, Thomas. 1265. *Summa Contra Gentiles.*

Calvin, John. 1845. *Institutes of the Christian Religion*. Translated by Henry Beveridge. Edinburgh: Calvin Translation Society.

1847. *Commentary on the Gospel according to John*. Volume 2. Translated by William Pringle. Edinburgh: Calvin Translation Society.

1850. *Commentaries on the First Book of Moses Called Genesis*. Volume 1. Translated by John King. Edinburgh: Calvin Translation Society.

1852. *Commentaries on the Four Last Books of Moses, Arranged in a Harmony*. Also published as *Harmony of the Law*. Volume 3. United Kingdom: Calvin Translation Society.

1856. *A Treatise on the Eternal Predestination of God*. In *Calvin's Calvinism*, part 1. Translated by Henry Cole. London: Wertheim & MacIntosh.

1857. *A Defence of the Secret Providence of God*. In *Calvin's Calvinism*, part 2. Translated by Henry Cole. London: Wertheim & MacIntosh.

Eilmann, Julian. 2017. *J.R.R. Tolkien: Romanticist and Poet*. Cormarë Series 37. Zurich and Jena: Walking Tree Publishers.

Eire, Carlos M.N. 1989. *War Against the Idols: The Reformation of Worship from Erasmus to Calvin*. Cambridge: Cambridge University Press.

Freeman, Austin. 2022. *Tolkien Dogmatics: Theology through Mythology with the Maker of Middle-earth*. Bellingham, WA: Lexham Press.

Hammond, Wayne, and Christina Scull. 2017. *The J.R.R. Tolkien Companion and Guide*. 3 vols. London: HarperCollins.

Helm, Paul. 1998. "John Calvin, the 'Sensus Divinitatis', and the Noetic Effects of Sin." *International Journal for Philosophy of Religion* 43.2: 87-107.

Lane, Belden C. 2011. *Ravished by Beauty: The Surprising Legacy of Reformed Spirituality*. Oxford: Oxford University Press.

LEWIS, C.S. 2014. "Preface." In John Behr (ed. and trans.). *Athanasius, On the Incarnation*. St. Vladimir Seminary Press, 9-15.

MCGRATH, Alister E. 2004. *The Intellectual Origins of the European Reformation*. Second Edition. Oxford: Blackwell.

MULLER, Richard. 2000. *The Unaccommodated Calvin: Studies in the Foundation of a Theological Tradition*. Oxford Studies in Historical Theology. Oxford: Oxford University Press.

SHERWOOD, Will and Julian EILMANN (eds.). 2024. T*he Romantic Spirit in the Works of J.R.R. Tolkien*. Cormarë Series 51. Zurich and Jena: Walking Tree Publishers.

TOLKIEN, J.R.R. 1977. *The Silmarillion*. Edited by Christopher Tolkien. Boston: Houghton Mifflin.

1980. *Unfinished Tales of Númenor and Middle-earth*. Edited by Christopher Tolkien. Boston: Houghton Mifflin.

1981. *The Letters of J.R.R. Tolkien*. Edited by Humphrey Carpenter with the assistance of Christopher Tolkien. Boston: Houghton Mifflin.

1986. *The Shaping of Middle-earth*. Edited by Christopher Tolkien. Boston Houghton Mifflin.

1987. *The Lost Road and Other Writings*. Edited by Christopher Tolkien. Boston: Houghton Mifflin.

1992. *Sauron Defeated*. Edited by Christopher Tolkien. Boston: Houghton Mifflin.

1993. *Morgoth's Ring*. Edited by Christopher Tolkien. Boston: Houghton Mifflin.

2004. *The Lord of the Rings*. 50th anniversary edition. Boston: Houghton Mifflin Harcourt.

2008. *Tolkien On Fairy-stories*. Extended edition. Edited by Verlyn Flieger and Douglas A. Anderson. London: HarperCollins.

2009. "Fate and Free Will." Edited by Carl Hostetter. *Tolkien Studies* 6: 183-88.

2014. *Beowulf: A Translation and Commentary together with Sellic Spell*. Edited by Christopher Tolkien. Boston: Houghton Mifflin.

2021. *The Nature of Middle-earth*. Edited by Carl Hostetter. New York: HarperCollins.

WOLTERSTORFF, Nicholas. 1983. *Until Justice and Peace Embrace: The Kuyper Lectures for 1981*. Grand Rapids, MI: Eerdmans.

Giuseppe Pezzini

Tolkien and Newman: Towards a Theology of History

Abstract

This chapter explores aspects of John Henry Newman's influence on J.R.R. Tolkien, focusing in particular on their shared perspectives on change and development, as well as the humble secrecy of divine action in history. Despite his significant biographical connections to the English Cardinal, Tolkien rarely refers to Newman directly in his texts, and the affinity between the two writers is often overlooked. However, Tolkien's view of change as "the law of the world under the sun" closely mirrors Newman's conviction that in human history, "to live is to change, and to be perfect is to have changed often." Both thus saw change, though often painful, as an essential part of life in this world. While they might sympathise with the reluctance of some to embrace change, as seen in the case of the Elves (the 'embalmers'), they expressed an attitude that was neither conservative nor progressive, but one that views change as renewal and development in continuity with the past. The chapter also examines the theme of secrecy in divine action, which is also central in Tolkien's literary works, where humble characters, like Hobbits, unexpectedly drive the course of history according to "the secret life in creation." This recalls Newman's insistence on the idea that God's providence manifests itself in a hidden and quiet way, often overlooked by the world, and reveals a shared belief in the power of the powerless, which can also be related to their affection for figures like Mary and St. Philip Neri.

The influence of John Henry Newman is one of the most important and yet mysterious aspects of Tolkien's work and personality, which has surprisingly received little attention in Tolkien scholarship.[1] This is certainly a tantalizing topic of research. On the one hand it is impossible to deny that

1 Cf. however the study by Fornet-Ponse 2010 (arguing for Tolkien's understanding of conscience in a Newmanian sense); also Tomko 2011 (esp. 217-18 on an "underlying structure of thought and approach to interpreting history shared by these writers within this same community [...] of seeing the struggles of eternal values in shifting temporal conditions"); Pearce (2014: 255-60; connecting Tolkien with the Catholic cultural revival "instigated" by Newman, and noting a shared concern for "the transcendent and objective nature of truth"; Pinsent (2022: 42526), suggesting that perhaps "the most significant aspect of Newman's thinking as far as Tolkien's fiction is concerned is related to the potential for holiness of the ordinary person doing ordinary things"; Imbert (2022: esp. 74-79) arguing for an influence of Newman's concept of the illative sense, and his related enhancement of the epistemological function of imagination, on Tolkien's theory of imagination and his thoughts on the aesthetic dimension of language invention. All these observations are taken into account in the present study.

there is an obvious biographical connection between John Henry Newman and John Ronald Reuel Tolkien: the Catholic conversion of Tolkien's mother, Mabel Suffield, was boosted by Newman's charism, first encountered in his 'Mission Church' at St Anne's in Birmingham, and she received a crucial support, both spiritual and material, from her close friendship with the Oratorian priest Francis Morgan, Newman's secretary in his final years; in 1904 Mabel died, and was buried in Rednal cemetery (not far from Newman's grave) and Father Francis became the guardian (or rather a proper 'second father') for Mabel's children, Ronald and Hilary. In the following years the Birmingham Oratory, Newman's most important foundation, became a home for the Tolkien boys, and there they became acquainted with other members of Newman's community, including Fr. John Norris and Fr. Ignatius Ryder;[2] that Tolkien remembered the Oratory and its members with great affection for all his life is confirmed by his decision in his will to donate to the Oratory the highest sum he bequeathed to any institution, in memory of Francis Morgan (Ordway 2023: 356). Moreover, in 1921 Tolkien moved to Leeds for his first academic job, and for the first months was hosted by Eleanor Mozley, Newman's great-niece, who would become Christopher Tolkien's godmother (Ordway 2023: 170-71). Finally, in the 1940s (and beyond), Tolkien became involved with the newly-founded Newman Association, whose activities in those years included a series of lectures on Newman's *The Idea of a University* and the promotion of Newman's canonization.[3] It would not be inappropriate to describe Newman as a sort of 'spiritual grandfather' for Tolkien (cf. Ordway 2023: 69).

On the other hand, there are almost no traces in Tolkien's published texts, whether fictional or non-fictional, which explicitly refer to Newman, apart from some minor circumstantial evidence, including a few occasional allusions (e.g. an indirect reference to Newman's famous epitaph in a work-diary dating

2 On Tolkien and the Birmingham Oratory see now the extensive study by Ordway 2023, esp. 62-77. also Imbert 2022: 1–22 for a reconstruction of Tolkien's Catholic background, in the context of the Catholic Literary Revival of the early 20th century, very much influenced by Newman's personality and thought.

3 One could also mention that on his 21st birthday, and coming to age, Tolkien apparently sent to his wife-to-be Edith, together with a passionate love letter, a copy of Newman's *Stations of the Cross* (Ordway 2023: 86); also, in 1954 Tolkien received an honorary degree from University College Dublin, the very University founded by Newman exactly 100 years before (438n7); in 1957 Tolkien's son, Fr. John, wrote the script for a film on Newman (250); finally Tolkien's memorial service in 1973 at Merton College concluded with Newman's famous hymn 'Praise to the Holiest in the Height' (356).

January 1913[4] or a possible hint at Newman's *Apologia* in his 1959 valedictory address[5]) and the Latinate name of Bilbo's grandfather, presumably derived from the eponymous protagonist of Newman's *Dream of Gerontius* (which, incidentally, Tolkien included in his curriculum for the National University of Ireland in 1949).[6] In sum, as put by one of the few scholars who wrote on Tolkien's Newmanian connection, "if Newman's indirect influence on Tolkien's early life is beyond question, the extent of his influence on Tolkien's work is not so easy to verify" (Pearce 2014: 256). The aim of this chapter is to give a (fore)taste of and pave the way to a 'verification' of Newman's influence on Tolkien's work. Given the constraints of space, I will focus on two discrete topics only, namely *change* and *secrecy*, which are arguably related as they subsume a very similar theology of history (both real and fictional, or 'primary' and 'secondary,' to use Tolkien's terminology): this is, I believe, one of the areas in which a comparison between Tolkien and Newman can be most productive, and in which one can identify a wide, hidden but pervasive Newmanian influence on his 'spiritual grandson,' but it is not the only one.[7]

Change: The Law of the World under the Sun

The first topic I will consider is 'change', and more specifically an ultimately positive outlook towards historical change, which despite its painful implications, is considered by both Newman and Tolkien as a necessary dimension of life in this world, to be embraced with courage.

Newman and Historical Change

Change and development are areas in which Newman was very much invested, for both biographical and intellectual reasons. Himself a life-long convert, from

4 *Per Umbras Et Imagines* echoing Newman's *ex umbris et imaginibus in veritatem* (cited and discussed by Ordway 2023: 102).

5 Tolkien writes: "I have not made any effective *apologia pro consulatu meo*, for none is really possible" (*MC* 238).

6 Pearce (2014: 255) connects Newman's vision of the afterlife in *The Dream of Gerontius* with that of Tolkien in "Leaf by Niggle" and "Mythopoeia." One could also mention that in a letter to Edith, written before their marriage, Tolkien used the expression "following the light", perhaps echoing Newman's famous hymn 'Lead kindly light' (as suggested by Ordway 2023: 120).

7 See above footnote 1. I hope to investigate systematically Tolkien's 'Newmanian spirituality' in a future work.

Evangelicalism to Anglo-Catholicism, and eventually to the Roman Catholic Church, Newman also shared with his Romantic contemporaries a great love for antiquity and nostalgia for the past – very similar, one might say, to that "heart-racking sense of vanished past" of which Tolkien speaks in his letters (*Letters* 159). An opposer of the ultramontanism and traditionalism of many of his fellow Catholics, and displaying a strong interest for (contemporary) literature,[8] an emphasis on subjective experience, and a direct engagement with modern discourses such as empiricism, Newman's personality was also characterized by a life-long commitment to the fight against theological liberalism and progressivism, the defense of the principle of dogma, and, after his conversion, a staunch devotion to the Catholic Church and its traditions, all tested and deepened through a series of serious personal sacrifices.[9]

Summing up this set of apparently opposite attitudes, one could say that Newman articulated a Christian response to modernity which was neither reactive to nor complacent with it, neither 'conservative' nor 'progressive,' keen to valorize, correct, and integrate the cultural changes introduced by modernity, rather than merely oppose them on ideological grounds. As rightly pointed out by Ian Ker (2014), in this respect Newman anticipated and indeed paved the way to the theological and pastoral advancements of the Second Vatican Council, which deliberately featured the contributions of many theologians who had themselves been directly influenced by Newman – from De Lubac to Ratzinger, from Congar to Guitton.

The problem of the relationship of Christianity and modernity is thus crucial to understand the trajectory of Newman's life and thought, which is indeed closely related to his understanding of change as a difficult but necessary stage of any 'living' human experience, and of Christianity above all. As Newman wrote in the first chapter of the treatise which he specifically dedicated to this topic (*Development of Christian Doctrine*):

> Whatever be the risk of corruption from intercourse with the world around, such a risk must be encountered if a great idea [i.e. Christianity] is duly to be understood, and much more if it is to be fully exhibited. […] It is indeed sometimes said that the stream is clearest near the spring. Whatever use may fairly be made of this image, it does not apply to the history of a philosophy or

8 See Pezzini 2023.
9 For an introduction to Newman's life and work see Ker 2009, Ker and Merrigan 2009.

> belief, which on the contrary is more equable, and purer, and stronger, when its bed has become deep, and broad, and full. [...] In time it enters upon strange territory; points of controversy alter their bearing; parties rise and around it dangers and hopes appear in new relations; and old principles reappear under new forms. It changes with them in order to remain the same. In a higher world it is otherwise, but here below to live is to change, and to be perfect is to have changed often. (Newman 1909: 40-41)[10]

To sum up this enlightening, emblematic passage: for Newman change *per se*, which necessarily involves the "intercourse with the world around," is not a "bane" to be opposed and resisted but rather is the only way any life, singular or collective, can grow and develop, and thereby maintain its vitality and (paradoxically) "remain the same."

Tolkien and Change: An Inner Conservatism?

Moving now from the nineteenth century theologian to the twentieth century writer, can one say that Tolkien's work expresses the same sort of 'positive' attitude towards change, as particularly regards periods of crisis, historical development, and the passing of Time in general, as well as, more specifically, the life of the Church and its relationship with modernity? I am convinced that many Tolkien readers and scholars would give a negative answer to this question: there is nowadays a widespread view that Tolkien had a deeply 'conservative' position towards history, culture, and politics, as well as Christianity and life in general. Scholars highlight for instance the supposed idealization of the Shire, as a model of rural, traditionalist, a-technological and autarchic community; or the idea of a 'return of the King,' construed as a restoration of a legitimate order against chaos. Tolkien has also been described as a man attracted to the myth of Old England, a nostalgic of the Middle Ages and its Christian framework, a defender of the West and its values: in sum a 'conservative' in a broad sense, "averse to change or innovation and holding traditional ideas and values" (*Oxford English Dictionary*).

Leaving aside the political implications, Tolkien's 'conservatism' seems to be confirmed by his fondness for a 'narrative of decline,' a vision of history that posits a gradual degradation (ontological, moral, social, and aesthetic) from an

10 All Newman texts quoted in this essay are freely available on the website *https://www.newmanreader.org*.

idealized Golden Age, going hand-in-hand with a detachment of God(s) from mortals and vice versa. We can trace this narrative in Tolkien's division of his world into ages, from a glorious First Age filled with Joy and Light, to a Third Age, described as "the first of the broken and changed world" (*Letters* 215). Take also his notorious perception of history as a "long defeat" (cf. *Letters* 368), related to the aforementioned "heart-racking sense of the vanished past" and longing for a lost Eden, which pervades Tolkien's works, and which he described as the emotion which moved him "supremely" and which he found "small difficulty in evoking" (cf. *Letters* 159).[11]

Change as the Unfolding of the Design of God

Narratives of decline are certainly present in Tolkien, together with a 'conservative' position and a perception of change as something inherently negative and painful: if history is a decline, creatures only try to preserve or restore the past, to delay or impede change. Novelties, and change in general, are perceived as evil, and related to an inescapable 'catastrophic' tendency of history and moral corruption. This negative outlook on change is present in Tolkien, and is probably due to his wounded sensitivity as a man who lived through moments of great crisis and loss.[12]

But, crucially, this is not his only perspective. Rather, within his secondary world 'conservatism' is presented as a 'partial' position, in the sense of both 'incomplete' and 'belonging to a part.' The part here belongs to the Elves, whose main "motive" is "the prevention or slowing of decay (i.e. 'change' viewed as a regrettable thing), the preservation of what is desired or loved, or its semblance" (*Letters* 212). Despite his own fondness for the Elves (cf. e.g. *Letters* 96), Tolkien is honest enough to admit that "the Elves are not wholly good or in the right [...] They wanted to have their cake and eat it: to live in the mortal historical Middle-earth because they had become fond of it [...] and so tried to stop its change and history, stop its growth" (*Letters* 293). For Tolkien the Elves' refusal of change, however understandable, is not right. Rather, it is an obsession: they "became obsessed with

11 Cf. Pezzini 2022. See also Honegger 2011 and Wiemann 2011.

12 Cf. e.g.: "Imagine the experience of those born (as I) between the Golden and the Diamond Jubilee of Victoria. Both senses or imaginations of security have been progressively stripped away from us. Now we find ourselves nakedly confronting the will of God, as concerns ourselves and our position in Time" (*Letters* 552).

'fading', the mode in which the changes of time (the law of the world under the sun) was perceived by them" (*Letters* 212). In fact "mere change as such is not represented as 'evil': it is the unfolding of the story and to refuse this is of course against the design of God. But the Elvish weakness is in these terms naturally to regret the past, and to become unwilling to face change" (*Letters* 342).

Just as for Newman, for Tolkien the changes of time, however dramatic and traumatic, are not catastrophes to avoid or bemoan, but rather "the law of the world under the sun," that is, the mysterious unfolding of the history of Creation, to be embraced with hope and courage, despite the possible sadness and pain. To try to arrest this unfolding, to refuse to engage with change, is a temptation to overcome; and this is why in *The Lord of the Rings* the Elves' redemption follows their acceptance that they must give up the power of their Rings, and accept the development of divine history.

Tolkien's (Newmanian) Way: Development, Maturation, Renewal

'Conservatism' is thus for Tolkien an understandable and yet wrong, 'partial' attitude. This of course should not lead anyone to affiliate Tolkien with the opposite party, and consider him as a sort of progressive or reformer, i.e. as someone seeking or invoking change as a means of power, in order to 'improve' the real world. As he loudly declared: "I am not a reformer nor an 'embalmer'! I am not a 'reformer' (by exercise of power) since it seems doomed to Sarumanism" (*Letters* 292). In fact, for Tolkien the error of the 'reformer' (epitomised in the wizard Saruman) is founded on the same temptation of the 'embalmer', consisting in the refusal to accept the 'inherent development' of reality: "the desire for Power [...] all use of external plans or devices [...] instead of development of the inherent inner powers or talents" (*Letters* 205). The correct attitude is thus, in Tolkien's view, the *via media*, or rather 'the Straight Way,' between these two errors.

This is where we can start seeing the influence of Newman in clearer terms. However, since Tolkien was an artist, and not a theologian, I will recount Tolkien's views of change with three images, rather than with an explicit argument. These images are different and yet similar, all implying the same Newmanian vision of life and history as 'development' and requiring the same attitude in the face of it.

The Growth of the Seed

The first image is the seed developing into a tree, which Tolkien uses to describe any individual human life, to be compared to "a seed with its innate vitality and heredity, its capacity to grow and develop. A great part of the 'changes' in a man are no doubt unfoldings of the patterns hidden in the seed" (*Letters* 346). The change envisaged by Tolkien is not thus the subversion of a pre-existing entity, nor the introduction into it of revolutionary external elements. Rather, it is a natural 'unfolding' of the 'patterns hidden in the seed.' Tolkien uses the same image in another letter, this time to describe the history and life of the Church:

> 'My church' was not intended by Our Lord to be static or remain in perpetual childhood; but to be a living organism (likened to a plant), which develops and changes in externals by the interaction of its bequeathed divine life and history – the particular circumstances of the world into which it is set. [...] The wise may know that it began with a seed, but it is vain to try and dig it up, for it no longer exists, and the virtue and powers that it had now reside in the Tree. [...] In husbandry the authorities, the keepers of the Tree [...] will certainly do harm, if they are obsessed with the desire of going back to the seed or even to the first youth of the plant when it was (as they imagine) pretty and unafflicted by evils. The other motive (now so confused with the primitivist one, even in the mind of any one of the reformers): aggiornamento: bringing up to date: that has its own grave dangers, as has been apparent throughout history. (*Letters* 553)

This is a key passage, in which Newman's 'ecclesiological' imprint is almost explicit, as is evident if one compares this passage with the excerpt from Newman's *Development of Christian Doctrine*, quoted above.

Intriguingly, this passage comes from a letter in which Tolkien directly engages in a criticism of the Second Vatican Council, or, to be more precise, of some its most progressive trends, including the idealization of primitive Christianity or the obsession with 'bringing up to date' Catholic doctrine (*aggiornamento*) with modernity. Again, we find in Tolkien the same Newmanian paradox of an attitude towards modernity which is not 'progressive,' but certainly not 'traditionalist' either. Indeed, as Tolkien continues: "I find myself in sympathy with those developments that are strictly 'ecumenical' [...] There are dangers (of course), but a Church militant cannot afford to shut up all its soldiers in a fortress" (*Letters* 554).

Therefore, in this letter Tolkien offers a balanced hermeneutics of the Second Vatican Council that implies and promotes a framework of development within continuity, precisely the same hermeneutics prophetically anticipated by Newman. Unfortunately, space does not permit us to delve more deeply into the Newmanian resonances of this key Tolkienian letter. Here I will only add that in the passages quoted above Tolkien refers to or implies a conception of (biological) 'heredity': the Church, just as any human life, is a living organism, which is bound to develop (if it is alive); but at the same time it has an inherited history, and thus a necessary link with the past. Change, in a living organism, is not a break with the past, but a development of/from it, as Newman explained in his *Development of Christian Doctrine.*

The Renewal of the Lineage and the collaboration with Modernity

This introduces the second image, of the (botanical) lineage renewed after centuries of apparent extinction. As the eagle announces to the city of Minas Tirith after the fall of Sauron: "the Tree that was withered shall be renewed, | and he shall plant it in the high places, | and the City shall be blessed" (*LotR* 693). The verb 'to renew' is a keyword in Tolkien, and is especially associated with the character of Aragorn, whose main epithet is that of "renewer" (*LotR* 170) and whose blade will be "renewed" (cf. 170), just like the "dignity of the kings of old" (*LotR* 1044) and the "kingship" in general (*LotR* 1057).

The renewal of the tree of Gondor is analogical to that of its kingship, as Gandalf explains to Aragorn in a key scene of the novel, when a new sapling of the ancient Tree is providentially found under the snow of the sacred mountain:

> Verily this is a sapling of the line of Nimloth the fair [...] though the fruit of the Tree comes seldom to ripeness, yet the life within may then lie sleeping through many long years, and none can foretell the time in which it will awake. [...] Here it has lain hidden on the mountain, even as the race of Elendil lay hidden in the wastes of the North. (*LotR* 971)

The renewal of the lineage, which is an expected yet mysterious event, is not an act of conservation: with Aragorn's return, the old, dead tree is replaced by the new sapling, and it is removed and "laid to rest in the silence" of the graves of the ancient kings (cf. *LotR* 972). It is a new tree that is born, a new story that begins, which yet belongs to and renews an old story, an ancient lineage.

Again, just as in Newman, the only way to preserve and recover the same vitality of old requires a change of situations, modes, circumstances – not a return to the past. More specifically, it involves a positive engagement with these new historical circumstances and all people who live in them, including those with very different sensitivities and spiritual depth than one's own (like Hobbits, in the case of King Aragorn).

To explain this important implication of Tolkien's vision, I will briefly refer to the short story "Leaf by Niggle" (reprinted in *TL*), which Tolkien considered an allegory of his own experience as a literary writer (*Letters* 492). The story focuses on the eponymous painter Niggle, who struggles to complete his masterpiece, the painting of a wonderful Tree. Apart from being naturally indolent and inconclusive (like Tolkien himself), Niggle is constantly interrupted by the requests of his neighbor Parish, who can be described as the prototype of the non-artistic man. Parish is completely indifferent to Niggle's work and is unable to catch the "glimpses" of a higher reality contained in it (*TL* 115). And yet, it is to this very non-artistic, materialistic man, whom "he did not like very much," that Niggle devotes himself, performing "a good many odd jobs," although begrudgingly, compelled by his "kind heart" (cf. *TL* 93-94).

Eventually, Niggle decides to attend to an annoying, petty request of Parish, which results in his fatal illness and complete artistic failure. In "Leaf by Niggle" the eponymous artist literally dies for the sake of his non-artistic, prosaic, and mundane neighbor.

The conflict and resolution between high (Christian) art and mundane (modern) life are also thematized in Tolkien's work on a secondary level, being especially evident in the lives of the Hobbits, who are described by Tolkien as exhibiting the "plain, unimaginative parochial man" (*Letters* 219n). It is significant that in Tolkien's stories Gandalf – an incarnate Angel, and the mediator of divine will in Middle-earth – is a great lover of hobbits and the fosterer of their heroism. He arrives at the point of accepting death in Moria for the sake of this kind of "parochial man" – a sacrifice for which he is then rewarded with an enhancement of power.[13] Similarly, it is only because of his 'gratuitous' acts of love for Parish, culminating in his own death for his neighbour's sake, that some mysterious

13 On the significance of Gandalf's death in Moria see further Pezzini 2025, Chapter 5.

Voices grant Niggle the chance "go to the next stage", that is, allegorically, to leave Purgatory for Paradise (*TL* 106-8), where he will be gifted with the vision of his Tree, completed at last (see below).

It is important to note that in the story Tolkien highlights the reciprocity of the relationship between Niggle and Parish: Niggle is not just worrying about Parish out of sheer altruism, but he is also ready to acknowledge his own gratitude to his neighbour and express his personal need for him; it is only after this acknowledgement that the First Voice is persuaded to let Niggle go "to the next stage."

This notion that the parochial characters (like Parish and the hobbits) are, themselves, necessary to more artistic and 'enlightened' characters (like Niggle and Gandalf) is crucial also in Tolkien's secondary world. In *The Lord of the Rings*, for instance, the 'high' Gandalf instructs the 'low' hobbits and sacrifices himself for them; yet, without the Hobbits, there would be no final victory. In the same way (moving to the primary world) Tolkien might have originally belittled the literary value of *The Hobbit* in contrast to his beloved higher mythology, but it is only thanks to *The Hobbit*'s intrusion into Tolkien's *legendarium* and the related success of *The Lord of the Rings* that his mythology was 'completed' and managed to 'descend to earth,' as he later acknowledged (cf. *Letters* 204). One could even take a step further and construe this reciprocal relationship between Niggle and Parish, and Gandalf and the hobbits, as reflecting for Tolkien that of Christian Art and secular modernity.[14] Parish is also, in many respects, the 'symbol' of the modern non-religious man, incapable of imagining the 'mountains' of divine transcendence (just as the Victorian-like hobbits, before Gandalf's 'education,' have forgotten the "memory of the high" *UT* 331). In contrast to some apologetic Christian art, Tolkien's mythology does not ignore or oppose modernity, but rather works with it, builds upon it, learns from it, enhances it, and re-integrates it into a higher vision.

That is to say, without the collaboration with modernity, with its apparently 'halved' humanity, culture and literature, there would be no *The Lord of the Rings* (Tolkien's own Tree, as he explicitly described it in *Letters* 454). In the same

14 On Tolkien's (complicated) relationship with modernity see esp. Curry 2004; Weinreich and Honegger 2006; Wood 2015.

way, at the end of his story, Niggle is rewarded with the gift of his Tree, fully finished and 'realized', just as he imagined it in his life, "with all of its leaves in the same style, and all of them different." This is Niggle's Tree, but also Parish's Tree, since "some of the most beautiful – and the most characteristic, the most perfect examples of the Niggle style – were seen to have been produced in collaboration with Mr Parish" (*TL* 110). And above all, this is also the Tree of the Voices, who have given reality to it, and integrated it into their Divine design. This introduces the third image.

The Infinite Blossoming of the One Tree

The final image is that of a single great Tree blossoming with infinite and ever-new leaves, symbolizing the artistic work of God, the story of Creation. For instance, in *Smith of Wootton Major* the eponymous hero Smith, symbol of the artist entering by grace into the depths of reality, sees at a certain point "the King's Tree springing up, tower upon tower, into the sky [...] and it bore at once leaves and flowers and fruits uncounted, and not one was the same as any other that grew on the Tree" (*SWM* 24). The idea of Creation as an organic ensemble of infinite individualities is central in Tolkien, and is developed especially in the cosmogonic myth "Ainulindalë," opening *The Silmarillion*: this tells of a primeval concert of angelic beings, who "like unto countless choirs singing with words" fashion the single theme of God, "with endless interchanging melodies" (*Sil* 15).

Newness and variety are necessary qualities of artistic creation, divine but also human, pointing out that the main aim of (human) art is to create "something new" (*TOFS* 68), and to pay tribute "to the infinity of [God's] potential variety" (*Letters* 283). At the same time, this ever-new variety is not autonomous or self-referential; rather, all individual stories, past, present, and future, are in relationship with each other, and all contribute to the same polyphonic music of Creation, which transcends time and space. There are infinite leaves, but they all belong to the same Tree, and as such they share the same archetypical pattern; just like all leaves of an oak tree are somehow similar, and yet none of them is identical to the other, because each one is called to blossom according to its own particular story, in springs that are ever-new, as an "unique embodiment of the pattern" (cf. *TOFS* 66).

Even as regards this third image, with its theological implications, one can trace a Newmanian ancestry: indeed, another key tenet of Newman's conception of development is the complementary conviction that any living idea, as it develops, must not lose its fundamental type, original principles, or vigor. An idea which loses this 'oneness' with its beginning, decays and eventually breaks up. For this reason 'oneness' within variety and development is a necessary feature of any 'living idea' and is indeed the most distinctive, most attractive feature of the Church. For Newman the history of the Church is in fact simply the development and flowering of what had already been promised from the beginning, lived out in every century. In the Church Newman saw, therefore, the characteristic of the most truly living of ideas – widespread influence in the hearts of individuals of every nation. The 'oneness' of the Church, across different times and places, shines in particular in the "wonderful unity of sentiment and belief in persons so dissimilar from each other, so distinct in their circumstances, so independent in their testimony" (Newman 1901: 292-93).[15] Or as Newman put it using a very Tolkienian metaphor: "[this] is the special glory of the Christian Church, that its members […] are, one and all, the births and manifestations of one and the same unseen spiritual principle of power, 'living stones' internally connected, *as branches from a tree*" (Newman 1907-9, IV: 11, emphasis added).

Novelty, Continuity, and the Ongoing Embracing of One's Tale

The images I discussed in the previous sections (the seed developing into a tree, the renewal of the lineage, and the Tree blossoming with infinite leaves) help clarify Tolkien's attitude in the face of historical change. This is essentially the same as Newman's, though expressed in the veiled form of literature. Tolkien has indeed an 'organic' and 'dynamic' vision of (divine) history, which develops through infinite, individual stories, embedded in always differing circumstances; new, individual, unique stories, and yet in continuity with the ones that precede them, in a narrative chain which ultimately has its center and origin in the Gospel story, the 'Primary Story' to which all human lives are called to conform.

15 Cf. also Newman (1909: 100): "All will agree so far as this, that […] the Baptist and St. Paul are in their history and mode of life […] in what is external and meets the eye […] more like a Dominican preacher, or a Jesuit missionary, or a Carmelite friar […] than to any individuals […] that can be found in other communions."

Historical change is thus inevitable and in fact positive and necessary, if construed and embraced as a providential development of the past – a past that is not to be preserved nor reformed (neither with the Elves nor Saruman), but renewed, through fully embracing one's own tale, in the present and ever-changing circumstances. This is why Tolkien could write to his young friends, after the horror of the Somme: "[We have] been granted some spark of fire [...] that was destined to kindle a new light, or, what is the same thing, rekindle an old light in the world; [...] to testify for God and Truth" (*Letters* 6). The conviction that kindling a new light is in fact the same as rekindling an old light sums up Tolkien's implicit theology of history, of clear Newmanian ancestry.

From a narrative point of view, this 'positive' position towards historical change is reflected in the characters' (expected) availability to live in the times they are given, and fully engage with the other people who live them, however different and alien to one's own preferences and images; to discover and tread the path that has been laid for them, as Galadriel says to the Fellowship of the Ring (cf. *LotR* 368), even when it leads to dark roads, together with whatever companions one has been assigned; and to allow God to bring their story to fulfilment, and eventually integrate it into His own great Story, the Great Story of the Great Author.[16] In Tolkien's vision to walk the path of one's history, with the courage and humility of a Hobbit and under the guide of incarnated Grace (Gandalf),[17] is thus the truest and most impactful way to rekindle a new light, and to "testify for God and Truth". All this is possible for those who know that there is a loving Author behind their story, an Author who simply needs the characters' decision "never to turn back", as Sam says to Frodo on the stairs of Cirith Ungol, in one of the most beautiful scenes of *The Lord of the Rings* (711-12); that is to say, to use a meta-literary analogy, the narrative availability of the characters to let the Author lead their own story (*fiat*). In fact, to tread one's own path, and thereby rekindle a new light in a changing world is not the result of a human project, but is rather only possible because "we have been granted [...] some spark of fire." This finally leads me to the second part of this chapter.

---

16 Cf. also Tolkien's commentary on this scene in *Letters* 151-52, referring to the "Whole Story".
17 Cf. *Letters* 174, where he alludes to Gandalf as grace "appearing in mythological forms."

Secrecy: The Power of the Powerless and the Wisdom of the One

The second concept I will discuss is that of 'secrecy', which is closely related to the role and agency of God in history – both primary and secondary. In fact, in Tolkien's view the blossoming of the Tree is not the product of a human effort, but rather an unexpected divine gift, to be recognized and received with humility; 'renewal' is not the result of a human strategy (even a Christian one) but a seed that germinates in hidden and unexpected places, planted and fostered by Someone else – which one is simply called to discover, protect, and nourish (like Aragorn with the new sapling of the Tree). In Tolkien's (and Newman's) view the acceptance of change is thus implicitly founded on a vision of history as the place where God can 'intrude', planting and fostering seeds of hope in the midst of the darkness of evil, in a way which is always secret and unexpected, defying human wisdom and any wordily logic of power. As Tolkien wrote in one of the darkest moments of the 20th century: "The future is impenetrable especially to the wise; for what is really important is always hid from contemporaries, and the seeds of what is to be are quietly germinating in the dark in some forgotten corner, while everyone is looking at Stalin or Hitler" (*Letters* 110).

Tolkien and the Secret Life in Creation[18]

In Tolkien's secondary world, the 'forgotten corner' of history, where the seeds of hope quietly germinate, is of course the Shire of the Hobbits; the Hobbits are indeed the characters whom Tolkien explicitly acknowledged as embodying this 'dominant motive' of his mythology:

> The Knowledge of the Creation Drama was incomplete [...] the Creator had not revealed all. [...] Here we meet among other things, the first example of the motive *to become dominant in Hobbits* that the great policies of world history, 'the wheels of the world', are often turned not by the Lords and Governors, even gods, but by the *seemingly unknown and weak – owing to the secret life in creation*, and the part unknowable to all wisdom but One, that resides in the intrusions of the Children of God into the Drama. (*Letters* 206-9, emphasis added)

18 This section re-elaborates material already published in Pezzini 2019 and expanded in Pezzini 2025 (chapter 3), to which I refer for a larger treatment.

To understand the content and implications of this passage, with its ultimate Hobbit reference, one should briefly recall Tolkien's secondary cosmogony; according to this, a single, superior Being (Eru or Ilúvatar) created a number of secondary divine powers (the Ainur, later Valar), with and through whom He subsequently brought into existence the World to which Middle-earth belongs (Arda). As explained in the "Ainulindalë," in Arda, the Valar "exercise delegated authority in their spheres" (*Letters* 206), in a fashion like the Greek gods (they are indeed the "Lords [...] Governors [...] gods" to whom Tolkien alludes in the quote above). The Valar also interact with the various anthropomorphic races inhabiting Arda,[19] including especially with the Elves and Men (the 'Children of Ilúvatar'); these are the special objects of the their love because they were created by Eru alone, without the Valar's participation, as free "intrusions [...] into the Drama."

The word "intrusion" is crucial, and epitomizes another important concept in Tolkien's 'secondary theology', which can be illustrated with a passage from another letter:

> the One [...] reserves the right to intrude the finger of God into the story [...] (a possible definition of a 'miracle'). According to the fable Elves and Men were the first of these *intrusions* [...] they were not therefore in any sense conceived or made by the gods, the Valar [...] and were for the Valar an incalculable element. (*Letters* 341, emphasis added)

The idea of 'intrusion' is thus strictly associated with Eru/Ilúvatar, who hides His plans from the Valar, thereby affirming His own creative freedom. This freedom goes well beyond the creation of His (free) Children and is revealed in other free "intrusions" within the history of Arda, in ways though that are always secret, beyond the understanding of other beings, divine or otherwise ("the Wise"). True wisdom is thus revealed and affirmed as an awareness of one's ultimate ignorance.[20] Finally, (returning to the passage quoted at the beginning of this section), the freedom of God is enacted especially in His enhancement of the role played by seemingly irrelevant characters and events ("the seemingly unknown and weak"). This motive ("the secret life in creation") is at the core of the narrative of *The Lord of the Rings*, where it is of course especially associated with the

19 See Pezzini 2021 for an overview of the different patterns.

20 Cf. in this respect Elrond's words in acknowledging the unexpected role of the Hobbits in the fight against Sauron: "Who of all the Wise could have foreseen it? Or, if they are wise, why should they expect to know it, until the hour has struck?" (*LotR* 270).

Hobbits: iconically small and reserved, neglected or despised by the Wise and the Powerful, they are revealed as unexpected heroes.

In this respect, as mentioned, it is significant that the great lover of the Hobbits is the incarnate angel Gandalf, who – in contrast with other 'Powers' like Sauron or Saruman – holds the Hobbits in high esteem, especially because of their surprising unpredictability,[21] which is indeed the mark of Eru's operation in the History of Arda, as seen. In fact, Gandalf's love for the Hobbits is not merely a narrative ornament: rather, Gandalf acknowledges that, by Eru's mysterious "wisdom", the Hobbits have been chosen as the secret instruments for the fulfilment of His narrative. This is reflected in his decision to entrust to the weak Frodo the 'secret mission' to destroy the Ring in Mordor – a decision which is counted as a "folly" according to the purely human wisdom of someone like Denethor,[22] but it is in fact a 'divine' folly, with strong biblical resonances.[23] All of these instances of folly and secrecy in *The Lord of the Rings* are thus ultimately dependent on and analogous to Eru's operation in the history of Middle-earth, which is always secret, unforeseen, and baffling to the reasoning of the Wise, and (to recall for the last time the passage quoted at the beginning of this section) always involves the unexpected enhancement of "the seemingly unknown and weak."

What has all this to do with Newman? The answer lies in the Marian subtext of this dominant Tolkienian motive of the 'enhancement of the weak', which, if it were not already obvious enough through its biblical resonances,[24] is openly acknowledged in a passage from a letter to Auden, where Tolkien allusively describes the "value of Hobbits" with a direct quote from the *Magnificat* (Luke 1:46-55):

> I myself saw the value of Hobbits, in putting earth under the feet of 'romance', and in providing subjects for 'ennoblement' and heroes more praiseworthy

21 Cf. the evaluation of Hobbit-lore as an "obscure branch of knowledge [...] full of surprises" (*LotR* 48) and Gandalf's reaction to Frodo's decision to take the Ring, noting that hobbits are "amazing creatures" that can "still surprise you at a pinch" (*LotR* 62).

22 Thus, Boromir vents his frustration at the "folly" of sending a hobbit to walk blindly into Mordor(*LotR* 398). Cf. also Celeborn, who judges Gandalf's decision to enter Moria as a fall "from wisdom to folly" (*LotR* 356).

23 Cf. "the wisdom of this world is folly with God, For it is written, 'He catches the wise in their craftiness'" (1 Cor. 3:19, quoting Job 5:13 and also recalling Luke 1:51).

24 Cf. especially: "This is the hour of the Shire-folk, when they arise from their quiet fields to shake the towers and counsels of the Great" (*LotR* 270), which can be compared with Luke 1:51: "he has scattered those who are proud in their inmost thoughts," which is another verse from the *Magnificat*.

> than the professionals [...]. Not that I am a 'democrat' in any of its current uses; except that I suppose, to speak in literary terms, we are all equal before the Great Author, *qui deposuit potentes de sede et exaltavit humiles*. (*Letters* 314).

The verse of the *Magnificat* (Luke 1:52), with all its implications as regards the theological significance of the Incarnation as the epitome of God's methodology, arguably encapsulates the nature and origin of Tolkien's conception of the "secret life in creation"; it is also useful to introduce Newman's Mariology, which I will discuss in the next, final section.

Newman: the 'Marian Turn' and the Love to be Unknown

The title of this section alludes to a recent contribution by Rebekah Lamb ("The Marian Turn in Newman's Idea of History"), on which I will here heavily rely to present this important aspect of Newman's thought; Newman's Mariology has often been neglected, but, as Lamb has demonstrated, it should indeed be considered as an important *tessera* in his theology of history; it can be fruitfully compared to and illuminate Tolkien's own 'implicit Mariology', as discussed in the previous section.

As a former evangelical and Anglican theologian, converted to the Catholic Church only as an adult (in 1845, when he was 44 years old), Newman might not appear as an obvious Mariological thinker; and yet, Newman's devotion for Mary (and his interest in her theological significance) can be traced to the late 1820s, also thanks to the influence of his friends John Keble (author of the influential prayer book *The Christian Year* (1827), which also included Marian hymns) and Richard Froude, the latter openly acknowledged in Newman's *Apologia pro vita sua* as an important source of his Marian devotion (25).

Moreover, as convincingly reconstructed by Lamb, the encounter with Mary should be considered as the natural development and fulfilment of an interest that Newman held since his early years in the value of the 'hidden life for history.' This can be illustrated for instance with a few verses from the poem "The Hidden Ones," originally written in 1829, and later reprinted in 1868 in his collection *Verse on Various Occasions*:

> Hid are the saints of God;—
> Uncertified by high angelic sign;
> Nor raiment soft, nor empire's golden rod
> Marks them divine.
> […]
> These are the chosen few,
> The remnant fruit of largely-scatter'd grace,
> God sows in waste, to reap whom He foreknew.

Among the 'seeds' of sanctitude planted by God in human history (which could indeed be compared to those "germinating in forgotten corners" mentioned by Tolkien) Mary stands out a special case, as Newman would realize in the following years. In fact, as put by Lamb (2003: 63): "Mary's status as patron of history is one which especially captured Newman's devotional imagination, informing his reflections on the place and value of hidden holiness in the outworkings of providence". Indeed, Lamb continues:

> in his turn to Marian dogma […] Newman saw that the lasting links between persons across history were created through the operations of divine grace. […] The animating force of history was not power politics for Newman […] his writings always hold a special affection for the ways in which, paradoxically, providence manifests the plans for salvation history in hidden ways, especially in the lives of saints who live in the outskirts of public life […]. (2003: 51)

As suggested by Lamb's perceptive words, this 'Marian turn' should thus be closely related to Newman's theology of history, and to his views on the nature and methodology of God's operation within it specifically, as presented in his *Development of Christian Doctrine* especially (in which Mary also receives a special mention), but also in other works. For Newman human history is in fact secretly and 'organically' guided by divine Providence; this also operates through the mediation of the Saints, who therefore also operate according to the same pattern of secret growth and organic development. For instance Newman wrote (in terms that could be easily applied to the way victory in *The Lord of the Rings* was achieved and the kingdom of Aragorn was restored) that St Benedict "found the world, physical and social, in ruins, and his mission was to restore it in the way, not of science, but of nature […] so quietly, patiently, gradually, that often, till the work was done, it was not known to be doing. It was a restoration, rather than a visitation, correction, or conversion" (Newman 1906: 410).

Therefore, in Newman's view Mary can be considered to be the 'patron of history' since, as the Queen of All Saints, she epitomizes both the operation of divine Providence in history ("*He hath regarded the lowliness of his handmaiden [...] and hath exalted the humble and meek*"), and the attitude required from human beings towards it, which is both of obedience (*fiat*) and of humble, patient 'exegesis,' aware of one's limitations in understanding God's designs (vs. the interpretative arrogance of the 'Wise' who "want to see all ends"); the *Magnificat* in this sense can be described as a model of human (self-)exegesis and Mary can be considered "the humble and holy reader of God's plan for her life, and by extension, for history himself" (Lamb 2023: 52).

Newman would further elaborate on such views in a sermon of 1868 on the Presentation of Christ in the Temple, appropriately titled "Secrecy and Suddenness of Divine Visitations." This can be here quoted at length:

> I say, we are today reminded of the noiseless course of God's providence, – His tranquil accomplishment, in the course of nature, of great events long designed; and again, of the suddenness and stillness of His visitations. [...] Now, there is evidently nothing great or impressive in this; nothing to excite the feelings, or interest the imagination. We know what the world thinks of such a group as I have described. *The weak and helpless*, whether from age or infancy, it looks upon negligently and passes by. [...] Such has ever been the manner of His visitations, in the destruction of His enemies as well as in the deliverance of His own people; – *silent, sudden, unforeseen*, as regards the world. [...] Men, who are plunged in the pursuits of active life, are no judges of its course and tendency on the whole. *They confuse great events with little*, and measure the importance of objects, as in perspective, by the mere standard of nearness or remoteness. [...] in every age the world is profane and blind, and *God hides* His providence, yet carries it forward. (Newman 1907-9, II: 109-14, emphasis added)

If one compares this with the passages by Tolkien quoted in the previous sections one can note striking points of similarity, especially in regard to the enhanced role of "the weak and helpless" and the secrecy with which God carries forward His Providence, in a way that baffles human wisdom, which normally pays attention to Stalin, Hitler, Augustus or Sauron, but forgets the "seeds germinating in the dark in some forgotten corner," from Nazareth to Birmingham and the Shire.

Although one should not altogether exclude it, it is probably incorrect to speculate about a direct influence of Newman on Tolkien as regards this aspect specifically and his theology of history in general; rather, I believe one should talk of a shared

'Newmanian spirituality,' passed on to Tolkien via osmosis through his experience at the Birmingham Oratory, and probably mediated by the figure of St Philip Neri, who attracted Newman especially because of his "love to be unknown" (*ama nesciri*) and to whom Tolkien was devoted to the point of choosing Philip as his confirmation name, and apparently integrating it into his monogram (as recently noted by Holly Ordway).[25] Philip Neri is indeed a Saint who best embodied the method of powerlessness, secrecy and humbleness ("the secret life in creation") so typical of God's operation in history and so dear to both Newman and Tolkien. As Newman pointed out in a sermon preached shortly after his move to Birmingham, with words that could be easily applied, *mutatis mutandis*, to the narrative arc of *The Lord of the Rings*:

> It is not by the enthusiasm of the multitude, or by political violence, – it is not by powerful declamation [...] not by sudden popularity, or by strong resolves, and demonstrations, or by romantic incidents, or by immediate successes, that undertakings commence which are to last. [...] So was it with the Lord of grace Himself, when He came upon earth; so it is with His chosen servants after Him. He grew up in silence and obscurity, overlooked by the world; and then He triumphed. [...] So was it in the beginning, so has it been ever since [...]
>
> [*Philip*] did not ask to be opposed, to be maligned, to be persecuted, but simply to be overlooked, to be despised. [...] We [*the community at Birmingham*] [...] have deliberately set ourselves down in a populous district, unknown to the great world, and have commenced, as St. Philip did, by ministering chiefly to the poor and lowly. [...] We have determined, through God's mercy, not to have the praise or the popularity that the world can give, but, according to our Father's own precept, "to love to be unknown." (Newman 1908: 218-19, 231, 241; emphasis added)

A final note: at the beginning of this very sermon Newman refers to a painting of St Philip Neri, a copy of a famous one by Guido Reni which is still visible in the Birmingham Oratory, and with which Tolkien was certainly very familiar. It may be not coincidental that this painting is surmounted by that very line of the *Magnificat* (*exaltavit humiles*) which Tolkien used in reference to the value of the Hobbits in his work,[26] and which in my view sums up this important mark of the spiritual affinity between Tolkien and Newman – an affinity still largely to be explored.

---

25 Cf. Ordway (2023: 34-35).
26 As noted by Ordway (2023: 244).

About the Author

Giuseppe Pezzini is Tutor and Fellow at Corpus Christi College, Oxford which he joined in 2021, after five years at St Andrews (2016-2021), and research fellowships in Oxford (2013-2015) and Princeton (2016). He has published especially on Latin language and literature, philosophy of language, and the theory of fiction, ancient and modern. He is the Tolkien Editor for the *Journal of Inklings Studies*, one the founders of the Oxford Tolkien Network, and the author of many publications on Tolkien, including a monograph on Tolkien's literary theory (Cambridge University Press 2025).

Bibliography

Curry, Patrick. 2004. *Defending Middle-Earth: Tolkien, Myth and Modernity.* 2nd edition. 1st edition 1997. Boston, MA: Houghton Mifflin.

Fornet-Ponse, Thomas. 2010. "Tolkien, Newman und das Oxford Movement." *Hither Shore* 7: 172-86.

Honegger, Thomas. 2011. "Time and Tide – Medieval Patterns of Interpreting the Passing of Time in Tolkien's Work." *Hither Shore* 8: 86-99.

Imbert, Yanick. 2022. *From Imagination to Faërie: Tolkien's Thomist Fantasy.* Eugene, OR: Pickwick Publications.

Ker, Ian T. 2009. *John Henry Newman: A Biography.* 2nd edition. 1st edition 1988. Oxford: Oxford University Press.

2014. *Newman on Vatican II.* Oxford: Oxford University Press.

Ker, Ian T. and Terence Merrigan (eds.). 2009. *The Cambridge Companion to John Henry Newman.* Cambridge: Cambridge University Press.

Lamb, Rebekah A. 2023. "The Marian Turn in Newman's Idea of History." In Michael D. Hurley and Rebekah A. Lamb (eds.) *Reading the Times: John Henry Newman.* Issue of *Religion and Literature* 55.1: 49-70.

Newman, John Henry. 1901. *Callista, a tale of the third century.* London and New York: Longmans. 1st edition 1855-1856.

1903. *Verses on Various Occasions.* London and New York: Longmans. 1st edition 1868.

1906. *Historical Sketches. Vol. II.* London and New York: Longmans. 1st edition 1840.

1907-1909. *Parochial and Plain Sermons.* Eight volumes. London and New York: Longmans. 1st edition 1868.

1908. *Apologia pro vita sua, being a History of his Religious Opinions*. London and New York: Longmans. 1st edition 1865.

1908. *Sermons Preached on Various Occasions*. London and New York: Longmans. 1st edition 1857.

1909. *An Essay on the Development of Christian Doctrine*. London and New York: Longmans. 1st edition 1845.

Ordway, Holly. 2023. *Tolkien's Faith: A Spiritual Biography*. Elk Grove Village, IL: Word on Fire Academic.

Pearce, Joseph. 2014. *Catholic Literary Giants: A Field Guide to the Catholic Literary Landscape*. 1st edition 2005. San Francisco, CA: Ignatius Press.

Pezzini, Giuseppe. 2019. "The Lords of the West: Cloaking, Freedom and the Divine Narrative in Tolkien's Poetics." *The Journal of Inklings Studies* 9: 115-53.

2021. "The Gods in (Tolkien's) Epic." In Hamish Williams (ed.). *Tolkien and the Classical World*. Cormarë Series 45. Zurich and Jena: Walking Tree Publishers, 73-103.

2022. "'Classical' Narratives of Decline in Tolkien: Renewal, Accommodation, Focalization." In Alicia Matz and Maciej Paprocki (eds.) *There and Back Again: Tolkien and the Graeco-Roman World. Thersites* 15: 25-51.

2023. "Newman on Art, Imagination, and the Classics: *Callista* revisited." In Michael D. Hurley and Rebekah A. Lamb (eds.) *Reading the Times: John Henry Newman. Religion and Literature* 55.1: 119-39.

2025. *Tolkien and the Mystery of Literary Creation*. Cambridge: Cambridge University Press.

Pinsent, Pat. 2022. "Religion: An Implicit Catholicism." In Stuart D. Lee (ed.). *A Companion to J.R.R. Tolkien*. 2nd edition. 1st edition 2014. Chichester: Wiley Blackwell, 424-36.

Tolkien, J.R.R. 1977. *The Silmarillion*. Edited by Christopher Tolkien. London: George Allen & Unwin.

1980. *Unfinished Tales of Númenor and Middle-earth*. Edited by Christopher Tolkien. London: George Allen & Unwin.

1988. *Tree and Leaf*. 1st edition 1964. 2nd edition. London: Unwin Hyman.

2004. *The Lord of the Rings*. 50th anniversary edition. 1st edition 1954-55. Boston: Houghton Mifflin.

2005. *Smith of Wootton Major*. 1st edition 1967. Extended edition prepared by Verlyn Flieger. London: HarperCollins.

2008. *Tolkien On Fairy-Stories*. Edited by Verlyn Flieger and Douglas A. Anderson. London: HarperCollins.

2023. *The Letters of J.R.R. Tolkien: Revised and Expanded Edition*. Humphrey Carpenter (ed.) with the assistance of Christopher Tolkien. 1st edition 1981. London: HarperCollins.

Tomko, Michael. 2011. '"An Age Comes On": J.R.R. Tolkien and the English Catholic Sense of History.' In Paul. E. Kerry (ed.). *The Ring and the Cross: Christianity and The Lord of the Rings*. Madison, NJ: Fairleigh Dickinson University Press, 205-23.

Weinreich, Frank and Thomas Honegger (eds). 2006. *Tolkien and Modernity.* Two volumes. Cormarë Series 9 & 10. Zurich and Berne: Walking Tree Publishers.

Wiemann, Dirk. 2011. "*Mundus senescit*: Tolkien and the Allure of Medieval Nostalgia." *Hither Shore* 8: 24-38.

Wood, Ralph C. (ed.). 2015. *Tolkien among the Moderns*. Notre Dame, IN: University of Notre Dame Press.

Zachary D. Schmoll

Tolkien and Chesterton: The Orthodoxy of Middle-earth

Abstract

In many ways, Tolkien and Chesterton were kindred spirits, sharing many similar perspectives on adventure, patriotism, and stories. Tolkien is known to have been familiar with the work of Chesterton, so while this chapter does not seek to prove a necessary causal connection between the two, it seeks to explore the ways in which elements of specifically Chesterton's *Orthodoxy*, one of Chesterton's works his works we know that Tolkien read, might have been an inspiration for the quest in Middle-earth.

Given Chesterton's sizable influence over British intellectual culture in the early 20th century, it is certainly no surprise that his work would be the stuff of conversations among groups like the Inklings.[1] Of the thirteen books written by G.K. Chesterton with which Oronzo Cilli reports J.R.R Tolkien was familiar, *Orthodoxy* seems to have been of special importance to him (Cilli 2019: 164).[2] As a young man in the 1908-1909 school year, Tolkien presented copies of both *Orthodoxy* and *Heretics* to his school library (Cilli 2019: 164). Holly Ordway suggests that Tolkien may have heard Chesterton speak in person when "he gave an evening lecture on the topic of 'Romance' at the Oxford Examination Schools in the Trinity term of 1914, when Tolkien was in residence" (2021a: 305). Ordway also notes that, according to Tolkien's daughter Priscilla, he was "steeped in" Chesterton's work (2021b). 'Romance'

1 Diana Glyer provides an account that does not involve J.R.R. Tolkien directly, but given his proximity to its main participants, it seems clear that Chesterton formed a part of the intellectual life of the Inklings. In 1936, C.S. Lewis missed a scheduled walk with fellow Inklings Owen Barfield and Cecil Harwood. Jokingly, they created a mock exam Lewis had to pass to gain readmittance to the walking club. Ultimately published in a very limited run, this exam was entitled *A Cretaceous Perambulator* and included the following essay prompt: "[Describe] an imaginary walking-tour lasting not less than 4 days with no more than 4 of the following." The list of potential walkers includes Father Ronald Knox, Mahatma Gandhi, G.K. Chesterton, Mary Pickford, Sigmund Freud, Sir William Morris, Lord Olivier and "Tha Dhali Llama of Thibet" [*sic*] (Glyer 2016: 137).

2 In a letter to his son Christopher in 1944, Tolkien did discuss Chesterton's poem, "The Ballad of The White Horse," and in a draft of a letter to Joanna de Bortadano from April 1956, Tolkien referred to Chesterton directly as well (*Letters* 92, 246). While these quotes do not directly relate to the thesis of this chapter, it is more direct evidence that Tolkien was quite aware of Chesterton's work broadly.

is, of course, a central theme in *Orthodoxy* and earns placement in the title of its penultimate chapter.

'Romance,' in the Chestertonian sense, is not to be confused with our contemporary definition of romance as passionate love or the movement of Romanticism. Chesterton defines 'romance' as follows,

> To show that a faith or a philosophy is true from every standpoint would be too big an undertaking even for a much bigger book than this; it is necessary to follow one path of argument; and this is the path that I here propose to follow. I wish to set forth my faith as particularly answering this double spiritual need, the need for that mixture of the familiar and the unfamiliar which Christendom has rightly named romance. (2009: 27)

Therefore, when Chesterton uses the term 'romance', the reader ought to be thinking of the connection between adventure and homecoming. It is the combination of the familiar and the unfamiliar. The Christian faith, as he continues to argue, is a romance because it is both comfortable and wild. Similarly, one can consider the story arc of *The Lord of the Rings* as a romance, an argument that will be drawn out throughout this chapter.

In a letter to Amy Ronald in 1969, J.R.R. Tolkien explicitly tied one of Gandalf's most famous lines to an image from *Orthodoxy*. He writes:

> Chesterton once said that it is our duty to keep the Flag of This World flying: but it takes now a sturdier and more sublime patriotism than it did then. Gandalf added that it is not for us to choose the times into which we are born, but to do what we could to repair them; but the spirit of wickedness in high places is now so powerful and so many-headed in its incarnations that there seems nothing more to do than personally to refuse to worship any of the hydras' heads [...]. (*Letters* 402)

In this letter, penned approximately four years before his own passing, Tolkien combines the wisdom of Chesterton with that of one of his wisest characters.

While it is not wise to read too far into one passing reference, it is still worth noting that Chesterton retained space in Tolkien's mind, even long after the show of boyish enthusiasm that led him to donate *Orthodoxy* to his school library so that others would pick it up and read it as well. This chapter will pursue this line of thought deeper into Tolkien's *legendarium*. In what ways was the spirit of Chesterton's *Orthodoxy* woven into the fiber of Middle-earth?

Other discussions of the similarities between Tolkien and Chesterton could be written as we know that Tolkien also read *Heretics* (mentioned above) and many others, but this discussion will be limited to *Orthodoxy* as it is arguably Chesterton's most direct discussion of the theme of romance.

An Adventure There and Back Again

Before J.R.R. Tolkien even introduced Bilbo Baggins's first name, the reader of *The Hobbit* is given a very brief plot summary. "This is a story of how a Baggins had an adventure, and found himself doing and saying things altogether unexpected. He may have lost the neighbours' respect, but he gained – well, you will see whether he gained anything in the end" (*Hobbit* 6). It is not surprising that Tolkien decided to write an adventure story. As Ordway has documented, Tolkien read a great deal of adventure literature throughout his life, from H. Rider Haggard and Edgar Rice Burroughs to J.M. Barrie and even Robert Howard's stories about Conan the Barbarian (2021a). Despite writing in a letter to Stanley Unwin, after the publication of *The Hobbit*, that "'Hobbit talk' amuses me privately (and to a certain degree also my boy Christopher) more than adventures", it is clear that Tolkien loved a good adventure story (*Letters* 36). However, he also titled his work "There and Back Again." The adventure was not only about going to an unfamiliar location, finding gold, and coming face-to-face with dragons; the adventure also included the return and some kind of hinted-at gain.

Chesterton also discusses an adventure that includes a return, albeit an unexpected one. He discusses an English yachtsman who ended up sailing off course, expecting to land somewhere else but finding himself back in England. Chesterton writes:

> What could be more delightful than to have in the same few minutes all the fascinating terrors of going abroad combined with all the humane security of coming home again? What could be better than to have all the fun of discovering South Africa without the disgusting necessity of landing there? What could be more glorious than to brace one's self up to discover New South Wales and then realize, with a gush of happy tears, that it was really old South Wales. (2009: 7)

The adventure provides a sense of excitement for the yachtsman, much like Tolkien's preview of a coming quest encourages the reader to turn to the next page. The yachtsman wants the adventure, but he is truly glad to return home when the adventure has come to its conclusion.

Even in these two very brief examples, Chesterton and Tolkien have begun constructing complementary theologies of place. There is value in helping others reclaim their homeland or in finding undiscovered islands. Adventures are not intrinsically evil and should not be avoided even though they might make one late for dinner. Nevertheless, the adventure is only complete and the profit, be it joy or gain, found when the hero has returned from his journey and finds himself back on familiar soil. The Chestertonian definition of romance encapsulates this combination of the familiar and unfamiliar making a complete and good story.

Chesterton expands on the importance of the return home as he writes: "We need so to view the world as to combine an idea of wonder and an idea of welcome. We need to be happy in this wonderland without once being merely comfortable" (2009: 21-22). Perhaps this was why, as Chesterton biographer Ian Ker notes, he enjoyed the work of Robert Louis Stevenson and believed it revitalized the adventure genre. Ker explains: "In Chesterton's view, it was this 'sharp return to simplicity, as the expression of the fiery thirst for happiness' that gave Stevenson an important place in the history of literature" (2011: 590). In another biography of Chesterton, William Oddie writes: "For Chesterton, the idea of 'Optimism' undoubtedly included Stevenson's notion of 'manly virtues' as an essential part of what was needed to overcome the dragon of 'pessimism': dragons, Chesterton believed, had to be confronted, sword in hand, not pusillanimously evaded" (2010: 139).

Adventure stories, or romances, reflect human desire. There is a simplicity to them: a combination of wonder at the obstacles overcome and the ultimate return to one's rightful place. In one of the most famous adventure stories, Odysseus seeks to find his way back to Ithaca. Despite the carnage that ensues when he arrives, it is important to him, his family, and even his city that he makes his way home. Readers are content when he returns home, even if they disapprove of his actions, because the adventure is now complete.

The Hobbit is a similarly simple story. It is an episodic narrative with increasingly higher stakes until it reaches the climactic Battle of the Five Armies, and then progresses to the ultimate return to the Shire. However, the Bilbo who returns to the Shire is not identical to the one that left it. Gandalf points out the change after Bilbo recites a poem extolling the virtues of adventure that could be titled, "Roads Go Ever On" (*Hobbit* 302). The timing in this situation is telling, though, as Bilbo breaks into verse immediately after he can see his Hill. As Tolkien puts it, he "stopped suddenly" and began to recite (*Hobbit* 302).

Bilbo's journey reflects that of the yachtsman. He goes on an adventure that he did not really want to join. He goes through many hardships but ultimately completes his journey and returns home. The narrator explains in the beginning that readers will have to judge if Bilbo gained anything from his journey. He did not bring home very much treasure, so his situation did not change all that much materially (despite what his neighbors ultimately said about him). Instead, he changed as a person; he gained virtue. In a Chestertonian sense, he gained all the benefits of going on an adventure with the pleasant surprise that his adventure brought him right back to where he started; it is a romantic tale. Not only that, but he is quite satisfied to be where he belongs, "and the sound of the kettle on his hearth was ever after more musical than it had been even in the quiet days before the Unexpected Party" (*Hobbit* 304).

The comparison of Bilbo and the yachtsman extends further, though, as the discussion of the yachtsman also extends into a meditation on fascination and comfort. Chesterton writes: "How can this queer cosmic town, with its many-legged citizens, with its monstrous and ancient lamps, how can this world give us at once the fascination of a strange town and the comfort and honour of being our own town?" (2009: 20-21). The tension present in this view of existence which Chesterton will go on to defend throughout the balance of *Orthodoxy* is very much like the tension that accompanies Bilbo's return. No one understands him. He is a Hobbit just like them, but he used to be an ordinary Hobbit that never went on any adventures or did anything unexpected. Upon his return, "[m] any shook their heads and touched their foreheads and said 'Poor old Baggins!' and though few believed any of his tales, he remained very happy to the end of his days, and those were extraordinarily long" (*Hobbit* 304). He both does and does not still belong in his old town. However, he is extraordinarily happy, much like those who, Chesterton would argue, actually begin to embrace the romance of orthodoxy. Even though many think he is losing his mind, he does not care because he has found the joy of adventure and has seen the benefits that a navigationally-challenged yachtsman can gain.

Sam Gamgee and the Flag of the World

The residents of Pimlico, an area in central London with a bad reputation at the time, were probably not thrilled when they read Chesterton's description of their abode, even if it was accurate:

> Let us suppose we are confronted with a desperate thing – say Pimlico. If we think what is really best for Pimlico we shall find the thread of thought leads to the throne or the mystic and the arbitrary. It is not enough for a man to disapprove of Pimlico: in that case he will merely cut his throat or move to Chelsea. Nor, certainly, is it enough for a man to approve of Pimlico: for then it will remain Pimlico, which would be awful. The only way out of it seems to be for somebody to love Pimlico: to love it with a transcendental tie and without any earthly reason. If there arose a man who loved Pimlico, then Pimlico would rise into ivory towers and golden pinnacles; Pimlico would attire herself as a woman does when she is loved. For decoration is not given to hide horrible things: but decorate things already adorable. A mother does not give her child a blue bow because he is so ugly without it. A lover does not give a girl a necklace to hide her neck. If men loved Pimlico as mothers love children, arbitrarily, because it is theirs, Pimlico in a year or two might be fairer than Florence. (Chesterton 2009: 102-3)

Chesterton's message is relatively straightforward. For something to become beautiful, the desire for its beauty must come first. Even a terrible place like Pimlico could become beautiful if somebody took the time to care for it. This love for a town, a place, a person, or a country that does not seem to deserve it is what Chesterton came to refer to as patriotism. He ultimately connects Christianity to *cosmic* patriotism, the devotion to a universe so broken and full of sin that believers ought to be moved to change it. He explains:

> The world is not a lodging-house at Brighton, which we are to leave because it is miserable. It is the fortress of our family, with the flag flying on the turret, and the more miserable it is the less we should leave it. The point is not that this world is too sad to love or too glad not to love; the point is that when you do love a thing, its gladness is a reason for loving it, and its sadness a reason for loving it more. (Chesterton 2009: 102)

Tolkien's similar commitment to loving the world despite its imperfections can be seen in many different ways, but Samwise Gamgee's love of the Shire shows true patriotism.

While recovering in the woods of Lothlorien, Sam is allowed to look into the Mirror of Galadriel. He is terrified by what he sees: "There's that Ted Sandyman a-cutting down trees as he shouldn't. They didn't ought to be felled: it's that avenue beyond the Mill that shades the road to Bywater. I wish I could get at Ted, and I'd fell him!" (*LotR* 362). Sam's outrage seems to channel Chesterton's line about the cosmic patriot: "He is ready to smash the whole universe for the sake of itself" (2009: 109). He is ready to take down whatever is happening in the Shire for the sake of the Shire. His ire grows as he realizes that the damage has gone even further, and he contemplates abandoning the quest altogether: "'I can't stay here,' he said wildly. 'I must go home. They've dug up Bagshot Row, and there's the poor old Gaffer going down the Hill with his bits of things on a barrow. I must go home!'" (*LotR* 363). Recall that Sam has been Frodo's most trustworthy companion and has sworn to continue wherever the path may lead. Even with that strong bond, which eventually remains intact, his sadness for the situation in the Shire causes him to love it all the more and to want to fix it. Again, channeling Chesterton, Sam could affirmatively answer this question, "Can he hate it enough to change it, and yet love it enough to think it worth changing?" (2009: 109). Stratford Caldecott writes: "For him to leave the Shire out of love for Frodo involves a great sacrifice. In a sense, he has to sacrifice the Shire itself – consciously so when he sees the threat to it in Galadriel's mirror but still determines to go on" (2012: 128).

Galadriel, in her wisdom, provides Sam with a present that ultimately allows him to do just that when he finally does return home, but one can see a Chestertonian spirit of patriotism shining through this obligation and commitment to the land and people that he loves. Caldecott expands on this gift: "Like Aragorn he has the power to heal his land of the hurts of war, and it is by this healing power that a true king is known, whether in Gondor or in Arnor. In Tolkien's intention, Sam is therefore paired with Aragorn as an 'heir of Elendil,' the archetypal Elf-friend" (2012: 129). After his vision in the mirror came true, Sam, not Frodo, turned out to be the one who would ultimately help set everything to the way it should have been.

As he ponders what to do with the gift from Galadriel, he realizes that, while it is his gift, it is also meant to be shared. He takes Frodo's advice to "[u]se all the wits and knowledge you have of your own, Sam [...] and then use the gift to help your work and better it. And use it sparingly. There is not much here, and I expect every grain has a value" (*LotR* 1023). His patriotism was not to himself, his own ambitions, or even his own garden. He was dedicated to the Shire. This is what causes Bradley Birzer to ultimately label him "the ultimate personification, representative, and defender of the Shire" (2009: 23).

His commitment and patriotism grow even deeper as he eventually marries Rosie Cotton, setting down roots for himself in the Shire in a way that would last for generations. Tolkien himself thought highly of this relationship, explaining in a letter to Milton Waldman: "I think the simple 'rustic' love of Sam and his Rosie (nowhere elaborated) is absolutely essential to the study of his (the chief hero's) character, and to the theme of the relation of ordinary life (breathing, eating, working, begetting) and quests, sacrifice, causes, and the 'longing for Elves', and sheer beauty" (*Letters* 161). Birzer quotes Charles Williams who said that Sam represents "freedom, peace, [and] ordinary life" (2009: 73). In fact, Sam would have been exactly the kind of person for whom Chesterton wrote *Orthodoxy*, for as he claimed: "If a man says that extinction is better than existence or blank existence better than variety and adventure, then he is not one of the ordinary people to whom I am talking" (2009: 21). As an ordinary Hobbit, Sam seeks to do the best he can for those around him.

He served as mayor, ceremonially hosting parties, for years. Being in charge of celebration, Sam had the opportunity to bring a sense of order and joy at appointed times around the year for his neighbors. He would affirm what Josef Pieper argued when he wrote: "To hold a celebration means to affirm the basic meaningfulness of the universe and a sense of oneness with it, of inclusion within it. In celebrating, in holding festivals upon occasion, man experiences the world in an aspect other than the everyday one" (2009: 49). Not only did Sam help make the Shire beautiful again, but as he presided over festivities for years and years, he affirmed the meaningfulness of various days. He affirmed the goodness of springtime and harvest. He affirmed the goodness of the way the world was at the same time as he helped the residents appreciate the different days that were specially set apart. Again, Sam's actions seem to resonate with the kind of person Chesterton was talking about when he wrote: "The ordinary man has always been sane because the ordinary man has always been a mystic" (2009: 46). He celebrated the special days, which were not extraordinary for any other reason than the Shire decided to celebrate them. Compared with Chesterton's maniac, who often is classified as a logician or mathematician, Sam exhibits the heart of a mystic, willing to celebrate the basic reality of a meaningful universe.

There is a sense in which his patriotism has achieved victory for the time being. Tolkien did start a quickly abandoned sequel to *The Lord of the Rings* entitled *The New Shadow*, where even after the defeat of Sauron, a new evil was rising. Birzer (2009: 107) connects this to a statement Gandalf made right before marching to the Black Gate:

> Other evils there are that may come; for Sauron is himself but a servant or emissary. Yet it is not our part to master all the tides of the world, but to do what is in us for the succour of those years wherein we are set, uprooting the evil in the fields that we know, so that those who live after may have clean earth to till. What weather they shall have is not ours to rule. (*LotR*: 879)

Nevertheless, as one comes to the book's final scene, as Sam returns home to his family, it is clear that everything is as it should be for the time being. That is the result of Chesterton's sense of patriotism: loving something enough that, even through suffering, it is not abandoned but embraced all the harder.

The Romance of Orthodoxy

As *Orthodoxy* provides an apologetic for the Christian faith, it is unsurprising that Chesterton ultimately raised the question of human choice. He wrote:

> All Christianity concentrates on the man at the crossroads. The vast and shallow philosophies, the huge syntheses of humbug, all talk about ages and evolution and ultimate developments. The true philosophy is concerned with the instant. Will a man take this road or that? – that is the only thing to think about, if you enjoy thinking. (Chesterton 2009: 204).

The result of a life of choices is a story, and Chesterton put his finger on why the Christian story was so exciting:

> It has in it so strong an element of will, of what theology calls free will. You cannot finish a sum how you like. But you can finish a story how you like. When somebody discovered the Differential Calculus there was only one Differential Calculus he could discover. But when Shakespeare killed Romeo he might have married him to Juliet's old nurse if he had felt inclined. And Christendom has excelled in the narrative romance exactly because it has insisted on the theological free will. (2009: 204-5)

Stories have power because readers do not know the end. Much like life itself, decisions have consequences. The drama of the 'what if' makes life the romance that Chesterton found orthodoxy itself to be.

Frodo and Sam have a conversation about stories (or rather 'tales') and their own place in them after Frodo laments that their path is laid in an accursed direction. Sam begins to talk about the stories that he remembers: "But that's not the way of it with the tales that really mattered, or the ones that stay in the mind. Folk seem to have been just landed in them, usually – their paths were laid that way, as you put it. But I expect they had lots of chances, like us, of turning back, only they didn't. And if they had, we shouldn't know, because they'd have been forgotten" (*LotR* 711). The best stories provide the unexpected situations for people to make the right decisions, and their stories are memorable when they make the right decisions.

However, there is another element to story, according to Chesterton. There can be wrong decisions, bad consequences, and even bad events outside of a person's control:

> But to a Christian existence is a story, which may end up in any way. In a thrilling novel (that purely Christian product) the hero is not eaten by cannibals; but it is essential to the existence of the thrill that he might be eaten by cannibals. The hero must (so to speak) be an eatable hero. So in Christian morals, in short, it is wicked to call a man 'damned': but it is strictly religious and philosophic to call him damnable. (Chesterton 2009: 203)

An adventure needs to have stakes; there has to be the opportunity for something to go wrong for people to recognize and appreciate all that has gone right. Sam recognizes the same quality in the good stories he loved:

> We hear about those as just went on – and not all to a good end, mind you; at least not to what folk inside a story and not outside it call a good end. You know, coming home, and finding things all right, though not quite the same – like old Mr. Bilbo. But those aren't always the best tales to hear, though

> they may be the best tales to get landed in! I wonder what sort of a tale we've fallen into? (*LotR* 711-12)

Frodo follows this comment, realizing: "You may know, or guess, what kind of a tale it is, happy-ending or sad-ending, but the people in it don't know. And you don't want them to" (*LotR* 712). The position espoused by Chesterton and Tolkien seems to be radically at odds with the way that many people prefer to live their lives. They crave regularity and predictability. They want to know that everything is going to be all right. Frodo and Sam seem to be saying that stories are better when there is drama and tension. When that realization is combined with the fact that human life, according to Chesterton, is a story and a romance, it must follow that humans might not be made for the regularity they seek. Instead, they are made for something more. Human life is perhaps at its fullest when the unknown and unpredictable have room to play.

As Frodo and Sam's conversation draws to a close, Frodo recognizes their current situation: "You and I, Sam, are still stuck in the worst places of the story, and it is all too likely that some will say at this point: 'Shut the book now, dad; we don't want to read any more'" (*LotR* 713). Sam's response shares a different side of human nature. "Maybe […] but I wouldn't be one to say that. Things done and over and made into part of the great tales are different" (*LotR* 713). Great stories, ones that are done and over to use Sam's terminology, can be safely finished because someone else has already shown courage. A modern-day Christian can read the testimony of martyrs, admire their courage, and still be comfortable. The situation is entirely different when people find themselves in the middle of their own great story. It is harder to endure pain than to hear about someone else's pain, even for the most empathetic listeners.

Facing a dangerous situation requires the virtue of courage, something that Chesterton highlighted about Christianity specifically. He writes: "Alone of all creeds, Christianity has added courage to the virtues of the Creator. For the only courage worth calling courage must necessarily mean that the soul passes a breaking point – and does not break" (Chesterton 2009: 206). Jesus Christ chose to endure a horrible experience for all of humanity, showing not only his great love but also courage. Reflecting on the beginning of Frodo and Sam's conversation, the best stories are the ones where the hero makes the right decision at the crossroads, even at the darkest moments. Courage is necessary.

As Chesterton begins to conclude his thoughts on the romance of orthodoxy, he asserts that Christianity "is the most adventurous and manly of all theologies" (2009: 207). Adventure makes for a good story. There must be stakes in order for the story to be compelling. For a right choice to be good and courageous, there has to be the potential for a wrong choice. Frodo and Sam have to be able to turn back, but they choose not to. Even, as discussed earlier in this paper, when Sam is shown the Shire in danger, he makes the courageous choice to complete his mission rather than quit early. Because of the decision he made, readers keep turning the pages. To live a thrilling life of adventure, specifically Christian adventure, decisions must also be made. While many shrink from decision-making out of fear, Chesterton saw these crossroads as what truly made Christianity special and unique, the story that people would remember.

Conclusion

Although this paper has sought to present similarities between the thematic elements of the work of J.R.R. Tolkien and G.K. Chesterton, it would not be appropriate to conclude that there must be a causal relationship between the two. Even though it is true that Tolkien read a great deal of Chesterton from his adolescence to his elder years, that does not mean that Chesterton necessarily influenced specific moments in Tolkien's *legendarium*.

That being said, it does seem reasonable to conclude that in several ways, Tolkien and Chesterton were kindred spirits, sharing many similar perspectives on adventure, patriotism, and stories. Drawing from a similar well of Christian inspiration, each man incorporated pieces of reality into his writing. Is it possible that Tolkien thought about some of what he had read from Chesterton as he was writing about Frodo and Sam? Hypothetically speaking, yes. However, it is probably most appropriate to remember what Tolkien said about the religious elements of his work as a way to think about how he may have been influenced by Chesterton.

Tolkien famously wrote a letter to Robert Murray in 1953:

> *The Lord of the Rings* is of course a fundamentally religious and Catholic work; unconsciously so at first, but consciously in the revision. That is why I have not put in, or have cut out, practically all references to anything like 'religion', to

> cults or practices, in the imaginary world. For the religious element is absorbed into the story and the symbolism. (*Letters* 172)

When considering Tolkien as a storyteller, one should never expect to see any Christianity presented explicitly. It would seem incredibly inappropriate to see Tolkien's characters directly pointing to Chesterton. Tolkien did not tell stories that way, so readers must consider his stories thematically.

In that respect, it is obvious that *The Lord of the Rings* is a religious work even though Tolkien hardly included any explicit trappings of religion in it. Thematically, religion shines through. In much the same way, readers familiar with both *Orthodoxy* and the *legendarium* can see significant similarities. The extent to which both of these men were drawing from a shared tradition that transcends both of them and incorporates creators today is remarkable.[3] Sam famously asks: "'Don't the great tales never end?' 'No, they never end as tales,' said Frodo. 'But the people in them come, and go when their part's ended. Our part will end later – or sooner.'" (*LotR* 712). The timeless elements contained within both Tolkien and Chesterton existed before them and will continue to exist long after them. This story will not end, and neither of them would want it to.

About the Author

Zachary D. Schmoll (PhD in Humanities, Faulkner University) is an adjunct faculty member at Houston Christian University and Southeastern University. He is the author of *Disability and the Problem of Evil* (Public Philosophy Press, 2020) and was the Founding Editor of *An Unexpected Journal*. His work has been published in a variety of places including the *Journal of Sociology and Christianity*, *Tolkien Studies*, *Christianity & Literature*, *Mythlore*, and *Cistercian Studies Quarterly*.

3 For additional religious similarities beyond what has been presented in this chapter, one would be wise to reference Alison Milbank's work, *Chesterton and Tolkien as Theologians*. She specifically endeavors to create a theology of fairy tales as "positive mediation" (Milbank 2009: 167).

Bibliography

Birzer, Bradley J. 2009. *J.R.R. Tolkien's Sanctifying Myth: Understanding Middle-earth*. Wilmington, DE: Intercollegiate Studies Institute.

Caldecott, Stratford. 2012. *The Power of the Ring: The Spiritual Vision behind The Lord of the Rings and The Hobbit*. New York: Crossroad Publishing.

Chesterton, G.K. 2009. *Orthodoxy*. Chicago, IL: Moody Publishers.

Cilli, Oronzo. 2019. *Tolkien's Library*. Edinburgh: Luna Press Publishing.

Glyer, Diana. 2016. *Bandersnatch: C.S. Lewis, J.R.R. Tolkien, and the Creative Collaboration of the Inklings*. Kent, OH: The Kent State University Press / Black Squirrel Books.

Ker, Ian. 2011. *G.K. Chesterton*. Oxford: OUP.

Milbank, Alison. 2009. *Chesterton and Tolkien as Theologians: The Fantasy of the Real*. New York: T & T Clark.

Oddie, William. 2010. *Chesterton and the Romance of Orthodoxy*. Oxford: OUP.

Ordway, Holly. 2021a. *Tolkien's Modern Reading: Middle-earth Beyond the Middle Ages*. Park Ridge, IL: Word on Fire Academic.

2021b. "Tolkien's Reading of Chesterton." *Gilbert*. Accessed December 26, 2023. https://www.chesterton.org/tolkiens-reading-of-chesterton/.

Pieper, Josef. 2009. *Leisure: The Basis of Culture*. San Francisco: Ignatius Press.

Tolkien, J.R.R. 1981. *The Letters of J.R.R. Tolkien*. Edited by Humphrey Carpenter, with the assistance of Christopher Tolkien. London: George Allen & Unwin / Boston: Houghton Mifflin.

1987. *The Hobbit*. 1st edition 1937. 50th anniversary edition. Boston: Houghton Mifflin.

2004. *The Lord of the Rings*. 1st edition 1954/55. 50th anniversary edition. Boston: Houghton Mifflin.

Lisa Coutras

Tolkien and Balthasar: Theological Aesthetics in Tolkien's Writings

Abstract

Tolkien and Hans Urs von Balthasar are both thinkers who emphasize the role of beauty as a transcendental alongside goodness and truth. This paper discusses how the affective element plays a role in faith and explores how Tolkien's two most prominent female characters, Galadriel and Éowyn, display their particular beauties. Galadriel is an echo of Mary's character, of the beauty of her soul. Likewise Éowyn, also physically beautiful, allows her physical form to be a translucent vehicle for inner beauty.

In the following discussion, I will bring J.R.R. Tolkien into dialogue with the Catholic theologian Hans Urs von Balthasar, whose theology of beauty offers a lens by which to examine Tolkien's narrative theology, or the overarching theological worldview woven throughout his narratives.[1] As Leland Ryken notes: "In the long run every writer's work shows a moral and intellectual bias" (1979: 85). It is not difficult to see that Tolkien's *legendarium* is preoccupied with various aspects of beauty, including its opposite. His own Catholic faith was rooted in beauty, finding expression through mystery and wonder. If Balthasar (1983: Foreword) is correct that beauty is a "main artery" crucial to theology, it would not be surprising to find it central to Tolkien's narrative theology as well. As such, the purpose of this paper is to demonstrate Tolkien's narrative theology through the lens of Balthasar's theological aesthetics. In particular I will utilize the narrative of Éowyn's encounter with the Witch-King as a case study to demonstrate his use of transcendental beauty as a weapon against evil, based upon the Marian archetype of beauty.

---

1 Not to be equated with postliberal theology.

Tolkien and Beauty

In *Tolkien and the Great War* (2003: 10), John Garth explores the imagination of the young Tolkien, highlighting the friendships of his youth that stoked his creativity. He and his three closest friends shared a common vision: to bring beauty to England through their imaginative work, which would act as a "great moral reformer" to "testify to God and truth" (Garth 2003: 180). His friend G.B. Smith wrote in a letter that, through their creativity, they would "re-establish sanity […] and the love of real and true beauty in everyone's breast" (Garth 2003: 105). For Tolkien and his friends, it was a story's beauty that "testified to God and truth." These young men perceived beauty and truth as interlinked. To express beauty through creativity would have a morally cleansing effect on England, for it was a reflective witness to the Creator and his truth.

Similarly, Tolkien wrote in a letter to his son Christopher: "The beauty of the story while not necessarily a guarantee of its truth is a concomitant of it, and one is meant to draw nourishment from the beauty as well as the truth" (*Letters* 109). He was referring to the Eden story, suggesting that those who disbelieve its historicity can nevertheless draw from its beauty, for beauty carries truth. Based on this belief, Tolkien endeavored to bring God's truth to England: by crafting stories that reflect, embody, and express beauty, he could enrich those who would read them.

Tolkien, however, did not set out to compose a sermon or a theological treatise. In his *Letters*, he writes:

> As for 'message': I have none really, if by that is meant the conscious purpose in writing *The Lord of the Rings*, of preaching, or of delivering myself of a vision of truth specially revealed to me! I was primarily writing an exciting story […]. But in such a process inevitably one's own taste, ideas, and beliefs get taken up. (*Letters* 267)

Tolkien made it clear that he did not consider himself a theologian or an evangelist. Rather, he was fashioning an imaginative world in which a story could unfold. By simply writing a story influenced by his own interests and life experiences, he subtly yet effectively demonstrated a view of reality and human nature. While he claimed no "message," he openly admitted that his stories were plainly "religious" and "Catholic," for his beliefs were naturally "absorbed into the story and the symbolism" (*Letters* 172). In order to draw out this theology from his narratives, one must therefore look to a theology of beauty.

A Theology of Beauty

Theological Aesthetics is founded upon the premise that God himself is beautiful. If God is beautiful, then it follows that beauty is integral to the Christian faith. Hans Urs von Balthasar, a Swiss Catholic theologian and contemporary of Tolkien, wrote extensively on beauty as an entry point to theology. While it is unclear whether these two men knew each other,[2] Balthasar's theology offers a compelling lens by which to extract and interpret Tolkien's overarching narrative worldview. In utilizing Balthasar's theological aesthetics, we can give words to Tolkien's images and expression to his intuition, providing a framework for understanding his most deeply held beliefs.

Tolkien's narrative theology is perhaps best described as a *transcendental* theology, as derived from a Catholic theological aesthetics. As I note elsewhere:

> The history of transcendental philosophy is ancient and complex, spanning from classical Greek philosophy, to Neoplatonism, to medieval scholasticism, to modern philosophy. While 'the one, the true, and the good,' have been named among the transcendentals from the time of Plato and Aristotle, it was Saint Bonaventure who formally added beauty. (Coutras 2016: 13)

To summarize, the so-called transcendentals are comprised of the good, the true, and the beautiful, as these qualities 'transcend' creation. Generally speaking, 'truth' refers to logic or philosophy; it engages reason. 'Goodness' refers to ethics or morality; it engages action. 'Beauty' refers to splendor or joy; it engages the imagination. In Balthasar's transcendental theology, he argues that beauty holds just as much weight as goodness and truth (1983: 17-18). The splendor, or transcendence, found within creation is suggestive of a transcendental beauty. This beauty transcends physical aesthetics and subjective taste (1983: 37). "The 'transcendental' qualities of being are so called because each of them holds sway over the totality of being [...] that which is beautiful and whole never lacks that which is morally sound or the radiance of truth,"

2 Caldecott notes that Tolkien and Balthasar shared a mutual friend, Louis Bouyer, who had a great appreciation for Tolkien's theological mythos. See Caldecott (2005: 141-42n32).

writes Balthasar (1989: 21). The transcendentals are the heart and structure of reality, the frame of existence. The transcendental reality is existence itself, otherwise known as "being." The good, the true, and the beautiful together comprise the whole of being.

If being refers to the whole of existence or reality, then God as Creator is the 'Absolute' Being. God declared his name to be "I AM WHO I AM" (Exod. 3:14), a reference to the Eternal Present (Schnackenburg 1968: 233). God exists – past, present, and future. His existence is utterly comprehensive. He is the Absolute Existence. Embodied in the Incarnation, he declared, "I am the way, the truth, and the life" (John 14:6). His eternally present life is also truth. God, as the Absolute Being is the Absolute Truth, the Absolute Goodness, the Absolute Beauty. In God, truth, goodness, and beauty are harmonious and identical, i.e., that which is beautiful must also be true and good. God, as the Absolute Being and Creator, is the Source of all being, for "[i]n him we live and move and have our being" (Acts 17:28). God, as the Absolute Beauty, is thus the ultimate source of beauty.

Balthasar defines beauty as the intersection of *form* and *splendor*. A form is something material and particular. Within this form is a reflection of the eternal, which Balthasar calls splendor or the "light of being." It is the eternal light of existence found within material creation that moves the heart with wonder. Beauty occurs when one encounters the eternal within a form and is enraptured by it.

This 'enrapturing' of the imagination occurs due to the eternal nature of the human being. Theologically, the human being has an immortal soul. When one's being, which is eternal, encounters the eternal in a material form, it is moving. To behold beauty is to be enraptured by the eternal; it involves the "whole person" (Balthasar 1983: 247). Given that beauty, as a transcendental, has its ultimate source in God, it has a transcendent quality. This quality engages the imagination and moves the heart. It is the presence of something eternal within something transient. It enlightens the mind and enraptures the heart.

This bears a striking resemblance to Tolkien's concept of the eucatastrophe. The eucatastrophe, or the "good" catastrophe, occurs when deliverance comes suddenly and unexpectedly, causing a "movement of the heart" and a "catch of the breath" so poignant it brings one to tears (*MC* 153-54). This movement of the heart is a testament to one's "true nature." Tolkien writes:

> It is a sudden glimpse of Truth, your whole nature chained in material cause and effect, the chain of death, feels a sudden relief as if a major limb out of joint had suddenly snapped back. It perceives – if the story has literary 'truth' on the second plane [...] – that this is indeed how things really do work in the Great World for which our nature is made. (*Letters* 100)

For Tolkien, the eucatastrophe is a witness to the gospel, a miraculous rescue that moves the soul with a glimpse of transcendent beauty. This is in keeping with Balthasar's belief that one may encounter God's transcendent beauty in the creative works of humankind, including stories. He writes: "Divine grace [...] is secretly at work in the whole sphere of history, and thus all myths, philosophies, and poetic creations are innately capable of housing within themselves an intimation of divine glory" (1991: 21).[3] To experience the eucatastrophe in a story is to encounter God's eternal beauty and truth.

Beauty is unique among the transcendentals in that it offers a connection between the physical world (form) and the transcendent (splendor). While true beauty has a transcendental quality, it is nevertheless expressed through the created order, i.e. through an action or object within the physical world. One encounters beauty in a material or natural form, and this form connects one to the supernatural. "The form of the beautiful appeared to us to be so transcendent in itself that it glided with perfect continuity with the natural into the supernatural world," writes Balthasar (1983: 34). By its very nature, true beauty expresses transcendence.

As one might expect, however, beauty has an inherent moral danger, for it can be deceptive. As Peter Kreeft notes, all throughout history one finds stories of beautiful women that have led heroes and kings to their demise. "A beautiful face often masks an ugly soul" (Kreeft 2005: 150). One example of deceptive beauty in Tolkien's writing would be the voice of Saruman, which casts an enchantment of beauty motivated by evil intention (*TT* 181-92). Conversely, the lack of physical beauty does not indicate the lack of inner beauty. When

3 For an engagement with Balthasar's approach to myth, see Christopher D. Denny's article "Greek Tragedies: From Myths to Sacraments?" (Denny 2006).

the Hobbits first encounter Strider, he "looks foul" but "feels fair." Strider's response is fitting: "All that is gold does not glitter" (*FR* 222).

Indeed, the outer appearance may not coalesce with one's inner beauty – or lack thereof. In Galadriel's case, her inner goodness shines through her physical beauty. In Saruman's case, he uses beauty bereft of goodness to weave deception. In Strider's case, his physical appearance does not clearly convey his actual inner goodness. Balthasar notes that beauty is typically treated with suspicion in theology precisely due to its moral danger. However, he advises that when beauty departs from the good, we must discern that it is no longer genuine beauty and immediately turn away from it (1983: 37). The lack of harmony between goodness and beauty is counter to creation's original design. Creation has fallen, and in a fallen world, beauty is not always as it should be.

Nevertheless, it is a profoundly Christian concept to reveal the beautiful within the unlovely and unlikely. At the heart of Christianity is the Suffering Servant, who "had no beauty or majesty to attract us to him; nothing in his appearance that we should desire him" (Isa. 53:2). And yet, embodied in this unlovely human form was God himself, the Absolute Beauty and source of all beauty. Thus, while a material form may express an eternal splendor or transcendent beauty, the form itself may not appear physically beautiful. The *inner* splendor is that which makes the form truly beautiful – an inner splendor radiant with goodness and truth.

Galadriel and the Transcendental Feminine

As a Catholic, Tolkien's understanding of beauty was ultimately derived from his reverence for the Virgin Mary. In his *Letters*, he writes that his "perception of beauty both in majesty and simplicity is founded" upon her (172). For Catholics, Mary embodies the beauty that Eve lost at the Fall. She possesses beauty that is both intrinsic (expressive of her own being) and reflective (expressive of the Absolute Being). Balthasar considers her beauty archetypal; the 'Eternal Feminine' ultimately points to her. He highlights the beauty of Beatrice in Dante's *Comedy*, showing that the enrapturing quality of her inner splendor is reflective of Mary. Beatrice "looks up to God, and her eyes mirror Heaven [...]. The Eternal Feminine that draws us up [...] extends, without break, up through all the gradations of reality [...] as far as Mary, the archetype and foundation" (Balthasar 1986: 102). Similarly, Tolkien's theology of beauty largely draws upon Mary. She was not only the archetype of feminine beauty but the foundation for his understanding of beauty holistically, from its simplicity to its grandeur.

Tolkien admitted that there were resonances of Mary throughout his writings, with the most recognizable being Galadriel in *The Lord of the Rings* (*Letters* 406). Stratford Caldecott (2005: 56) references Dwight Longenecker's prayerful encounter with Marian Beauty, which Longenecker describes as a "purity [...] soft as moonlight and as hard as diamonds." Similarly, the Hobbit Samwise Gamgee describes Galadriel as "Beautiful [...]! Hard as di'monds, soft as moonlight" (*TT* 288).

This mineral metaphor appears more than once. When Gimli encounters the queenly Elf, he regards her as an enemy. However, the 'splendor' of her goodness is revealed as physical beauty. He looks into her eyes and sees "love and understanding" that entrances him. He declares: "The Lady Galadriel is above all the jewels that lie beneath the earth!" and later remarks that he had beheld in her "that which was fairest" (*FR* 371, 394). Dwarves were known for their love of treasure and greed for gold; however, Gimli raises the beauty of Galadriel above his earthly desires. Her beauty moves his heart with awe and adoration. In this case, Gimli associates the inner splendor of her goodness with her physical beauty.

Tolkien, however, is careful to differentiate Galadriel from Mary. While she possesses Marian qualities, she is not an allegory of Mary, nor is she sinless. Rather, Galadriel is a "penitent" with a dark past, who is eventually "pardoned because of her resistance to the final and overwhelming temptation to take the Ring for herself" (*Letters* 406). Nevertheless, in her renunciation of power, she displays Marian qualities revealed in splendor: self-giving, courage, and sorrow. She humbly gives up her personal dreams of control, as well as the hope of Lothlórien's longevity. It will cost her dearly, yet she courageously chooses the good. In the resilience of her humility, she reveals her power and strength through beauty and light.[4]

In Mary, we see these same qualities of self-giving, courage, and sorrow. When she encounters the angel Gabriel, Mary humbly yet courageously offers herself to serve the Lord, willing to receive the angel's word (Luke 1:38). She experiences an intensity of love and sorrow because of the child she would bear (Luke 2:34-35). Indeed, she is known throughout history as the "Handmaid of the Lord," denoting her humility; the "Woman of Valor," denoting her courage; and the *Mater Dolorosa*, the Mother of Sorrows (Pelikan 2005: 85, 168).

Tolkien's understanding of beauty is, perhaps, most clearly displayed through feminine beauty. For his female characters, their beauty is most moving when expressed through heroic courage and resilient sorrow. This is a complex blend of Marian self-giving and heroic fortitude, characterized by beauty and light. It is a 'soulish' self-giving: a courageous resolve and love drawn from the depths of being.

Éowyn and the Splendor of Being

In keeping with the Marian archetype, Éowyn's narrative is one defined by beauty, courage, and sorrow. When we first encounter her, she is described as physically beautiful, yet bold and resilient: "Very fair was her face [...] but strong she seemed and stern as steel, a daughter of kings" (*TT* 119). Tolkien describes her beauty and strength as illumined by a transcendent quality, for she is compared to the Elves: Faramir declares that she is beautiful beyond Elven language (*RK* 242), while Aragorn likens her to a "white flower [...] wrought by elf-wrights out of steel" (*RK* 142). In Tolkien's mythology, the Elves are the epitome of beauty. By describing her beauty as exceeding Elven language or her strength as forged by Elven smiths, he assigns a transcendent quality to her beauty and courage. Indeed, her mortality serves to enhance the splendor of these immortal qualities, creating a tragic blend of beauty, courage, and sorrow. This holistic beauty is shown to stir the hearts of many; it haunts Aragorn with

4 For a fuller treatment of Galadriel's splendor, see "The Transcendental Feminine" in Coutras (2016: 217-30).

shame, pierces Legolas with grief, holds Merry in awe, and moves Faramir to pity (*RK* 143, 150, 68).

The holistic nature of Éowyn's beauty is profound precisely because it expresses an integrity of being. She resolutely conforms herself to an "inner law," a framework of something greater than herself. Balthasar calls this inner law a "life form"; or a form that is courageously lived out over a narrative trajectory.[5] To steadfastly conform to this life form may be costly, but the sheer grit of integrity has the potential to reveal one's inner splendor – much like the tragic hero that stands fast in the face of certain defeat.[6] Éowyn's narrative arc is singly defined by this framework: she is a shieldmaiden. As a shieldmaiden, she grieves her uncle Théoden, inwardly torn by his disgrace and powerlessness. As a shieldmaiden, she loves Aragorn, admiring his nobility and power. As a shieldmaiden, she loves and defends Rohan, yet suffers the shame of powerlessness.

To be sure, Éowyn holds to her identity of shieldmaiden in all things. Her courage is described as "stern as steel," yet her love is as fierce as her courage, whether her love for Théoden, for Aragorn, or for Rohan. Her heartbreak – fueled by the intensity of her resolve – is the catalyst for desiring glory and death in battle. It drives her to despair: as a shieldmaiden, she believes that a warrior's glory through death is her only remaining option.

While this framework defines her decisions and actions, she nevertheless holds to something greater than this inner law. In particular, her love for Théoden reveals her true courage, for it is a love drawn from the depths of being. It is a 'soulish' outpouring of resolve and fortitude, involving her whole being. In this instance, her courage is not for herself or her warrior status, but rather for Théoden, the man she loves like a father. While her self-identity as shieldmaiden drives her to despair, it is love that raises her above despair. In love, she stands between Théoden and the Witch-King, whose very presence exudes evil. This 'soulish' fortitude – a courage and love that involves her whole being – expresses a holistic integrity of being. The sheer intensity of her resolve reveals her splendor.

---

5 e.g. "Marriage" or "the Christian life" Balthasar (1983: 24, 27).
6 See Tolkien's discussion on the "theory of courage" (*MC* 5-48).

Aragorn later describes her transcendent courage: "She was pitted against a foe beyond the strength of her mind or body. And those who will take a weapon to such an enemy must be sterner than steel, if the very shock shall not destroy them" (*RK* 242). Aragorn notes the enormity of her enemy's power, highlighting the greatness of her will, strength, and courage as exceeding that of mortals. However, the Witch-King openly mocks her courage, for he knows that no "mortal man" can bring his downfall. At this point, Éowyn declares her identity as a woman and a daughter of kings, revealing her splendor: "The helm of her secrecy had fallen from her, and her bright hair, released from its bonds, gleamed pale gold upon her shoulders. Her eyes grey as the sea were hard and fell, and yet tears were on her cheek. A sword was in her hand, and she raised her shield against the horror of the enemy's eyes" (*RK* 116). In this moment, there is an intersection of beauty (as she reveals her golden hair), courage (as she confronts the horror of the enemy's eyes), sorrow (as the tears fall upon her face), and love (as she protects Théoden). As she takes her physical stand against the enemy, a moment of transcendent beauty occurs.

Balthasar (1983: 119) writes: "Only through [physical] form can the lightning-bolt of eternal beauty flash. There is a moment in which the bursting light of spirit as it makes its appearance completely drenches the external form in its rays." The unveiling of such beauty is experienced only by "the few who [...] bear the weight of the whole on their shoulders," whose "courage to embrace this [transcendence] will raise everything else into the light along with itself: the true, the good, and the beautiful" (1983: 26). In love, Éowyn resolutely bears a horror of evil so great that it exceeds mortal courage, eliciting something *immortal* within her: the splendor of her being. This splendor is enrapturing, revealing the "lightning-bolt of eternal beauty," stirring the being of another. The Hobbit Merry lies nearby, paralyzed with terror. Yet when he looks up to see Éowyn's splendor, he is "raised up into the light": "Pity filled [Merry's] heart and great wonder, and suddenly the slow-kindled courage of his race awoke. [...] He clenched his hand. She should not die, so fair, so desperate! At least she should not die alone" (*RK* 116). Her beauty captivates his heart and fills him with courage, ultimately driving him to action. Released from the paralysis of terror, he stabs the Witch-King, enabling Éowyn to strike the final blow. In Éowyn's soulish resolve of holistic integrity, we see the light of transcendental beauty reflective of the Marian archetype: self-giving love drawn from the depths of being.

Conclusion

In conclusion, the dialogue between J.R.R. Tolkien and Hans Urs von Balthasar provides a rich exploration of the intersection between theology and narrative through the lens of beauty. Tolkien's theology, deeply rooted in his Catholic faith, intertwines themes of beauty, courage, and sorrow throughout his works, drawing inspiration from his reverence for the Virgin Mary. Balthasar's theological aesthetics offer a framework to interpret Tolkien's overarching narrative worldview, highlighting the transcendental nature of beauty and its intrinsic connection to truth and goodness.

Tolkien's portrayal of beauty extends beyond mere physical appearance, encompassing inner qualities such as courage, self-giving love, and resilience in the face of evil. Characters like Galadriel and Éowyn exemplify this holistic beauty, embodying both physical grace and love-driven fortitude. Éowyn's narrative arc, in particular, displays the transformative power of beauty as she confronts the Witch-King with courage and love, ultimately inspiring Merry to action through the transcendent beauty of her being.

Through the exploration of Tolkien's narrative theology and Balthasar's theological aesthetics, we gain deeper insights into the interplay between beauty, truth, and goodness within Tolkien's *legendarium*. For Tolkien, as for Balthasar, beauty is the radiance of truth. In creating beautiful stories, he sought to nourish the reader's imagination with a deep sense of God's truth. The immense power of beauty represents redemptive grace as splinters of light in a dark world. Beauty is a "moral reformer" precisely because it is the primary weapon against evil – whether in Galadriel's resistance to absolute power or in Éowyn's steadfast love. Tolkien does not hide the stark reality of evil, of loss, and of the human condition. But he demonstrates the greater power of transcendental beauty. He leaves space for the eucatastrophe, the splendor of a moment that moves the heart with wonder.

About the Author

LISA COUTRAS is a theologian and scholar specializing in the intersection of theology, philosophy, and literature. She holds a Ph.D. in Theology and Religious Studies from King's College London, where she conducted groundbreaking research on the theological aesthetics of J.R.R. Tolkien. Dr. Coutras is known for her book, *Tolkien's Theology of Beauty: Majesty, Splendor, and Transcendence in Middle-earth* (Palgrave MacMillan, 2016). She currently teaches theology as adjunct faculty at Houston Christian University. She also serves as adjunct faculty at West Virginia University in the Department of Behavioral Medicine & Psychiatry, contributing to new interdisciplinary research on the intersection of addiction psychiatry and the writings of Tolkien.

Bibliography

BALTHASAR, Hans Urs von. 1983. *The Glory of the Lord: A Theological Aesthetics I: Seeing the Form.* Edinburgh: T&T Clark.

1986. *The Glory of the Lord: A Theological Aesthetics III: Studies in Theological Style: Lay Styles.* Edinburgh: T&T Clark.

1989. *The Glory of the Lord: A Theological Aesthetics IV: The Realm of Metaphysics in Antiquity.* Edinburgh: T&T Clark.

1991. *The Glory of the Lord: A Theological Aesthetics VI: Theology: The Old Covenant.* Edinburgh: T&T Clark.

CALDECOTT, Stratford. 2005. *The Power of the Ring: The Spiritual Vision behind The Lord of the Rings.* New York: Crossroad Publishing.

COUTRAS, Lisa. 2016. *Tolkien's Theology of Beauty: Majesty, Splendor, and Transcendence in Middle-earth.* New York: Palgrave Macmillan.

DENNY, Christopher D. 2006. "Greek Tragedies: From Myths to Sacraments?" *Logos: A Journal of Catholic Thought and Culture* 9, no. 3: 45-71.

GARTH, John. 2003. *Tolkien and the Great War: The Threshold of Middle-earth.* New York: Houghton Mifflin.

PELIKAN, Jaroslav. 2005. *Jesus through the Centuries, Mary through the Centuries.* New York: History Book Club.

KREEFT, Peter J. 2005. *The Philosophy of Tolkien: The Worldview behind* The Lord of the Rings. San Francisco: Ignatius Press.

RYKEN, Leland. 1979. *Triumphs of the Imagination: Literature in Christian Perspective.* Lisle, IL: InterVarsityPress.

SCHNACKENBURG, Rudolf. 1968. *The Gospel According to St. John. Herder's Theological Commentary on the New Testament.* London: Burns & Oates.

Tolkien, J.R.R. 1954. *The Fellowship of the Ring.* London: George Allen & Unwin.

1954. *The Two Towers.* London: George Allen & Unwin.

1955. *The Return of the King.* London: George Allen & Unwin.

1981. *The Letters of J.R.R. Tolkien.* Edited by Humphrey Carpenter, with the assistance of Christopher Tolkien. London: George Allen & Unwin / Boston: Houghton Mifflin.

1983. *The Monsters and the Critics and Other Essays.* London: George Allen & Unwin.

Łukasz Neubauer

Tolkien and John Paul II: The Civilisation of Death and Its Resonances in Arda

Abstract

This paper investigates how Pope John Paul II's idea of the 'civilization of death', which is characterized by abortion and euthanasia, sets itself against the 'civilization of life' that prioritizes human flourishing before God. While Tolkien and John Paul likely never had direct intellectual contact, Tolkien's condemnation of Denethor's suicide and the newly-published details of Elvish childbirth in *The Nature of Middle-earth* are in alignment with John Paul's traditional Roman Catholic condemnation of abortion and euthanasia.

At the risk of stating the obvious, there is, of course, absolutely no way that Tolkien could have heard of anyone called 'John Paul II,' since the Polish bishop (since 1958) and cardinal (since 1967) Karol Wojtyła did not become pope until 16 October 1978, more than five years after Tolkien's death. Moreover, even before 1973, they almost certainly never met in person.[1] On the other hand, it is not improbable that Tolkien might have heard of Wojtyła from his Polish friend Przemysław Mroczkowski (1915-2002), the Cracow-based Professor of English Philology, whose family knew the future pope well.[2] However, provided that such had really been the case, it is not known whether the two great men, Mroczkowski and Tolkien, both devout Catholics and scholars of medieval literature (with, nonetheless differing views on, for instance, the reforms of the

1 To begin with, Tolkien never went to Poland. They could not have met in Italy either. While Tolkien was touring it with his daughter Priscilla (31 July-13 August 1955; Scull and Hammond 2017: 488-99), Karol Wojtyła was kayaking with some of his students on the River Drawa (Boniecki 1983: 138). And the latter did not visit Britain until 1982, his only pastoral visit there, nine years late for Tolkien to take any part in it.

2 I am indebted for this information to Przemysław Mroczkowski's daughter, Prof. Katarzyna Mroczkowska-Brand, who kindly answered my questions in connection with her father in the spring of 2022. For an in-depth look at Przemysław Mroczkowski and his friendship with Tolkien, see my article 'The "Polish Inkling": Professor Przemysław Mroczkowski as J.R.R. Tolkien's Friend and Scholar' (2020: 149-76).

Second Vatican Council),[3] ever had an opportunity to talk about the theological writings of Karol Wojtyła.[4]

Even if they did talk about his works, it is not very likely that Karol Wojtyła ever had any noticeable impact upon the writings of Tolkien. By 1958, his two most famous works of fiction had already been published – *The Hobbit* in 1937, and *The Lord of the Rings* in 1954-55. Besides, Tolkien was not the kind of man to be easily influenced, although C.S. Lewis's assertion that "[n]o one ever influenced Tolkien. You might as well try to influence a bandersnatch" (Lewis 2007: 1049) seems somewhat exaggerated if one should consider the sheer number of authors, both modern and premodern, whose works are in one way or another echoed in his fiction.

Why, then, this comparison? Curiously, there are at least a few things in the writings of Tolkien which visibly resonate with some of the concepts developed by Karol Wojtyła/John Paul II. What is more, there are certain passages, not only in *The Hobbit* and *The Lord of the Rings*, which could be used as good illustrations of what, years after they had been written, John Paul II would call the 'Civilisation (or 'Culture') of Life' and the 'Civilisation (or 'Culture') of Death.'

The reasons for this are multiple. First of all, both Tolkien and John Paul II were devout sons of the Church of Rome, and so must have read many works by the same authors (the latter, as a theologian, doubtlessly more than the former), and been familiar with more than just the main trends in theology and philosophy (once again, John Paul II, who studied both subjects, must have been more knowledgeable in this area).[5] Moreover, both lived in roughly the same period of time (Tolkien was born in 1892, Wojtyła in 1920), and could

3 Whereas John Paul II (at that time still as Archbishop Karol Wojtyła) took part in the Second Vatican Council (1962-65), making a significant contribution to the drafting of the Constitution *Gaudium et Spes*, Tolkien is known to have been rather unwilling (to say the least) to embrace some of its liturgical reforms (Birzer 2002: 48-49).

4 Prior to 1958, the year when Mroczkowski met Tolkien, Wojtyła had published only individual articles in various theological and philosophical periodicals. In 1959, his first monograph came out in print, an analysis of Max Scheler's system of values. This was soon followed by *Love and Responsibility* (1960, *Miłość i odpowiedzialność*), one of his most famous works, republished many times and translated into a number of languages, including English (1981). The surviving body of correspondence between Tolkien and Mroczkowski (as yet unpublished), however, makes absolutely no mention of either Wojtyła or any of his works.

5 Other notable analogies between J.R.R. Tolkien and Karol Wojtyła/John Paul II are that they both studied philology, were polyglots, and wrote poetry, although, understandably, at least in the first two areas the former is generally regarded as being more prominent than the latter.

therefore be considered as first-hand witnesses to some of the problems (ethical, social etc.) which afflicted not only the Catholic Church, but, in fact, the entire world in the first half of the twentieth century (and beyond). On a more personal note, but clearly having a more or less direct bearing on their attitude to life, they both experienced the horrors of war[6] and lost their parents early in life.[7] It should come as no surprise, then, that the two would be so much alike in their views upon the matters of ethical concern, particularly with regard to the sanctity and dignity of human life.

The Civilisation of Death

However, before we turn our attention to the practical application of John Paul II's terminology in the sub-created world of Arda and its implementation in the study of Tolkien's fiction, we shall first consider what the pope actually meant by the now frequently used terms 'Civilisation (or 'Culture') of Death.'[8] Taken at face value, the words 'civilisation' (or 'culture'), on the one hand, and 'death,' on the other, may give the impression of being mutually exclusive. After all, the latter (in the sense of 'disastrous collapse' or 'downfall') is clearly antithetical to each of its two predicates.[9] What John Paul II meant by this, though, is

6 Tolkien fought in the First World War (1916), and, at the time of the Second, was an anxious father of three sons, two of whom, John and Christopher, were called up for military service. Karol Wojtyła was not only born after the Great War, but he was also too young to have any memories of the Polish-Soviet War of 1919-21. However, under the German occupation of Poland (1939-45), the future pope was forced to work as a manual labourer (Moskwa 2010: 44-46), studied at the clandestine underground seminary (61-64), and, in August 1944, had to flee Cracow in order to avoid the upcoming wave of arrest of young men which came to be known as 'Black Sunday' (69).

7 Arthur Tolkien died in 1896 and his wife Mabel in 1904, when their elder son was, respectively, 4 and 13 years old. Karol Wojtyła's parents died in 1929 (mother Emilia) and 1941 (father Karol), when their younger son was 9 and 21, respectively. Likewise traumatic must have also been the loss of his elder brother Edmund, who passed away in 1932, when Karol Wojtyła was 12 years old.

8 In the *Evangelium vitae*, the encyclical which will constitute the conceptual basis of our study, John Paul II invariably speaks of the "culture of death" (§12ff; *mortis cultura*). It is, however, frequently juxtaposed there with the "culture of life" (§6; *cultus vitae*; §21ff; *cultura vitae*) and its three derivatives: the "civilization of truth and love" (§6; *veritatis amorisque* […] *humanita*[*s*]), the "civilization of love and life" (§27; *amoris vitaeque cultu*[*s*]), and the "civilization of life and love" (§100; *vitae et amoris cultu*[*s*]). Therefore, it may be assumed that, in the papal argument concerning human life and dignity, the words 'culture' and 'civilisation' ('of death') are used synonymously. Besides, in his 1994 *Letter to Families*, the pope himself uses the term "civilization of death" (§21), no doubt to the same effect as the "culture of death" in the *Evangelium vitae*.

9 I should like to avoid the need to draw any greater distinction between 'civilisation' and 'culture,' even though the latter term is actually broader in its semantic coverage. Suffice it to say that here the two will be used as "essential synonyms […], denot[ing] somewhat distinguishable grades of degree of the same thing" (Kroeber 2011: 11).

'death' as, literally, (1) 'the termination of life' and, more figuratively, (2) 'the end, conclusion, finale,' including on the more global level.[10] Likewise figurative, albeit chiefly on the principle of semantic reversal, is the pope's use of the other two words. Combined with 'death,' both stand in clear opposition to what we would normally regard as 'civilisation' and 'culture,' in their sense being closer to 'barbarity' or 'savagery.' Hence, in the moral parlance, the terms 'Civilisation (or 'Culture') of Death' could be used interchangeably, as direct opposites to (or negatives of) the 'Civilisation (or 'Culture') of Life,' that is to say, the vision of our world in general compliance with God's commandments.

The concept of the 'Culture of Life' was first discussed at length in John Paul II's encyclical the *Evangelium vitae* (25 March 1995), the eleventh pastoral letter (of fourteen) promulgated during his long pontificate (1978-2004).[11] Its focal point is the sanctity (or, from the viewpoint of ethics, inviolability) of human life,[12] particularly in the face of increasing (individual and national legislative) support for such counter-ethical issues, "opposed to life itself" (*Evangelium vitae*, henceforth *EV*, §3),[13] as abortion and euthanasia.[14] In this way, it reaffirms the position of the Roman Catholic Church with regard to these issues, bringing together, on the one hand, the medical perspectives and, on the other, the ethical stance of Christian theology throughout the ages.

In chapter III, for instance, quite appropriately titled 'You shall not kill' (*Non homicidium facies*), John Paul II quotes the words of the early Christian author Tertullian, who, in his *Apologeticum*, asserts that abortion "is anticipated murder

---

10 After all, performed on a more and more massive scale, the former could evidently be the mainspring of the latter.

11 The two terms "the culture of life" (*cultura vitae*) and "the culture of death" (*mortis cultura*) first appear in chapter I of the encyclical (§19). As has been noted, apart from these two, it also uses terms like "the culture of human life" (§6; *cultus vitae humanae*), "the civilization of truth and love" (§6; *cultus veritatis amorisque*), and "the civilization of love and life" (§27; *amoris vitaeque cultus*).

12 The full title of the encyclical is '*Evangelium vitae*, to the Bishops Priests and Deacons Men and Women religious lay Faithful and all People of Good Will on the Value and Inviolability of Human Life' (*Evangelium Vitae, litterae encyclicae episcopis, presbyteris et diaconis religiosis viris et mulieribus christifidelibus laicis universisque bonae voluntatis hominibus de vitae humanae inviolabili bono*).

13 *ipsi vitae adversantur.*

14 By 1995 abortion on request was legal in as many as 46 countries (66 in 2022), with many more places in the whole world in which it could be practised with certain restrictions. Moreover, about 45.5 million unborn children are estimated to have been killed globally in 1995 alone (Singh, Henshaw and Berentsen 2002: 23), which makes abortion – both then and now – by far the most common cause of human death. Although euthanasia is still way behind, in some countries, such as Belgium, it has recently climbed the statistical ladder, accounting for as many as 2,656 (of all 9,786) deaths (more than 27%) in 2019 (den Hartogh 2022: 225).

to prevent someone from being born; it makes little difference whether one kills a soul already born or puts it to death at birth. He who will one day be a man is a man already" (*EV* §61).[15] Tertullian's stance is sometimes criticized as being absolutist, but the fact that he looked at this critical issue in a binary way should not be seen in a negative light. After all, as Christ reminds us in the Gospel according to Matthew: "All you need say is 'Yes' if you mean yes, [ναὶ, ναί] 'No' if you mean no [οὒ, οὔ]; anything more than this comes from the Evil One" (5:37). Nowhere is this statement truer and more needed than in the face of the now long-standing debate concerning the onset of human life (or the so-called 'beginning of human personhood'),[16] an issue which has recently been subject to much ideological distortion. Various people, including those in the medical profession, continuously push the imagined boundary of when human life begins, often with little or no regard for scientific facts.[17] Human life, however, as Brookes and Zietman explain in very plain terms, "begins with conception by the union of gametes or sex cells [...]. Growth and development continue thereafter" (qtd. in Fisher 2012: 139).[18]

When it comes to euthanasia, John Paul II's stance was just as firm as in the case of abortion. Although here the encyclical does not reference any earlier Christian authors, it is fair to say that in this particular instance the pope hardly needed to rely upon anyone else's authority. More than five years in Poland under the German occupation (1939-45) made him acutely aware of the fact that, for some people, human life had no intrinsic value, particularly when those who were euthanized or subjected to other comparable practices, were seen as less deserving to live than those of the race of *Übermenschen*.[19] "Euthanasia,"

---

15 *Homicidii festinatio est prohibere nasci, nec refert, natam quis eripiat animam an nascentem disturbet. Homo est et qui est futurus.* In fact, in the *Evangelium vitae,* abortion is treated on a par with infanticide (§61ff.).

16 For an insightful discussion on this topic, see, in particular the third chapter of Christopher Kaczor's book *The Ethics of Abortion*, provocatively titled 'Does Personhood Begin at Birth?' (2023: 41-63).

17 Quite recently, for instance, the American politician and activist Stacey Abrams argued that the heartbeat of a six-week-old child in a prenatal period is only a "manufactured sound designed to convince people that men have the right to take control of a woman's body" (Nerozzi 2022).

18 It is interesting to note that John Paul II's mother, Emilia Wojtyła, was herself advised by the gynecologist to terminate her pregnancy on the grounds of medical indications (Kindziuk 2013: 135-38). Had she listened to the doctor, her son Karol, the future Pope John Paul II, would not have been born.

19 Euthanasia took its toll in Germany and the German-controlled states of Austria, Poland, and the Protectorate of Bohemia and Moravia, where, between 1939 and 1945, as result of the *Aktion T4* campaign up to 300,000 disabled people (physically as well as mentally) were put to death (Hohendorf 2014: 272-73).

the encyclical says, being, "in the strict sense [...] understood to be an action or omission which of itself and by intention causes death, with the purpose of eliminating all suffering" (*EV* §65)[20] is "sometimes [perversely] justified by the utilitarian motive of avoiding costs which bring no return and which weigh heavily on society" (§15).[21] This position, however, cannot be defended should we agree that "human life is sacred because from its beginning it involves 'the creative action of God'" (§53).[22]

Not surprisingly, this firm papal stance with regard to abortion and euthanasia earned John Paul II a number of opponents, not only in the left-liberal circles.[23] In the Catholic circles, too, there have been more and more claims that his teaching in this area is far too idealised, detached from the reality of the late twentieth and early twenty-first centuries, that the pope's vision of the world is not quite in accord with the spirit of the time.[24] This is all the more surprising given that the whole text of the encyclical is based not only upon the recurrent appeals to Scripture,[25] but also the centuries-old apostolic tradition, as well as, no less importantly, the medical knowledge and the natural law. Nonetheless, nearly thirty years on, the legacy of the *Evangelium vitae* seems lasting, its promulgation in many ways constituting a foundation of numerous pro-life movements in the world.

Much in the same vein, almost ninety years earlier, Matthew Arnold wonders what has happened to "the Sea of Faith" ("Dover Beach" l. 21), what has caused its ever more observable retreat. Some such changes happen practically overnight, others come about as a result of longer, not always easily observable, processes, often in conjunction with the ever-new (though, in many ways, still the same)

20 *proprioque sensu accipitur actio vel omissio quae suapte natura et consilio mentis mortem affert ut hoc modo omnis dolor removeatur.*

21 *defenditur interdum ex certae utilitatis aestimatione, ob quam nempe nimia pro societate impendia infructuosa declinari debeant*

22 *humana vita pro re sacra habenda est quippe quae inde a suo exordio Creatoris Dei actionem*

23 For a good overview of the current state of Christian (both Catholic and non-Catholic) positions in the fields of medicine and genetics, see, for instance, the final chapter in *The Cambridge Companion to Christian Ethics* (Childress 2014: 287-303).

24 At this point, it is hard not to invoke the words of G.K. Chesterton: "We do not want [...] a church that will move with the world. We want a church that will move the world" (qtd. in Pearce 2015: 279).

25 One example of that might be the reproachful words of God in communication with Cain, "the voice of your brother's blood cries to me from the ground" (Gen 4:10); words which constitute the encyclical's moral theme (Conley 2008: 36) and are used as the title of its first and, in many ways, most important chapter.

ideological conventions.[26] Typically, they are disguised as being beneficial to the people, masquerading under the cloak of 'common good' or 'societal happiness.' This, however, is easily deceptive, for, as we know not only from the works of George Orwell and Aldous Huxley, whenever some revolutionary idea of sweeping social consequences is implemented, there are always more victims than beneficiaries.

Today, upon hearing the word 'euthanasia' (εὐθανασία, literally, if somewhat obliquely, meaning 'good death') some people may be inclined to think of the various forms it has taken in the last few decades or so. Others, who, like Tolkien and Wojtyła, lived at the time of the Second World War, may recall the *Aktion T4*, the campaign of systematic murder of those people (mostly elderly and disabled) who were incurably sick, and thus unable to take care of themselves. As has been said, it was enforced in Germany (and other German-controlled countries) under the National Socialist regime in September 1939 and ran practically until the end of the war, claiming the lives of around 300,000 people.

The history of euthanasia is, however, considerably longer and goes back to the times of Ancient Greece and Rome, with some of the greatest minds of the age, including Plato and Seneca the Elder (but not, it seems, Hippocrates and the Pythagoreans), at least in some measure justifying the practice of 'medically assisted death' (Carrick 2001: 94-95, 189). In the sixteenth century, the utilitarian Francis Bacon actually coined the term *euthanasia exterior* (as opposed to *euthanasia interior*, or mental preparation for death), by which he explicitly meant the physical termination of one's life (von Engelhardt 2018: 114). In more recent times, its leading proponents included the surgeon John Collins Warren, lawyer and orator Robert Green Ingersoll (both Americans), as well as German philosopher and ethicist Felix Adler. In Britain, the Voluntary Euthanasia Legalisation Society (still in existence under the name of 'Dignity in Dying'), campaigning for the legalisation of euthanasia, was founded in 1935 by the physician Charles Killick Millard. Although active euthanasia is still illegal there, since 1957 it has been possible to cause a patient's death through the intensified administration of lethal drugs normally used to alleviate the

26 The latter form of development (or 'progression,' in the liberal-left understanding of it) is best summarised in the words of the German communist activist Rudi Dutschke: *der lange Marsch durch die Institutionen* (qtd. in Gerhardt 2018: 62).

pain, or through withholding medical treatment, nutrition, and/or hydration (Whiting 2002: 42).

Abortion has an even longer history, with some of the earliest known references to be found in ancient Chinese, Indian, and Egyptian sources (King 2013: 47). Throughout the history, various people had different attitudes to it. Despite his views on the so-called 'ensoulment' (a theory later revived by Saint Thomas Aquinas), Aristotle, for instance, appears to be generally in favour of various means of population control (Riddle 1994: 18). Even in the Roman Catholic Church, there was, for a long time, no strict consensus with regard to when the human soul actually begins its existence. It was not until the sixteenth century that, notwithstanding the stage of pregnancy, abortion was fully condemned by the Church of Rome, placing it on a par with the act of homicide (Stensvold 2015: 69). Within the next three centuries or so, this position would be subject to some investigation and debate. Today, however, the official stance of the Vatican, as stated in the *Catechism of the Catholic Church* (promulgated by John Paul II in 1992, three years before the *Evangelium vitae*), is that

> Human life must be respected and protected absolutely from the moment of conception. From the first moment of his existence, a human being must be recognized as having the rights of a person – among which is the inviolable right of every innocent being to life. [Therefore], abortion willed either as an end or a means, is gravely contrary to the moral law (*Catechism of the Catholic Church* 2270-71).

In Britain, abortion was, for many years, illegal in accordance with the Offences Against the Person Act 1861. This is still the definitive law there, despite the Abortion Act which was passed by the Parliament in 1967 (Lee 2003: 82). The former act succeeded in penalising abortion – without, however, defining any moral basis for such legal regulations (Lee 2003: 82). The latter made it legal on a wide number of grounds, in practice up to the twenty-eighth week of gestation, even though the document itself makes no mention of any temporal restrictions. Not surprisingly, it did not take long to see the consequences of this new legal situation. While in the first half of the 1960s there were fewer than 20,000 'illegal operations' (as abortions were then euphemistically termed) annually, by 1973, the year of Tolkien's death, these figures had increased tenfold, with as many as 167,149 pregnancies terminated in the light of the new law.

The Conflict of Civilisations in the Works of Tolkien

In the penultimate chapter of *The Lord of the Rings*, Samwise Gamgee voices his despair over the ruin that was once his beloved Shire. "This is worse than Mordor!" he says, "Much worse in a way. It comes home to you, as they say because it is home, and you remember it before it was all ruined" (*RK* 1018). "Yes, this is Mordor," replies Frodo. "Just one of its works" (*RK* 1018).

Reading *The Lord of the Rings*, or in fact any other work of Tolkien within the *legendarium*, it is sometimes tempting to use John Paul II's terminology and think of the two conflicting sides as the 'Civilisations' of 'Life' (collectively referred to as 'the West') and 'Death' (Sauron in the East and his many vassals and allies in the South). Of course, this clear-cut (and only ostensibly Manichean),[27] division is wholly justified, even if, at first glance, it seems to have little to do with what is put forth in the *Evangelium vitae*. What is more, just as in the papal encyclical, here the term 'Civilisation of Death' could only be used antithetically, in strict opposition to what is known about the general ways of those peoples who are known to be highly skilled (Dwarves), live in perfect harmony with the natural world (Elves), or simply "love peace and quiet and good tilled earth" (*FR* 1; Hobbits). After all, as we are reminded by Frodo, when Sam finds him in the Tower of Cirith Ungol, "the Shadow [...] can only mock, it cannot make: not real new things of its own" (*RK* 914). Logically, then, none of the numerous works of Morgoth, Sauron, and, later, Saruman could really be referred to as products of what we would normally call a 'civilisation.'[28]

On the more ethical level, perhaps the best illustration of what some four decades later John Paul II would call the 'Civilisation of Life' is the oft-quoted words of Gandalf, as he instantly rebukes Frodo for wishing Gollum dead. "He is as bad as an Orc, and just an enemy. He deserves death" (*FR* 59), exclaims Frodo, upon hearing that Bilbo had an opportunity to kill the vile creature

27 For a convincing refutation of 'Manichean dualism' in the works of Tolkien, see Christopher Garbowski's chapter on 'Evil' in *A Companion to J.R.R. Tolkien* (2014: 424-26).

28 Here, again, I use the term 'civilisation' in one of the loosest possible ways, meaning a complex, and therefore not always easily definable, structure of societal relations.

long ago.[29] To this, the wizard astutely replies, "Deserves it! I daresay he does. Many that live deserve death. And some that die deserve life. Can you give it to them? Then do not be too eager to deal out death in judgement. For even the very wise cannot see all ends. I have not much hope that Gollum can be cured before he dies, but there is a chance of it" (*FR* 59).

Fleming Rutledge rightly observes that Gandalf's response echoes the argument of Saint Paul that, in one way or another, we are all under the power of sin (2004: 66). In his Epistle to the Romans, Paul asks rhetorically, "are we any better off?" (3:9), the ensuing answer being, of course, in the negative (9-11). Frodo would probably not be able to understand its significance in its entirety until the moment the Ring gets destroyed in the fire of the Cracks of Doom.[30] However, it is, I believe, also possible to read the words of Gandalf in the light of the three theological virtues: "faith, hope and love" (1 Corinthians 13:13);[31] namely, (1) the faith in Ilúvatar's plan for Middle-earth, (2) hope for some kind of alteration in Gollum's crooked ways, and (3) love for Gollum as a (fallen) child of Eru. The first one is rather general, but the other two stem directly from the fact that all the sentient creatures are the offspring of the Lord, "created [...] in the image of [...] God" (Gen 1:27).[32]

Passing any such condemning 'sentence' upon Gollum is, of course, unworthy of a child of God, regardless of its ultimate outcome, which is utterly independent of Frodo's will. First of all, it inevitably rejects any hope which may still be left for Gollum, a hope nonetheless shattered by Sam on the steps of

29 "Bilbo almost stopped breathing, and went stiff himself. He was desperate. He must get away, out of this horrible darkness, while he had any strength left. He must fight. He must stab the foul thing, put its eyes out, kill it. It meant to kill him. No, not a fair fight. He was invisible now. Gollum had no sword. Gollum had not actually threatened to kill him, or tried to yet. And he was miserable, alone, lost. A sudden understanding, a pity mixed with horror, welled up in Bilbo's heart: a glimpse of endless unmarked days without light or hope of betterment, hard stone, cold fish, sneaking and whispering" (*Hobbit* 81).

30 Frodo's moral failure at the end of his quest does, however, serve as a powerful reminder of our fallibility, and that, in the end, only the grace of God can restore man to his original condition before the Fall.

31 By the last of the three, ἀγάπη, Saint Paul evidently means the kind of love which God has for each of us, and which we, *in imitatio Christi*, can (and in fact should) bestow upon others.

32 The encyclical *Evangelium vitae* makes numerous references not only to the book of Genesis, but also to Wisdom 2:23: "For God created man for incorruption, and made him in the image of his own eternity" (*EV* §34), and Psalm 139:13[-14]: "For you formed my inmost being[, knit me together in my mother's womb. [...] a wonder am I, and all your works are wonders]" (*EV* subsection heading between paragraphs 43 and 44).

Cirith Ungol, when, deep in his heart, he seems to accuse the poor creature of "pawing at master" (*TT* 714). Secondly, killing Gollum only because he is both malicious and vulnerable would constitute a serious abuse of his dignity as a creation of God.

In the same vein, in our world, one or both of the parents might wish their unborn child dead for the sole reason that he or she is (terminally) ill, in this way (1) rejecting the hope that the child can still be cured (even if it requires a miracle), and (2) forgetting that man, even fatally ill, or deemed to be suffering for months or years to come, is not an injured animal that, with no big ethical qualms, could be put down to alleviate its suffering. Every man (or other humanoid creature in the world of Tolkien), therefore, has the same right to live as anybody else, "from conception to natural death" (*EV* §93).[33]

Against Euthanasia: Denethor's Pyre

The above-quoted words of Gandalf are, of course, very general in their meaning and application. In fact, they could be brought up in just about any context involving the act of killing a human being – healthy or disabled, born or preborn. There is, however, an episode in *The Lord of the Rings* which could be used as a perfect illustration of the papal arguments against the practice of euthanasia. Interestingly, it also involves the character of Gandalf, Tolkien's regular voice of reason.[34]

Overcome with grief, remorse, and despair as a result of being gradually poisoned by Sauron's powers through his sustained use of the *palantír*, Denethor, the Ruling Steward of Gondor, loses any remaining shreds of hope that he might

---

33 *a conceptione ad usque naturalem mortem*. Pivotal in John Paul II's reflections upon human life and dignity is the person of Mary (both as the *Virgo* and Θεοτόκος), who not only lives in fear of potential ostracism at the time of Her pregnancy (Matthew 1:18-20), but also, later in life, experiences the horror of seeing Her Son die upon the Cross (John 19:25-27).

34 Gandalf is a complex character whose portrayal hints at a number of inspirations, ranging from the more mythical and legendary ones (Odin, Merlin), through literary-historical (Byrhtnoth, albeit in reverse), to implicitly Christian (angel, Christ). It could be argued that, in him, Tolkien also appears to mimic certain Socratic traits and methods of conversation by means of thought-provoking (and sometimes genuinely elenchic) dialogues between the wizard (note that at the root of this word lies the Old English adjective *wīs* 'wise') and his interlocutors.

still be able to save (or, at any rate, efficiently defend) his realm and its people.[35] Consequently, he resolves to set himself as well as his only living (but critically wounded) son Faramir on fire, crying, "Why should we wish to live longer? Why should we not go to death side by side?" (*RK* 852-53). Placing oneself upon a funeral pyre obviously qualifies as suicide, a horrid act in itself, being not only an abuse of the natural law, but also a major offence against God, who, in the Christian teaching, alone can claim sovereignty over life. Likewise, killing a helpless person (and, as a matter of fact, one's own child) is, according to the *Evangelium vitae*, "a grave violation of the law of God" (§65).[36]

In his inability to cope with the looming crisis, the siege of Minas Tirith, Jane Chance says, Denethor "fails as a father, a master, a steward, and a man" (2001: 175).[37] What is more, she continues in connection with the first of the four failures, he is very much like Shakespeare's Lear, who "measures the quality and quantity" (175) of his offspring. As a result, in the eyes of his father, the more studious and insightful Faramir turns out to be perceptibly inferior to his pugnacious and quick-tempered brother Boromir. This evaluative mindset of Denethor as a parent is thus startlingly revelatory of his flawed understanding of the worth of human life, a primary concern also in the now long-standing debate over euthanasia (and abortion).

Denethor's wish that he and his son should perish in flames might also evoke the numerous pyres set on fire in the works of early Germanic literature (*Beowulf*, *Vǫlsunga saga* etc.).[38] In fact, even the Steward himself declares that he and his son "will burn like heathen kings before ever a ship sailed hither from the West" (*RK* 825). As always, Gandalf sees the bigger picture of the situation, sensibly reminding Denethor that the heathen kings he speaks of were "under

35 Tolkien himself observes that "Denethor *was* tainted with mere politics" (*Letters* 241; emphasis original), and therefore his "prime motive [is] to preserve the polity of Gondor" (241). Once this not-quite-elaborate structure is broken, he is left with nothing but the acute feeling of defeat.

36 *gravem divinae Legis esse violationem.*

37 By this last one she means 'rationality' (176), but, in fact, its semantic contours could be stretched to mean 'humanity' etc.

38 Amongst those whose bodies are buried, albeit almost always *post mortem* (the only notable exception to this is Brynhild, who wishes to die with the man she loved), are the two great heroes Beowulf and Sigurd. It is quite possible, though, that, writing this chapter in 1946-47 (Scull and Hammond 2017: 324-28), at the back of his mind Tolkien had the terrifying news of the crematoria which Germans used in their Extermination Camps at the time of the Second World War.

the domination of the Dark Power" (*RK* 853),[39] killing themselves "in pride and despair," and, he adds, "murdering their kin to ease their own death" (853). Alexei Kondratiev has pointed out that

> Tolkien's view of suicide as presented [here] is different from that of the source cultures he was drawing from (Anglo-Saxon, for instance), in which suicide was an honorable way out for a man who, like Denethor, had lost everything he most cared for. While the trappings of Middle-earth come from pagan cultures, Christian elements enter in when you come to ethical structures. (qtd. in Hammond and Scull 2014: 573)

Speaking through Gandalf, Tolkien thus explicitly argues that, since the incentive comes from "the Dark Power" (*RK* 853), such actions can never be reconciled with the laws of God. What is more, unlike the proponents of euthanasia,[40] he also explicitly uses the word 'murdering,' a present participle whose substantive form is 'murder.' It hardly needs to be added that the Old English equivalent of the latter happens to be *morðor*,[41] intentionally or not, resounding in Tolkien's name for the land of the Dark Lord.[42]

Gandalf's third argument against euthanasia (and other related practices) is to be found in his assertion that the "heathen kings" of the past killed their kin in order "to ease their own death" (*RK* 853). Indeed, many such (or similar) rituals are also well documented in the history of our world.[43] A good description of this kind of practice is outlined in Ahmad ibn Fadlan's account of the time he

39 Tolkien's somewhat ambiguous use of the word 'heathen' with regard to the world which appears to have little or no established religious practices has provoked some discussion (Shippey 2000: 177; Dickerson 2007: 266-67). Perhaps closest to the truth is the position of the latter scholar, who argues that "Tolkien may have had in mind [the] more literal, nonreligious, [but] certainly derogatory meaning [of it]" (2007: 267). Either way, it cannot be ruled out that Gandalf's argument also echoes one of the commandments of the Mosaic law, namely the prohibition to practice child sacrifice (by incineration) to the Canaanite god Moloch (Leviticus 18:21, 20:2-5; Deuteronomy 12:31).

40 See, for instance, the concluding words of one of the chapters in the book *Asking to Die: Inside the Dutch Debate about Euthanasia:* "Euthanasia is not murder: it is mercy" (Thomasma et al. 1998: 302). In *The Encyclopedia of Libertarianism*, Ronald Hamowy also argues, clearly reducing the status of a human to that of a wounded animal, that "euthanasia is not murder because the killing done in euthanasia is done with the intention of alleviating pain and suffering, not inflicting it" (2008: 157).

41 As Bruce R. O'Brien explains, in pre-Norman England, the terms *morð* and *morðor* were used to mean (1) "a kind of killing for which there could be no compensation" and (2) "a crime of betrayal against one's lord and the sympathetic punishment for such treason" (1996: 345-46). In addition to these, as is argued by Kenneth R. Brooks, the word *morðor* might connote any kind of violence, as well as 'evil' in general and 'deadly sin' in particular (1961: 62).

42 Within the *legendarium*, Mordor is said to be a Sindarin compound name, comprised of *mor* 'dark' (*Sil* 334) and *dôr* 'land' (*Sil* 330), and thus meaning "Black Land" (*Letters* 178).

43 See, for instance, the Mosaic Pentateuch, where Yahweh explicitly forbids the Israelites to practice child sacrifice (by incineration) to Moloch (Leviticus 18:21, 20:2-5; Deuteronomy 12:31).

spent amongst the Rus. In it, the tenth-century Arab traveller provides an account of the burial of a Scandinavian chieftain, an important element of which is the ritual slaying of a thrall girl, who, it was deemed, would accompany her master in the afterlife.[44] What really matters here, though, is the 'argument' that the sorrow resulting from one's demise could be somehow eased through the act of killing another person. Similarly, the proponents of euthanasia contend that terminating someone's life could actually be a 'blessing,' as it helps to alleviate the suffering (physical and/or mental) of a patient (as well as his or her family and friends).[45] However, as Gandalf reminds Denethor, "authority is not given to you [...] to order the hour of your death" (*RK* 853).[46] No doubt, to this, one might as well add 'and that of your seriously wounded son,' the very kind of killing which, in modern parlance, is now more and more frequently euphemistically referred to as 'assisted (or 'friendly') death.'[47]

Against Abortion: Childbearing Laws and Customs among the Eldar

Unlike the fellow Inkling C.S. Lewis, who, in his response to a letter from Mary Van Deusen (7 February 1951) explicitly addresses the issue of what he calls a "sin" and, like Tertullian, puts side-by-side with "infanticide,"[48] Tolkien is not known to have ever openly expressed his views on abortion. It is, however, hard to imagine that, as with euthanasia, he would not have a fully formed opinion about it, doubtlessly in compliance with the moral

44 That part of Ahmad Ibn Fadlan's *Risala* which deals with the funerary practices of the Rus in the first part of the tenth century has been discussed at length in a great number of publications, e.g. Judith Jesch's book *Women in the Viking Age* (2001: 119-23).

45 Note, again, the dubious ethical stance of one of the authors of the book *Asking to Die*: "Euthanasia is not murder: it is mercy" (Thomasma et al. 1998: 302).

46 As has been pointed out a number of times by a great many scholars, Tolkien's use of no-subject passive often suggests some kind of divine agency and providence.

47 Other, similarly cynical terms used as synonyms of euthanasia include: 'medical aid in dying,' 'medically-assisted dying,' 'physician-assisted suicide,' 'putting one out of their misery,' etc.

48 "It is certainly not wrong to try to remove the natural consequences of sin provided the means by which you remove them are not in themselves another sin (e.g. it is merciful and Christian to remove the natural consequences of fornication by giving the girl a bed in a maternity ward and providing for the child's keep and education, but wrong to remove them by abortion or infanticide). Where benevolent planning, armed with political or economic power, becomes wicked is where it tramples on people's rights for the sake of their good" (*CL3* 1951).

teachings of the Roman Catholic Church.[49] In fact, it appears that, in some measure, Tolkien's stance on abortion (or, at any rate, his pro-life commitment) could be extrapolated from his fiction, from a text which, interestingly, does not directly deal with what in the *Evangelium vitae* is set in opposition to the "culture of human life" (§6).[50]

"The Laws and Customs among the Eldar" (*MR* 207-53) sheds light upon some of the domestic practices and rituals of the Elves, including child-naming, marriage etc. Tolkien also provides insight into the nature of Elvish immortality, the ongoing consumption of their *hröa* (body) by the *fëa* (spirit). However, what seems most pertinent with regard to the present discussion is the information concerning their begetting and bearing of children. According to Tolkien, "a year passes between the begetting and the birth of an elf-child, so that the days of both are the same or nearly so, and it is the day of begetting that is remembered year by year" (*MR* 212). It must be stressed here that, since they do not *always* fall on the same day, what the Elves in point of fact celebrate is not their child's birthday, but the day when he or she was conceived. This might seem to recall the traditional East Asian age reckoning, whereby a person's age is determined by the year of his or her conception. That is to say, he or she is born already "at the age of one" (Cong 2016: 29). However, as is not hard to calculate, this does not perfectly reflect one's prenatal development, since human pregnancy lasts about 40 weeks, not 52.[51]

This obviously stands in stark opposition to what is sometimes (against the medical facts) claimed about the origins of life and/or one's 'personhood.' It is, for instance, often argued that the pro-life view on when human life begins is, for the most part, based upon "religious arguments" (Hamowy 2008: 2),[52] or the *feeling* that "once a zygote is formed" it has the same rights as the mother (Hamowy 2008: 2). In reality, however, in order to facilitate the decision to terminate a pregnancy,

49 Issued in 1908 and translated into English in 1910, the so-called Catechism of Saint Pius X (*Catechismo della Dottrina Cristiana*), the pope whom Tolkien is known to have held in high esteem (Birzer 2007: 87), makes no mention of abortion *per se*. It does, however, explicitly urge parents to "love, support and maintain their children" (Fourth Commandment, Q4).

50 *cultus vitae humanae.*

51 Of course, as is revealed in *The Nature of Middle-earth*, the Elvish years are different from those of Men. In reality, "from conception to birth they lay in the womb 9 *löar*" (29), that is 9 mortal-years.

52 Characteristically, whenever some such claims are made, it is rarely (if ever) explained what the author really means by 'religious arguments' (or 'sentiments').

the imagined boundary is constantly being pushed, so much so that today even the mother's womb can no longer be seen as the only place where an unwanted child could be put to death. In some hospitals and clinics, abortion survivors are either instantly killed (typically by strangulation), or left in trays to die, even if they are already capable of surviving outside of the womb.[53]

In other words, what for some might seem to be merely a 'clump of cells,' zygote, embryo, foetus, or, at best, a 'potential person,' for Tolkien already is a person and the "time [spent] in the womb" is included in the child-growth (*NME* 68). Moreover, it is explicitly "an elven-child" (and, we may presume, those of other humanoid races in Middle-earth would not be treated any differently) who "is borne in its mother's womb" (*NME* 22), not some indefinable 'foetal tissue.' Or, on a more personal level, it is Fëanor, not some 'Elf-to-be,' who is reported to have "remained in the womb [of his mother] for one growth-year" (*NME* 22). The reasons for this are clearly biological, but, as in the *Evangelium vitae*, the fact that an Elvish child in his or her prenatal stage should be treated as a person has its eschatological foundations in Tolkien's assertion that "the provision of a bodily house for a *fëa*, and the union of *fëa* [spirit] with *hrondo* [body], was committed by Eru to the Children, to be achieved in the act of begetting" (*MR* 221).

Once again, none of this has anything to do with the problem of abortion *per se*. However, by presenting his readers with so much vital (*nomen est omen*) information concerning the life of Elves prior to their birth and, not only in the case of Fëanor, by providing them with prenatal personhood, Tolkien demonstrates that, in the long-standing conflict between the 'Civilisation of Life' and the 'Civilisation of Death,' his stance is perfectly consistent with the pro-life ethic, and therefore in harmony with the moral teachings of the Roman Catholic Church, both at the time of his life (1892-1973) and in 1995, when the *Evangelium vitae* was promulgated by Pope John Paul II.

---

53 Many such instances are regularly reported around the world. See, for instance, the high-profile case of the annual report on abortions performed in Minnesota, which states that in 2021 five children were denied even the most basic medical care, having survived their own abortion (Terzo 2022).

Conclusion: John Paul II and J.R.R. Tolkien on the Matters of Life and Death

As is stated in the beginning, there is practically no way that the teachings of Karol Wojtyła – ethical, social, or other – could have reached, and thus have any kind of influence upon Tolkien, either directly or indirectly. However, it looks as though, at least in some measure, his (and, of course, the pope's) strict adherence to the Catholic stance on euthanasia and abortion might have been a reaction to the rapidly changing attitudes to these practices in the twentieth century.

We have already seen how the legal restrictions in Britain came to be loosened in the 1950s and 1960s. In Poland, the situation was only roughly analogous. Unlike in Britain, the radical liberalisation of abortion laws was always imposed from the outside: first, at the time of the German occupation (1943), and then under the Soviet-controlled Communist regime (1956).[54] Also, in contrast with Britain, euthanasia was never a matter of any serious debate in Poland, and it was only at the time of the Second World War that, under the *Aktion T4* programme, mentally and physically disabled people could be 'legally' put to death in a medically induced way.

Notwithstanding these discrepancies, both Tolkien and Wojtyła appear to have been of one mind with regard to abortion and euthanasia, with heavy hearts anticipating what was soon to happen in increasingly post-Christian Europe (and beyond). The former, as was frequently the case, expressed his concerns (in this case ethical) through fiction, the latter – as a priest, bishop, cardinal, and finally Pope John Paul II – by means of more explicit pastoral methods: a sermon, lecture, article, letter, or encyclical.

All these ethical reflections must have been additionally triggered and/or strengthened by the reading of various works in the fields of Christian eth-

54 Since then, the Polish law on abortion has been successively limited to two (as of February 2023) cases: (1) when the pregnancy is a result of a criminal act and (2) when the woman's life or health is in danger.

ics and, possibly, social sciences and medicine.[55] The case of Karol Wojtyła/ John Paul II does not, I think, call for any special evidence. As a qualified theologian and philosopher (in fact, an Associate Professor of Philosophy at the Catholic University of Lublin since 1954), he was doubtlessly well-read in a great number of publications on the subject, in Polish and at least some of the seven foreign languages he knew.[56] Tolkien was, of course, a philologist specialising in medieval literature and languages. However, as is argued by A.R. Bossert, he was also "an intellectually sophisticated and orthodox Catholic, […] exhibiting awareness of early twentieth-century Church policies" (2006: 53).[57] Tolkien's reading list, for instance, is known to have included the works of Saint Thomas Aquinas (Cilli 2019: 287)[58] and Christopher Dawson (67).[59] Not only for that reason, he seems likely to have been also familiar with at least some of the ethical concepts discussed by the most prominent nineteenth- and early-twentieth-century British theologians: Cardinals John Henry Newman and Henry Edward Manning, Frederick William Faber, Henry Nutcombe Oxenham, and John Dobree Dalgairns, as well as Austin Farrer and Ronald Knox, both of whom Tolkien knew personally.[60] Moreover, in the early 1930s, being already a father of four, Tolkien could also have read (or, at least, heard about) the encyclical *Casti connubii* (1930), in which Pope Pius XI explicitly

55 This does not mean, of course, that Tolkien was an avid reader of medical books. However, unlike his friend and colleague C.S. Lewis, he was not averse to the media, regularly read conservative newspapers (most notably *The Daily Telegraph*), and so, more than once, may have come across news articles, interviews, and commentaries dealing with the more medical side of euthanasia and/or abortion, particularly in the 1930s and onwards, when the debates over the former, and, most of all, the latter were becoming more and more intense.

56 Apart from Polish, John Paul II was fluent in English, French, German, Italian, Latin, Russian, and Spanish.

57 Bossert seems a bit overcautious in his claim that Tolkien's awareness of Church policies was (particularly? only?) noticeable "later in his life" (2006: 53). For many years, he regularly, often daily, attended the Mass (as well as said the Rosary and prayed in front of the Host). Why would he have done all this in at least some kind of isolation from the Catholic policies concerning the ethics of life and death?

58 It is important to note that his edition of the *Summa Theologica* (in seven volumes) features "many notes in pencil (gray, blue and red) and in purple ink" (Testi 2019: 58). It is, however, unclear whether these annotations are actually in Tolkien's own hand (58).

59 In *On Fairy-stories* Tolkien makes two references to Dawson's 1929 book *Progress and Religion: An Historical Inquiry* (44, 72).

60 Many of them were, like Tolkien, Catholic converts. Unlike the above-listed, though, the future writer became a Catholic early in his life, at the age of eight (along with his mother Mabel, brother Hilary and aunt May Incledon).

voices his condemnation of abortion.[61] Likewise, in 1943, he may have become acquainted with the position on euthanasia advocated by Pius XII in his encyclical *Mystici corporis Christi*.[62]

It is obviously impossible to track down the development of Tolkien's understanding of the dignity of human life in the context of abortion and euthanasia. Nonetheless, given the above evidence – a small selection from *The Lord of the Rings*, *Morgoth's Ring*, and *The Nature of Middle-earth* – it does not differ in any noticeable way from that which, in 1995, led John Paul II to formulate his concepts of the 'Civilisation (or 'Culture') of Life' and the 'Civilisation (or 'Culture') of Death.' As we have seen, both terms can perfectly illustrate the general ethical dimensions in Tolkien's *legendarium*. Moreover, narrowing the scope of our investigation to the sphere of pre- and postnatal dignity of man, we can see that, with their roots in Scripture, the Christian tradition, and numerous works in the fields of theology and ethics, John Paul II's arguments concerning the sanctity and inviolability of human life are nothing short of universal. As such, they should therefore be considered as valid and applicable under all circumstances, also in the subcreated world of Arda, where, indeed, they are. For in this way too, in spite of being fictional, it retains what in *On Fairy-Stories* Tolkien calls "the inner consistency of reality" (59ff.).

---

61 In §63 of the encyclical, Pius XI argues that "the taking of the life of the offspring hidden in the mother's womb" (*vita prolis, in sinu materno reconditae, attentatur*) is "very grave crime" (*gravissiumum* [...] *est facinus*). The argument then continues in the following paragraphs (64-71).

62 "Conscious of the obligations of Our high office We deem it necessary to reiterate this grave statement today, when to Our profound grief We see at times the deformed, the insane, and those suffering from hereditary disease deprived of their lives, as though they were a useless burden to Society" (§94; *Quam quidem gravissimam sententiam Nos in praesens, pro altissimi conscientia officii, quo obstringimur, iterandam reputamus, dum magno cum maerore cernimus corpore deformes, amentes patriisque morbis infectos, utpote molestum societatis onus, vita interdum privari*).

About the Author

Łukasz Neubauer received his PhD in English philology from the University of Łódź. He is a researcher and lecturer at the University of Szczecin, Poland, where he teaches a number of literary courses. Apart from his publications dealing with various medieval as well as Christian influences and resonances in *The Lord of the Rings*, he has written papers on *The Battle of Maldon*, *Beowulf*, *Hêliand*, Icelandic sagas and the so-called 'beasts of battle' trope in, particularly but not exclusively, Old Germanic poetry. His most recent publications include a monograph *The Long Shadow of Fáfnir: Dragons in the Works of J.R.R. Tolkien and C.S. Lewis. A Christian Perspective* (2023) and book of essays *The Songs of the Spheres: Lewis, Tolkien and the Overlapping Realms of their Imaginations* (2024).

Bibliography

Arnold, Matthew. 2004. "Dover Beach." *Victorian Poetry: An Annotated Anthology*. Ed. Francis O'Gorman. Malden, MA: Blackwell, 312-13.

Birzer, Bradley. 2002. *J.R.R. Tolkien's Sanctifying Myth: Understanding Middle-earth*. Wilmington, DE: ISIS Books.

2007. "Roman Catholicism." In Michael D.C. Drout(ed.). *J.R.R. Tolkien Encyclopedia: Scholarship and Critical Assessment*.. New York, NY and London: Routledge, 85-89.

Boniecki, Adam. 1983. *Kalendarium życia Karola Wojtyły*. Kraków: Wydawnictwo Znak.

Bossert, A.R. 2006. "'Surely You Don't Disbelieve': Tolkien and Pius X: Anti-Modernism in Middle-earth." *Mythlore* 25.1: 53-76.

Brooks, Kenneth R. (ed.). 1961. *Andreas and the Fates of the Apostles*. Oxford: Clarendon Press.

Carrick, Paul. 2001. *Medical Ethics in the Ancient World*. Washington, DC: Georgetown University Press.

Catechism of the Catholic Church. 2006. London: Burns and Oates.

Catechism of the Christian Doctrine for First Communicants in Conformity with the Encyclical of Pope Pius X. 1918. Philadelphia, PA: John Joseph McVey.

Catholic Bible: Revised Standard Version. 2006. San Francisco, CA: Ignatius Press.

Chance, Jane. 2001. *Tolkien's Art: A Mythology for England*. Lexington, KY: University of Kentucky Press.

Childress, James F. 2014. "Christian Ethics, Medicine and Genetics." In Robin Gill (ed.). *The Cambridge Companion to Christian Ethics*. Cambridge: Cambridge University Press, 287-303.

Cong, Xiaoping. 2016. *Marriage, Law and Gender in Revolutionary China 1940-1960*. Cambridge: Cambridge University Press.

Conley, John J. SJ. 2008. "Philosophy and Anti-Philosophy: The Ambiguous Legacy of John Paul II." In Nancy Mardas Billias, Agnes B. Curry and George F. McLean (eds.). *Karol Wojtyla's Philosophical Legacy*. Washington, DC: The Council for Research in Values and Philosophy, 33-43.

Dickerson, Matthew. 2007. "Heathenism and Paganism." In Michael D.C. Drout(ed.). *J.R.R. Tolkien Encyclopedia: Scholarship and Critical Assessment.*. New York, NY and London: Routledge, 266-67.

Engelhardt, Dietrich von. 2018. "Scientific Progress in Socio-Cultural Context: Natural Science, Medicine and Myth after Nuremberg." In Ulrich Tröhler and Stella Reiter-Theil (eds.). *Ethics Codes in Medicine: Foundations and Achievements of Codification Since 1947*. Oxford and New York, NY: Routledge, 109-18.

den Hartogh, Govert. 2022. *What Kind of Death: The Ethics of Determining One's Own Death*. New York, NY and London: Routledge.

Fisher, Anthony. 2011. *Catholic Bioethics for a New Millennium*. Cambridge: Cambridge University Press.

Garbowski, Christopher. 2014. "Evil." In Stuart D. Lee (ed.). *A Companion to J.R.R. Tolkien*. Chichester: Wiley-Blackwell, 418-430.

Gerhardt, Christina. 2018. *Screening the Red Army Faction: Historical and Cultural Memory*. New York, NY: Bloomsbury.

The Greek-English Interlinear ESV New Testament. 2019. Wheaton, IL: Crossway Books.

Hamilton, Victor P. 1995. *The New International Commentary on the Old Testament. The Book of Genesis, Chapters 1-17*. Grand Rapids, MI: William B. Eerdmans.

Hammond, Wayne G. and Christina Scull. 2014. *The Lord of the Rings: A Reader's Companion*. London: HarperCollins.

Hamowy, Ronald (ed.). 2008. *The Encyclopedia of Libertarianism*. Los Angeles, CA, London, New Delhi, Singapore: SAGE Publications.

Hohendorf, Gerrit. 2014. "Die nationalsozialistischen Krankenmorde zwischen Tabu und Argument. Zur aktuellen Debatte über die Sterbehilfe." In Wolfgang Bialas and Lothar Fritze (eds.). *Ideologie und Moral im Nationalsozialismus*. Göttingen: Vanderhoeck & Ruprecht, 267-92.

Jesch, Judith. 2001. *Women in the Viking Age*. Woodbridge: The Boydell Press.

Johannes Paulus II. 1995. *Evangelium vitae*. Roma: Libreria Editrice Vaticana.

John Paul II. 1995. *The Gospel of Life: Evangelium Vitae. The Encyclical Letter on Abortion, Euthanasia, and the Death Penalty in Today's World*. New York, NY: Random House.

2015. *Letter to Families*. Bedford, NH: Sophia Institute Press.

Jones, David Albert. 2008. "John Paul II and Moral Theology." In Michael A. Hayes and Gerald O'Collins SJ (eds.). *The Legacy of John Paul II*. London and New York, NY: Burns and Oates, 79-109.

Kaczor, Christopher. 2023. *The Ethics of Abortion: Women's Rights, Human Life, and the Question of Justice*. New York, NY and London: Routledge.

Kindziuk, Milena. 2013. *Matka papieża. Poruszająca opowieść o Emilii Wojtyłowej*. Kraków: Znak.

King, Margaret L. 2013. "Children in Judaism and Christianity." In Paula S. Fass(ed.). *The Routledge History of Childhood in the Western World*. London and New York, NY: Routledge, 39-60.

Kroeber, A[lfred] L[ouis]. 2011. *Checklist of Civilizations and Culture*. London and New York, NY: Routledge.

Lee, Ellie. 2003. *Abortion, Motherhood, and Mental Health: Medicalizing Reproduction in the United States and Great Britain*. New York, NY: Aldine de Gruyter.

Lewis, Clive Staples. 2007. *The Collected Letters of C.S. Lewis. Vol. III. Narnia, Cambridge and Joy. 1950-1963*. Ed. Walter Hooper. San Francisco, CA: Harper San Francisco.

Moskwa, Jacek. 2010. *Droga Karola Wojtyły. Vol. 1. Na Tron Apostołów 1920-1978*. Warszawa: Świat Książki.

Nerozzi, Timothy. 2022. "Planned Parenthood edits fact sheet to say no heartbeat at 6 weeks of fetal development." https://foxwilmington.com/politics/planned-parenthood-edits-fact-sheet-to-say-no-heartbeat-at-6-weeks-of-fetal-development/. 22 September 2022. Accessed 10 October 2022.

Neubauer, Łukasz. 2020. "The 'Polish Inkling': Professor Przemysław Mroczkowski as J.R.R. Tolkien's Friend and Scholar." *Mythlore* 39.1: 149-76.

O'Brien, Bruce R. 1996. "From Morðor to Murdrum: The Preconquest Origin and Norman Revival of the Murder Fine." *Speculum* 71: 321-57.

Pearce, Joseph. 2015. *Wisdom and Innocence: A Life of G.K. Chesterton*. San Francisco, CA: Ignatius Press.

PIUS XI. 1931. *On Christian Marriage [Casti connubii]. In the original Latin with English translation*. New York, NY: The Barry Vail Corporation.

PIUS XII. 1943a. *De Mystico Iesu Christi Corpore deque nostra in eo cum Christo coniunctione « Mystici Corporis Christi»*. Romae: Apud Aedes Pont[ificiae] Univ[ersiatis] Gregorianae.

1943b. *Mystici corporis: Encyclical Letter of Pope Pius XII on the Mystical Body of Christ*. Washington, DC: National Catholic Welfare Conference.

RIDDLE, John M. 1994. *Contraception and Abortion from the Ancient World to the Renaissance*. Cambridge, MA and London: Harvard University Press.

RUTLEDGE, Fleming. 2004. *Battle for Middle-Earth: Tolkien's Divine Design in* The Lord of the Rings. Grand Rapids, MI: William B. Eerdmans Publishing Company.

SCULL, Christina and Wayne G. HAMMOND. 2017. *The J.R.R. Tolkien Companion and Guide. Chronology*. London: HarperCollins.

SHIPPEY, Tom. 2000. *J.R.R. Tolkien: Author of the Century*. Boston, MA and New York, NY: Houghton Mifflin Company.

SINGH, Susheela, Stanley K. HENSHAW and Kathleen BERENTSEN. 2002. *The Sociocultural and Political Aspects of Abortion: Global Perspectives*. Ed. Alaka Malwade Basu. Westport, CT and London: Praeger, 15-48.

STENSVOLD, Anne. 2015. *A History of Pregnancy in Christianity: From Original Sin to Contemporary Abortion Debates*. New York, NY and London: Routledge.

TESTI, Claudio A. 2019. 'Tolkien and Aquinas.' *Tolkien and the Classics*. Eds. Roberto Arduini, Giampaolo Canzonieri and Claudio A. Testi. Zurich and Jena: Walking Tree Publishers, 57-71.

TERZO, Sarah. 2023. 'Minnesota report reveals five babies born alive after abortion in 2021.' https://www.liveaction.org/news/minnesota-babies-born-alive-abortion/. Accessed 21 March 2023.

THOMASMA, David C., Thomasine Kimbrough KUSHNER and G.L KIMSMA (eds.). 1998. *Asking to Die: Inside the Dutch Debate about Euthanasia*. Dordrecht, Boston, MA and London: Kluwer Academic Publishers.

TOLKIEN, J[ohn] R[onald] R[euel]. 2007. *The Hobbit*. London: HarperCollins.

The Letters of J.R.R. Tolkien. 1981. Ed. Humphrey Carpenter with the assistance of Christopher Tolkien. London, Boston, MA and Sydney, NSW: George Allen & Unwin.

2005. *The Lord of the Rings. Vol. 1. The Fellowship of the Ring*. London: HarperCollins.

2005. *The Lord of the Rings. Vol. 2. The Two Towers.* London: HarperCollins.

2005. *The Lord of the Rings. Vol. 3. The Return of the King.* London: HarperCollins.

2003. *The History of Middle-earth. Part Three. X. Morgoth's Ring.* Ed. Christopher Tolkien. London: HarperCollins.

2021. *The Nature of Middle-earth.* Ed. Carl F. Hostetter. London: HarperCollins.

2008. "On Fairy-stories." *Tolkien On Fairy-stories. Expanded edition, with commentary and notes.* Eds. Verlyn Flieger and Douglas A. Anderson. London: HarperCollins, 25-84.

2006. *The Silmarillion.* Ed. Christopher Tolkien. London: HarperCollins.

Whiting, Raymond. 2002. *A Natural Right to Die: Twenty-three Centuries of Debate.* Westport, CT and London: Greenwood Press.

Holly Ordway

Tolkien in His Contemporary Context: Among the Oratorians and the Jesuits

Abstract

As an English Catholic Christian of the 20th century, with his roots in Birmingham and most of his adult life in Oxford, Tolkien had more interaction with contemporary theologians than can readily be estimated from references in his writing. This essay focuses specifically on Tolkien's interactions with the Oratorians and the Jesuits. In his childhood and youth, he was formed by the spirituality of the Congregation of the Oratory of St. Philip Neri at the Birmingham Oratory, for which Robert Eaton, one of the Oratorian priests in Birmingham in Tolkien's youth, stands as an example. At Oxford as a student and later a professor, he interacted with a number of Jesuit theologians; this essay considers Joseph Rickaby, C.C. Martindale, and Martin D'Arcy. A detailed consideration of biographical context helps scholars to consider the chronology of possible influences on the theological and spiritual elements of the *legendarium*, to establish the relative importance of certain influences and ideas, and to exercise appropriate caution in making arguments from silence. Appreciating Tolkien's place among his contemporary theologians helps us better to understand his world, and therefore better to understand, and fruitfully explore, his work.

This volume as a whole considers Tolkien 'among the theologians'; not surprisingly, many of the authors have focused on Tolkien's literary interaction or intellectual resonance with the work of major figures in the history of theology, such as Augustine, Aquinas, Boethius, and Calvin. However, as an English Catholic of the 20th century, with important connections to Birmingham and Oxford, Tolkien was also part of a dynamic contemporary theological scene. Placing him within this cultural and intellectual context, and attending to the specific connections he had with individual theologians during his life, especially during the personally and creatively formative years of his youth and the decades leading up to the writing of *The Lord of the Rings*, will help us to gain a fuller, more nuanced picture of Tolkien's religious formation and the influences on his theology, which will in turn help us to understand more fully both his academic and imaginative writings.

From the mid-nineteenth century to the early twentieth century, significant cultural shifts in the religious landscape of the United Kingdom included the Oxford Movement in the Church of England, the restoration of full civil rights to Catholics through the various Relief Bills and other acts, the corresponding anti-Catholic protests such as the Gordon Riots, and the English Catholic revival, centered around John Henry Newman's exceptionally high-profile conversion from Anglicanism to Catholicism. It was at the Birmingham Oratory, founded by John Henry Newman, that Tolkien spent the formative years of his youth. He probably never met G.K. Chesterton in person, but from an early age read and appreciated his apologetics works.[1] As a professor at Oxford, he was part of an intellectual scene that included such notable Anglican and Catholic thinkers as Martin D'Arcy, Austin Farrer, Ronald Knox, C.S. Lewis, C.C. Martindale, Evelyn Waugh, Hilaire Belloc, Charles Williams, and Francis de Zulueta (to name just a few), all of whom Tolkien knew personally, and some of whom he counted among his close friends.

Some of these figures have, for us, receded into the shadows of historical footnotes and out-of-print books; others are well known in themselves, but their connection to Tolkien has been overlooked or underappreciated. All, however, present the opportunity to gain a more complete picture of Tolkien's theological engagement by placing him in his intellectual and cultural environment.

We can get a glimpse of Tolkien's place in that context in a letter he wrote to E.V. Gordon regarding Gordon's translation of the Middle English poem *Pearl*. Tolkien says that he is willing to assist with the project, and remarks that if he did so, "I will tackle the theological parts first. Because they interest me least. Because if I am a partner, I shall have to be specially responsible for any 'bad theology'. Because I can fairly easily get advice, Dominican, Benedictine and Jesuit" (*Letters* 32). This comment, though brief, is productive of insights. First, his passing remark that the "theological parts" of *Pearl* are the least interesting to him is a reminder that Tolkien was not professionally a theologian nor, unlike his friend C.S. Lewis, did he have an interest in explaining the subject to a popular audience. Tolkien was an attentive reader of Scripture and

1 George Sayer recalled that Tolkien appreciated Chesterton's apologetics book *The Everlasting Man* and said that he felt its arguments to be "absolutely valid" (Carpenter, Sayer, and Kilby 1984: 21).

had volumes of theology in his personal library, including Aquinas's *Summa Theologica*, a full set of which he acquired in the 1920s (Cilli 2023: 287), and his letters and imaginative writings show that he had a solid knowledge of Catholic theology and a keen interest in exploring theological ideas through his *legendarium*.[2] However, his professional interests were primarily literary and linguistic, not theological; the fact that he was a serious Catholic himself does not mean that he would automatically be interested in the theological aspects of every literary work that he studied. He certainly was interested in the theological elements in some of the works he studied, as we can see in his discussion of Gawain's confession in the Middle English poem *Sir Gawain and the Green Knight*, as well as his awareness of the theological underpinnings of the *Old English Exodus* (*SGGK*; *OEE*). In the instance of *Pearl*, it seems he simply found the "theological parts" of *Pearl* less compelling than its literary and linguistic elements.

Second, even though he was not particularly interested in writing about the theological content of *Pearl*, he took it seriously; it is notable that he felt that he would be "specially responsible" for any errors in theology in an edition he co-edited. Although we lack the fuller context of the discussion with Gordon that would enable us to know precisely what he meant by this remark, it is not unlikely that it reflects Tolkien's awareness that as one of only four Catholic professors at Oxford University and a role model for other Catholics at the university, anything he wrote that touched on matters theological would be scrutinized.[3]

The last part of his comment is most relevant for our discussion in this chapter, as it shows how Tolkien felt able to turn "fairly easily" for advice from a variety of Catholic theologians: "Dominican, Benedictine and Jesuit." Those three religious orders undoubtedly came immediately to his mind because they all had a presence in Oxford: the Dominicans at Blackfriars, the Benedictines at St. Benet's Hall, and the Jesuits at Campion Hall. The Dominican priest Gervase Mathew was also a fellow member of the Inklings. We should not take this threefold listing as exhaustive, however. Throughout his life, Tolkien counted a number of theologians among his mentors, colleagues, and friends. These

2 See, for instance, the contents of *The Nature of Middle-earth*.
3 For more on Tolkien as a Catholic academic, see Ordway (2023: 184-95).

included Catholics who were not members of a religious order, such as Ronald Knox and Douglas Carter, the scholarly parish priest of St. Gregory and St. Augustine (cf. Ordway 2023: 250-51), and non-Catholic theologians such as the Anglicans C.S. Lewis, Charles Williams, and Austin Farrer. Writing to Austin and his wife Katharine Farrer in 1962, Tolkien offered his thanks for Austin's "booklet on the Rosary," noting that he had "derived profit and encouragement from it" and that it was "a great delight to know that others whose virtue and learning is far above mine are companions" (*Letters* 456).[4]

The constraints of space do not permit a full listing, let alone a full treatment, of the many theologians whom Tolkien knew throughout his long life. This chapter, therefore, focuses on two specific groups of theologians – the Oratorians and the Jesuits – and, within those, a small number of individuals who are particularly interesting or significant as possible influences on Tolkien's theological understanding.

The Oratorians

Tolkien quite literally spent his formative years 'among the theologians.' His earliest formation as a Catholic was at the Birmingham Oratory. In 1903, just shy of his twelfth birthday, he had his First Holy Communion and received the sacrament of confirmation, taking the confirmation name "Philip" after St. Philip Neri.[5] After his mother's death, he and his brother Hilary became the wards of Fr. Francis Morgan, a priest of the Oratory. From that time until 1911 when he matriculated at Exeter College, Oxford, Tolkien recalled that he "had the advantage [...] of a 'good Catholic home' – '*in excelsis*' [in the highest]: virtually a junior inmate of the Oratory house, which contained many learned fathers (largely 'converts')" (*Letters* 554).

These "learned fathers" at the Birmingham Oratory were members of the Congregation of the Oratory, a religious congregation founded in the sixteenth

4 The "booklet" in question was a short volume (under a hundred pages) titled *Lord I Believe: Suggestions for Turning the Creed into Prayer*, first published in 1955 (London: Church Union), reprinted in an expanded second edition in 1958 (London: Faith Press and London, S.P.C.K.). Chapter IX, "The Heaven-sent aid" and Chapter X, "Twenty mysteries," address the use of the rosary in prayer.

5 Personal communication with Priscilla Tolkien, October 2, 2020. For more on the significance of "Philip" in Tolkien's life, see Ordway (2023: 34-35).

century by the Italian priest Philip Neri. Born in 1515 in Florence, Italy, Philip came to Rome as a young man, where he was ordained a priest and gathered around himself a company of other men, all seeking holiness of life. He had a considerable and long-lasting reforming effect on the Catholic clergy and laity of 'the eternal city' and was declared a saint only a few years after his death in 1595.

Philip's community in Rome was initially formed from the young men who were drawn to his approach to the Christian life, and was then formally recognized as the Congregation of the Oratory. New Oratories were founded, in Italy and beyond. Oratorians are technically a congregation, not a religious order, because although the men who join a particular Oratory live in community, they do not take vows, they retain their own personal property, and they are free to leave at any time. Oratories exist worldwide; each is independent of the others, but they have in common that they all follow the Oratorian Rule and take their spiritual father, St. Philip Neri, as their model. Oratories are always established in cities, and they have a particular mission to the more highly educated in the community.[6]

The Oratory in Birmingham was the first to be established in England, founded in 1852 by John Henry Newman (later Cardinal Newman); he was its Superior until his death in 1890. Before his entrance into the Catholic Church, Newman had been one of the leading lights of Oxford; he was Fellow of Oriel College, Oxford, and Vicar of the University Church. After he became a Catholic and was ordained a priest in Rome, he returned to England with his friends who had converted and been ordained alongside him to set up a religious community. Newman decided that the model of community and outreach offered by the Oratory of St. Philip Neri was the one best suited for English culture, and for his particular talents and those of his friends, all of whom were well-educated converts from Anglicanism. His choice of the Oratorian Rule for this new community was based in part on the fact that it "allowed the retention of personal property, such as books, and it encouraged scholarly pursuits among its members" (Jacob 2016: 95).

---

6 See, for instance, Bertram 2015, Bouyer 1995, Oxford Oratory 2016, Robinson 2015, Türks 1995.

Tolkien therefore had his early spiritual and intellectual formation in an environment whose spirit and ethos was grounded in the spirituality of St. Philip Neri, as articulated in English culture by Newman, the foremost English theologian of the nineteenth century. In fact, there was only one generation separating Tolkien and Newman, for his guardian Francis Morgan had been taught by Newman as a young man and served as Newman's personal secretary (Birmingham Oratory, "Fathers and Brothers"; Ferrández Bru 2011: 57; cf. Newman 1976a, Newman 1976b). Many of the other Oratorian Fathers had known Newman well and worked with him for many years. Newman remained the central figure of the Oratory after his death; his room was, and indeed still is, kept exactly as it was during his life, and the Fathers continued to refer to him affectionately as 'Our Cardinal.' The influence on Tolkien of Newman's thought[7] is a major subject, far beyond the scope of this essay; here we will attend only to Oratorians whom Tolkien had occasion to know personally.

It is important to keep in mind that although Oxford now has its own Oratory, this was not established until 1990; during Tolkien's lifetime, what is now the Oxford Oratory was simply the parish church of St. Aloysius, run by the Jesuits. However, Tolkien did retain a connection with several of the Birmingham Oratory Fathers into his adult life: most notably, his guardian Francis Morgan, but also Fr. Vincent Reade (Ordway 2023: 64-65).

Among the "learned fathers" at the Birmingham Oratory were gifted theologians whose sermons Tolkien would have heard, and whose friendship and mentoring he received.[8] Following both the model of St. Philip Neri and John Henry Cardinal Newman, the spirituality of the Birmingham Oratory was characterized by an attention to beauty (especially in music and in the liturgy of the Mass), Eucharistic devotion, an emphasis on honoring the Virgin Mary (the Oratory church is in fact the Parish Church of the Immaculate Conception, a Marian

7 We do not as yet have any details of Tolkien's direct engagement with Newman's writings, but, in addition to his immersion in the Newmanian atmosphere of the Birmingham Oratory, he was in later years involved with the Newman Society at Oxford and the national Newman Association (see Ordway 2023: 190-93).

8 His guardian, Fr. Francis Morgan, was a cultured and well-educated man, but not a theologian; his particular gifts were more pastoral in nature.

title), a particular emphasis on the sacrament of reconciliation (confession), and an emphasis on humor and humility in the spiritual life.[9]

Fr. Robert Eaton, Cong. Orat.

The most prolific theological and spiritual writer among these Fathers, whose work encompassed many of these themes, was Robert Ormston Eaton (1866-1942), headmaster of St. Philip's Grammar School during the few months that Tolkien attended, and a dynamic presence at the Oratory during Tolkien's entire time there. A skilled boxer and cricketer as a young man, Fr. Robert, called "Burby" by his students at The Oratory School (Oratory School Society 1999: 76), was also a talented amateur actor, who continued as a priest to coach student actors in Latin plays, a tradition of The Oratory School. John Ronald Tolkien would thus have had a Catholic mentor to encourage him both in his love of sport (in his case, rugby) and his acting in classical plays, two passions which he developed at King Edward's School. Eaton's interest in music led him to a long involvement with the Oratory choir and, eventually, to his work as Director of Music for the Birmingham Catholic Choir (Birmingham Oratory, "Fathers and Brothers").

Eaton was also the author of many theological and devotional works. Most of these were published in the years after Tolkien's time at the Oratory, and we cannot at present identify any specific titles which he knew, but they are nevertheless valuable in representing the theological material that Eaton (and other Oratorian Fathers) would have brought to his preaching and mentoring at the Oratory.

One aspect of this is an approach to the exposition of the Bible that is both scholarly and accessible, in line with the Oratorians' emphasis on the intellectual life for Catholics. Works in this vein include *Sing Ye to the Lord: Expositions of Fifty Psalms* (1915), *The Man of Sorrows: Chapters on the Sacred Passion* (1921), which explores in detail the events of the last days of Christ's earthly life, and *The Forty Days: Chapters on the Risen Life of our Lord* (1926), which explores the

9 For more on these elements of Oratorian spirituality, and how they influenced Tolkien, see Ordway 2023.

significance of the ministry of Christ in the forty days between his Resurrection from the dead and his Ascension into heaven. With reference to Eaton's 1930 study *The Apocalypse of St. John*, T.E. Bird, the Professor of Sacred Scripture at Oscott College in Birmingham, notes that the work is "based on sure scholarship" while also "expressed with admirable simplicity" (Eaton 1930: 7-8).

Oratorian spirituality places a strong emphasis on the value of regular participation in the sacrament of reconciliation (confession), a view which Tolkien shared. In *The Ministry of Reconciliation: Chapters on Confession* (1925), Eaton provides a theologically informed exploration of this sacrament as "the sacrament of mercy" (Eaton 1925: 172), considering the working of the conscience and the sense of contrition, the effects of sin, and the practice and effects of a good confession.

Eaton's writings also reflect the importance of the Eucharist in Oratorian spirituality. Tolkien's personal devotion to the Blessed Sacrament as "the one great thing to love on earth" is well attested (*Letters* 74). In 1944, he recalled "spending half an hour [...] before the Blessed Sacrament when the Quarant' Ore was being held" (*Letters* 140). The *Quarant'ore*, or Forty Hours Devotion, consists of approximately forty hours of Exposition of the Blessed Sacrament for prayer and adoration – corresponding to the forty hours that Jesus's body lay in the tomb – in a single church or sometimes in a sequence of churches. It began in Italy in the sixteenth century and was encouraged by the Oratory of St. Philip Neri. By means of the Oratorians, it made its way to England in the nineteenth century, although it was held by only a tiny fraction of English Catholic churches in Tolkien's day. Tolkien would have first encountered the *Quarant'ore* at the Birmingham Oratory. His participation in the *Quarant'ore* in later years in Oxford indicates that he had, at least to some extent, integrated this characteristically Oratorian devotional practice into the adult practice of his spirituality.

Eaton's 1927 *The Divine Refreshment: Chapters on the Blessed Sacrament* focuses on the sacrament of the Eucharist, exploring the significance and effects of the reception of Holy Communion. Although this particular book was published after Tolkien was an adult, it illustrates the way that the Oratorians were at the forefront of encouraging a shift in Catholic spiritual practices that was unfolding during Tolkien's youth. Francis Cardinal Bourne, the Archbishop of Westminster, observes that Eaton's book is particularly valuable because the Eucharist, "in consequence of the growing frequency of reception of Holy Communion, holds a place of importance in the spiritual life unequalled in the past" (Eaton 1927: vii).

Bourne is referring to the new emphasis on frequent communion initiated by Pope Pius X. Although Catholics, in both Tolkien's day and today, are obligated to attend Sunday Mass each week if it is possible to do so, they are only required to receive communion once a year. As late as 1920, it was common for even devout Catholics to receive the Sacrament no more than once a month, a few times a year, or even only at Easter (Crichton 1979: 21). The practice of frequent or even daily communion was brought about through the work of Pope Pius X. In 1905, the pope approved the decree "*Sacra Tridentina*: On Frequent and Daily Reception of Holy Communion" and began to encourage the practice of daily communion. Tolkien thoroughly approved of these reforms, writing in 1963 that Pius X had established "the greatest reform of our time," one that he felt was sorely needed: "I wonder what state the Church would now be but for it" (*Letters* 476).

Another of Eaton's works which is helpful in understanding Tolkien's theological formation is *Auxilium Infirmorum*, published in 1908 when Tolkien was a young man at the Oratory. Its Latin title, 'help of the sick,' is one of the epithets given to the Virgin Mary in the Litany of Loreto. Eaton notes that the book is comprised of pieces originally written for "one who at length crowned a painful illness of eight years' duration by a death precious in the sight of God"; published at her request, the book seeks "to illustrate some of the phases and trials of the times of sickness, and to encourage those who suffer and mourn to make all things work together for good, exercising in fullest measure the difficult apostleship of pain entrusted to them by our Lord" (Eaton 1908: v).

This book is particularly notable as we consider the formative elements in Tolkien's life. Eaton shows in this book his experience with the pastoral care of the sick and dying, and his understanding of the "dark days," the "temptations," the "difficulties at prayer" and the suffering experienced by the sick. Tolkien's mother Mabel died in 1904 from diabetes, a disease which at that time was poorly understood and untreatable, and which would have caused her much pain before her eventual lapse into a coma and her death. Theological questions regarding suffering and sickness – perhaps especially the suffering and death of someone who was a faithful Catholic – would have been very much on the forefront of Tolkien's mind. Eaton's handling of it in *Auxilium Infirmorum* provides insight into the characteristics of the pastoral guidance and spiritual formation that Tolkien would have been receiving at that time – care that contributed to an adult spirituality that could come to terms with sorrow and loss, without rejecting his faith or becoming angry or resentful toward God or the Catholic Church.

Given that we know Tolkien to have developed a strong devotion to the Blessed Virgin Mary, it is notable that Eaton takes his title from the Litany of Loreto (from which Tolkien would later take another Marian epithet, *Consolatrix Afflictorum*, as the title of a poem he wrote in the trenches of the Great War; (Scull and Hammond 2017: 97; Ordway 2023: 147-50), and makes direct connections to Mary's experiences in seeing the suffering of her son. For instance, Eaton takes in one chapter the suffering that Jesus experienced when, before his crucifixion, he was scourged by the Roman soldiers. He writes, "Imagine, if you can, the anguish of our Lady" on hearing that her son was to be scourged, knowing that "her Child, who had been subject to her for thirty years [...] was to be in a hall alone, with brutal men around, infuriated with drink and malice, who would tear from His aching body the clothes she herself had woven for him, and then with scourges rend the flesh from those sacred limbs, and cause the blood to flow in streams" (Eaton 1908: 77). Mary's sorrow and suffering during the events of the Crucifixion, so vividly evoked here, was a point that also moved Tolkien greatly as an adult (Ordway 2023: 145).

Whether or not Tolkien read any of Eaton's published writings, he would have encountered Fr. Robert's presentation of these ideas through his sermons over the years at the Oratory. In any case, Eaton's writing is valuable as offering insight into the theology being preached, taught, and expressed in pastoral care at the Birmingham Oratory in the first decade of the twentieth century.

The Jesuits

Tolkien's religious identity as a young man was formed primarily in the context of Oratorian spirituality, but by his undergraduate years, he had evidently developed some interest in Jesuit spirituality. One indication of this is his use of the abbreviation AMDG in his Oxford work-diary, which he began in January, 1913. It served as an "account book" of his time, with the promised reward from Edith of kisses for hours put in at his studies (McIlwaine 2018: 149), and it also contained "notes (in red ink) of the performance of religious duties and saints' days" (*Tolkien: Life and Legend* 1992: 27). Most notably for our purposes, its heading is "JRRT and EMB [Edith Mary Bratt] in account together, AMDG" (*Tolkien: Life and Legend* 1992: 27). AMDG stands for *ad majorem Dei gloriam*, Latin for 'to the greater glory of God,' which is the motto of the Jesuits, the Society of Jesus founded by Ignatius of Loyola in the sixteenth century.[10]

Like the Oratorians, the Jesuits place a strong emphasis on education and the intellectual life. Unlike the Oratorians, who, as we have observed, were new arrivals on the English Catholic scene, the Jesuits had a deep history in England, having provided the largest share of missionary priests during the centuries following the Reformation, when Catholicism was proscribed. When the penal laws were lifted, the Jesuits developed into "the most vigorous religious order in the country, and they received the lion's share of converts from the Oxford Movement" (Sire 1997: 18). One of these converts was the poet Gerard Manley Hopkins, in whose work Tolkien later took an interest (*Letters* 182; cf. Ordway 2023: 153). Hopkins was received into the Catholic Church by John Henry Newman himself, but rather than joining Newman's Oratorians, he was ordained as a Jesuit priest. The parish church of St. Aloysius in Oxford, which would become a regular place of worship for Tolkien from his undergraduate

10 Interestingly, in December of 1913, Tolkien's brother Hilary, while studying at an agricultural college in Aberdeen, became a member of the Arch-Confraternity of the Blessed Sacrament, a devotional society for laypeople founded by Jesuits, as indicated by the motto AMDG on Hilary's certificate of admission (Gardner and Holford 2010: 70-71). It may be that the two brothers encountered Jesuit spirituality independently; it is also possible that Tolkien, with his early devotion to the Blessed Sacrament, encouraged his younger brother in this aspect of his spiritual life.

years onward, was at that time run by the Jesuits; Hopkins briefly served as a curate (assistant priest) there.[11]

Tolkien was probably first introduced to Jesuit spirituality while still at the Birmingham Oratory. One piece of evidence for this is that his guardian, Francis Morgan, had in his library the book *Nova et Vetera* by the Jesuit priest George Tyrrell; it has Francis's bookplate and is dated 1907 (Ferrández Bru 2018: 79n12). George Tyrrell (1861-1909) was a controversial figure: a noted English theologian, he came to dispute some of the Church's teachings, especially Pope Pius X's condemnation of modernism, and was eventually excommunicated (Rafferty 2009). However, *Nova et Vetera* was not one of his controversial works, but rather a collection of spiritual meditations; it received an 'Imprimatur' and 'Nihil Obstat' from the English Catholic hierarchy (Tyrrell 1905), meaning that it contained nothing contrary to the faith. Its meditations are on a range of subjects, such as the example of specific saints (St. Andrew, St. Martin, Sts. Peter and Paul, and others), "Giving to the Poor," "Christ, Our Sun," the Virgin Mary as "Mother of Mercy," "Death," "Fellowship in Suffering," "Uncovenanted Mercies," and the suffering of Christ on the Cross.

Once Tolkien arrived at Oxford University, he had the opportunity to get to know more of the Jesuits. From 1896 onward, the Jesuits had what is called a 'private hall' at Oxford University, which allowed for Jesuit undergraduates to study for degrees. Private halls are named for their current 'master' or head, so it was first known as Clarke's Hall (after Fr. Richard Clarke) and then Pope's Hall (after Fr. O'Fallon Pope). The Jesuits were also in charge of the parish of St. Aloysius. Tolkien presumably had at least some interactions with Fr. Frederick O'Hare, SJ, who served as rector of St. Aloysius from 1908-1921 (Bertram 2000: 45). The Jesuit connection continued in later years. During the Great War, Tolkien was assigned to the 11th Lancashire Fusiliers, whose senior chaplain was Fr. Henry Gill, a Jesuit priest (Hagerty 2017: 135).[12]

A more lasting connection was formed when Tolkien returned to Oxford from Leeds to take up his professorial chair. In 1918, the Jesuit private hall gained

11 St. Aloysius would not become the Oxford Oratory until 1990.

12 I am indebted to John Garth for sharing with me his research notes identifying the chaplains who ministered to Tolkien's battalion. For more on Tolkien's spiritual life under wartime conditions, see Ordway (2023: 129-55).

official status as a Permanent Private Hall, and its name was changed from Pope's Hall to its present name of Campion Hall. In 1936, after years of using a leased property, the Jesuits built a substantial new building on Brewer Street, designed by Sir Edwin Lutyens. Tolkien and Edith attended the opening of this new building in 1936, a gala affair whose guest-list included the Earl of Oxford and Asquith and the novelist Evelyn Waugh (Martindale 1936). The Jesuits had an important role in the Catholic academic scene at Oxford. Tolkien himself was one of only four Catholics to hold a full professorial chair, and the number of Catholics doing any lecturing at the University was small enough that, starting in 1938 and continuing for about a decade, the *Catholic Herald* published lists of each term's Catholic lecturers at Oxford. Among the lecturers appearing on these lists are the Jesuit priests Martin D'Arcy (whom we will discuss below), Leslie Walker, Lewis Watt, John Rogers, and V.G. Turner (*Catholic Herald* 1939, 1940a, 1940b, 1941a, 1941b, 1949). Tolkien's own diligence as a lecturer is indicated in the fact that he is the only don who appears in every extant lecture-list.

Having established this background sketch of the Jesuit presence in Tolkien's life, we now turn to considering individual figures of note.

Fr. Joseph Rickaby, S.J.

As an undergraduate at Oxford, Tolkien would certainly have known of, and very probably personally encountered, one of the most notable Jesuits of the day, Fr. Joseph Rickaby (1845-1932). Rickaby was highly regarded in his day as a retreat director, preacher, scholar, and the author of thirty-three books and many articles (Feeney 2001: 170), and played an important role in English Catholic education during a time of new opportunities and new challenges for Catholics.

From the Reformation until 1854, all matriculating students at Oxford had been required to assent to the Thirty-Nine Articles, a specifically Anglican declaration of faith that excluded Catholics and Nonconformists. The passing of the Universities Test Act in 1854 removed this requirement, such that Catholics could now study at Oxford.[13] However, with Catholics a tiny minority in a still largely hostile Anglican environment, the Catholic hierarchy was hesitant to encourage Catholics to study there; as a result, at first Catholic students wishing to study at Oxford had to receive special permission from their bishop to do so. In 1895, this restriction was lifted, and university chaplaincies were established to supply weekly 'conferences' or lectures to support the faith of Catholic students. Rickaby participated in this project early on; his Oxford and Cambridge conferences from 1897-1899 were published in 1899 and reprinted in 1915 as *The Lord My Light*. Topics in his Oxford sessions included theological issues such as "Natural and Supernatural Virtue," "Inspiration and Historical Accuracy of Holy Scripture," "Faith distinct from Reason," and "The Value of Reason along with Faith" (Rickaby 1899).

His books include *The Divinity of Christ* (1906), *Waters that Go Softly: Thoughts for Time of Retreat* (1906), *Scholasticism* (1908), and *An Index to the Works of John Henry Cardinal Newman* (1914). Rickaby had been a friend and classmate of the poet Gerard Manley Hopkins during their seminary training at St. Beuno's College in North Wales, later recalling how they "took long walks together, and conversed intimately" (quoted in Feeney 2001: 170). One of his contemporaries recalled that Rickaby "was rather short, had untidy grey hair, steel-rimmed spectacles, and a half-smile playing about his lips as though he was enjoying a little private joke of his own. Perhaps he was, for he was a man with an abiding sense of fun" (quoted in Sire 1997: 27-28).

Tolkien would have first encountered Rickaby at the official opening of the Cardinal Newman Memorial Church in 1909.[14] This event was of major importance for the Birmingham Oratory community. The Oratory church building that Tolkien and his mother Mabel had known had become too small for the needs of the parish, and had been gradually replaced with a much larger, classical-style basilica, designated the Newman Memorial Church. It was officially opened on December 8, 1909 (Tristram 1934: 35), the Solemnity of the Immaculate

13 Since the oath was required at matriculation, not at the conferral of degrees, students such as Gerard Manley Hopkins who began their studies as Anglicans and then converted to Catholicism could still receive their degree; however, until further legislation in 1871, such students could not go on to hold university fellowships as their Anglican counterparts could.

14 I am indebted to Peter Gilliver for calling my attention to Fr. Rickaby's sermon at the Newman Memorial Church and his prominence as a scholar, thus setting in train my further research.

Conception of the Virgin Mary, a date of particular significance in the Catholic liturgical calendar and also the Birmingham Oratory's patronal festival. It is almost certain, then, that the young Tolkien would have been present at this event, with its significance for his Marian piety, its liturgical solemnity, and its importance for the community of which he was a part.

Rickaby preached the first of the two sermons on that occasion, a detailed exploration of Newman's intellectual and spiritual life, ending with an impassioned vision of Newman's legacy as a living and dynamic force in English Catholic culture:

> I augur that from this Cardinal Newman's Memorial Church, from this his Oratory of St. Philip, from this his Oratory School, and from these the many volumes of his writings [...] good shall flow [... that] in this city and diocese of Birmingham, at Oscott, and even in far-off Oxford, there shall grow up and be perpetuated a school of Newman's thought [...] I augur that from this spot, the central city of our isle, shall be wrought out, not perhaps the conversion of England, but what the Cardinal, with his distrust of a popular religion, loved rather to contemplate, the conversion of Englishmen. I augur that Catholics, sore tempted in faith, shall here be strengthened in the same, first by prayer and Mass and Sacraments, then by what I have long considered the best philosophy for an English Catholic layman, the teaching of John Henry Newman, taken as a whole – I say, 'taken as a whole,' the whole gist and spirit and mind of the man. (1910: 24-25)

His exhortation in 1909 to carry on the work of Newman was grounded in his own efforts to provide an intellectually robust as well as doctrinally sound theological formation for Catholics in England's two greatest universities. In fact, in 1912, Rickaby returned to Oxford and, along with another Jesuit, Fr. Alban Goodier, provided the 'conferences' for the Chaplaincy during the Trinity Term of Tolkien's second year at Exeter College ("University Notes" 1912).

Fr. C.C. Martindale, S.J.

Cyril Charles Martindale (1879-1963) was another of Britain's leading Jesuit scholars. He studied at Pope's Hall (as Campion Hall was then known) in Oxford, later teaching at the University for a few years before taking up a post in London at Farm Street Church (Van Goethem 2019). Martindale's diverse and extensive literary output included a volume of short stories, *The Goddess of Ghosts* (1915); a biography of the Catholic novelist and priest Robert Hugh Benson (1916); *The Vocation of Aloysius Gonzaga* (1929) about the saint for which St. Aloysius's Church, Oxford, is named; *Catholic Thought and Thinkers: Introductory* (1920); *The Religions of the World* (1931); *Does God Matter for Me?* (1937); *The Queen's Daughters: A Study of Women Saints* (1951), and several entries for the *Catholic Encyclopedia*.

During Holy Week of 1946, Martindale gave a series of six talks on BBC Radio's Home Service under the title "Creative Love," on the love of God and God's love for humanity, a topic that would have been all the more compelling given that he had only recently returned from five years of captivity by the Nazis: while traveling, he had been caught up in the German invasion of Denmark and detained for the duration of the war (Van Goethem 2019; Martindale 1946).

Martindale only overlapped with Tolkien at Oxford for two years (1925-27), but their paths crossed again later, as he was an Honorary Vice-President of the Newman Association alongside Tolkien in the 1950s (Palace Green Archives D1/J/1/1/1). Tolkien certainly would have known of Martindale, given the Jesuit's high profile as a Catholic academic and literary figure. We now know that Tolkien read at least one of Martindale's works: the booklet *Bernadette of Lourdes* (Catholic Truth Society, first published 1934), as he notes in a 1945 letter that he read it immediately after seeing the film *The Song of Bernadette* (*Letters* 155).

Fr. Martin D'Arcy, S.J.

At Oxford Tolkien also had the opportunity to get to know Martin Cyril D'Arcy (1888-1976), who served as Master of Campion Hall from 1933 to 1945. D'Arcy was a major part of the Oxonian Catholic scene, then going on to serve as Provincial of the English Province of the Jesuits. D'Arcy was a "charismatic" and striking figure, with "bristling eyebrows and flashing eyes [...] Quick of movement, he spoke with great animation [...] There was something almost birdlike about him [...] He had a splendid sense of humor and was quick to smile and laugh" (D'Arcy 1991: xviii).

D'Arcy was one of the few Catholics among Tolkien's academic colleagues. D'Arcy, who was the Master of Campion Hall, appears in the *Catholic Herald* lecture-lists for 1938, 1939, and 1941. D'Arcy's subjects were Aristotle's *Nicomachean Ethics*, "Introduction to Moral Philosophy," and the theology of Thomas Aquinas.[15]

The two men would certainly have met in the context of university work, and as part of the small Oxonian Catholic world; for instance, they overlapped briefly in their memberships in the Oxford Dante Society.[16] Certainly, D'Arcy knew Tolkien well enough to describe him, in his memoir, as "a very good Catholic" (1991: 112). We can get a glimpse of their informal interactions in a comment that Tolkien made in a 1944 letter; regarding the poet Roy Campbell, who turned up unexpectedly at an Inklings gathering at The Eagle & Child, Tolkien remarked in his favor that "Martin D'Arcy vouches for him, and told him to seek us out" (*Letters* 137).

D'Arcy's magnum opus, which helped to earn him the sobriquet 'the philosopher of love,' is *The Mind and Heart of Love: A Study in Eros and Agape* (1945). But in the inter-war years, D'Arcy also engaged deeply with the problem of suffering and pain, in *The Pain of this World and the Providence of God* and the shorter *The Problem of Evil*, both published in 1929. D'Arcy took seriously the question of suffering, which was all the more pressing after the slaughter and destruction of the Great War. In *The Problem of Evil*, he puts it forthrightly: "Why does God permit suffering, mental and physical, and the moral evil of sin in this world which He has created and governs?" (2017: 11).

The most interesting connection with this Jesuit scholar is that Tolkien had in his library a copy of D'Arcy's *The Nature of Belief* (1931), which he received as a Christmas gift in the year of its publication.[17] Why might his friends choose this volume for him? Perhaps it is because of its strong connection to the thought of

15 *Catholic Herald*, 22 April 1938, 11; 28 April 1939, 10; 13 October 1939, 10; 17 January 1941, 7.

16 D'Arcy was a member from May 1939 to November 1945; Tolkien joined the Society in February 1945 (Oxford University Dante Society 1965: 147).

17 The givers were "Rene and Jack Eccles" (Cilli 2023: 72): Irene Frances Eccles and John Carew Eccles, an Australian couple living in Oxford. The latter, subsequently Sir John, came to Oxford in 1925 as a Rhodes Scholar, earning a PhD in 1929; in 1931 he was a Junior Research Fellow of Exeter College. He went on to win the Nobel Prize in Medicine in 1963 (Curtis and Andersen 2001) This friendship, not previously noted in Tolkien scholarship, is indicative of Tolkien's wide range of acquaintances and interests.

John Henry Newman. The book is an extended, complex, and detailed consideration of how religious beliefs are formed. After initial chapters providing cultural context for the issue at hand, and a philosophical defense of objective truth and the possibility of belief grasping such truth, D'Arcy moves into an extended critique, analysis, and application of Newman's highly significant work on that subject, *An Essay in Aid of a Grammar of Assent* (1870), usually called simply, as D'Arcy does, *The Grammar of Assent*. Here, D'Arcy engages in depth with Newman's concepts of "notional" and "real" assent and of the "illative sense." Tolkien had certainly encountered Newman's thought in his youth at the Oratory; he participated throughout his working years in organizations devoted to Newman's legacy, namely the Newman Society in Oxford and the national Newman Association (Ordway 2023: 190-93, 338); here is further indication of his sustained interest in Newman's intellectual work and legacy.

As it happens, Martin D'Arcy, like C.C. Martindale, was also one of Tolkien's fellow Honorary Vice-Presidents in the Newman Association (Ordway 2023: 423n25). And so we find a link back to the place where we began: John Henry Newman and the Oratory which he founded.

Conclusion

Tolkien's youth was spent among the theologians of the Birmingham Oratory; once he arrived at Oxford, he would go on to meet and befriend theologians, both Anglican and Catholic, laypeople and priests, throughout the rest of his life. In this essay, we have focused on two groups of theologians whose influence was strongest in the years leading up to his magnum opus, *The Lord of the Rings*, but recently published volumes such as *The Nature of Middle-earth* remind us that Tolkien continued to work on the *legendarium*, including theological aspects of it, all the way to the end of his life. It is therefore worth attending to all of his theological connections, even those in his later years.

As an English Catholic Christian of the 20th century, with his roots in Birmingham and most of his adult life in Oxford, Tolkien interacted socially and professionally with many of the most notable theological figures of his day. Tracing these connections reveals that Tolkien had a great deal more interaction with both professional and amateur theologians than can readily be estimated from references in his writing. We lack a complete listing of his personal library, but we know that his shelves contained at least some volumes of theology and apologetics, and that he owned these because of personal rather than strictly professional interest. We have barely begun to plumb the depths of the richly textured, dynamic, sometimes tense, always complex culture of academic Oxford with regard to matters theological. Whether it was at meetings of the Dante Club, the Newman Society, or the Inklings, over a meal at a college High Table, during a casual conversation in a Senior Common Room, at Catholic social and liturgical events, and so on, Tolkien had many day-to-day opportunities to speak with some of the finest theological minds of his generation. What we do know indicates that there is more to discover and assimilate.

The argument of this essay is simply this: that in addition to working backward from Tolkien's literary output to the ideas of well-known theological figures such as Aquinas and Augustine, it is valuable to work forward, as it were, from the context of Tolkien's life, both in general terms and in the specific personal connections, and experiences he had. This context helps us, for instance, to consider the chronology of possible influences in terms of the development of the *legendarium*, and establishes the relative importance of certain influences and ideas. Having a better sense of his contemporary context, including details that are not immediately apparent from reading his writings, reminds us to be cautious about making arguments from silence or apparent silence. And, in short, appreciating Tolkien's place among his contemporary theologians helps us better to understand his world, and therefore better to understand, and fruitfully explore, his work.

About the Author

Holly Ordway is the Cardinal Francis George Professor of Faith and Culture at the Word on Fire Institute, and Visiting Professor of Apologetics at Houston Christian University. She holds a PhD in English from the University of Massachusetts and is a subject editor for the *Journal of Inklings Studies*. She is the author of the award-winning *Tolkien's Modern Reading: Middle-earth Beyond the Middle Ages*, and has contributed chapters on Tolkien, C.S. Lewis, and the Inklings to volumes such as *C.S. Lewis in Poets' Corner*, *The Inklings and King Arthur*, and *C.S. Lewis's List*. Her book *Tolkien's Faith: A Spiritual Biography* was released in 2023, in time for the 50th anniversary of Tolkien's death.

Bibliography

BERTRAM, Jerome. 2000. *St Aloysius' Parish: The Third English Oratory: A Brief History and Guide, 1793–2000.* 2nd edition. Oxford: Oxford University Press.

2015. *St Philip Neri and the Oxford Oratory.* Oxford: The Oxford Oratory.

BIRD, T.E. "Preface" to Robert Eaton. 1930. *The Apocalypse of St. John, with Expositions of Each Chapter.* London: Sands & Co.

BIRMINGHAM ORATORY. "Fathers and Brothers." Accessed 12 July 2024. <https://www.birminghamoratory.org.uk/fathers-and-brothers/>.

BOUYER, Louis. 1995. *St. Philip Neri: A Portrait.* Herefordshire, UK: Gracewing.

CARPENTER, Humphrey, George SAYER, and Clyde S. KILBY. 1984. "A Dialogue." *Minas Tirith Evening-Star* 13.1: 20-24.

Catholic Herald. 1939. "Catholic Lectures at Oxford." 13 Oct 1939: 10.

1940a. "New Names Among Catholic Lecturers at Oxford." 12 Jan 1940: 9.

1940b. "Catholic Lectures at Oxford." 19 April 1940: 7.

1941a. "Lecturers at Oxford University." 17 January 1941: 7.

1941b. "Lectures at Oxford University." 10 Oct 1941: 7.

1949. "Catholic Lecturers." 14 Jan 1949: 7.

CILLI, Oronzo. 2023. *Tolkien's Library: An Annotated Checklist.* 2nd revised and expanded edition. Edinburgh: Luna Press Publishing.

CRICHTON, J.D. 1979. "1920-1940: The Dawn of a Liturgical Movement." In J.D. Crichton, H.E. Winstone, and J.R. Ainslie (eds.). *English Catholic Worship: Liturgical Renewal in England since 1900.* London: Geoffrey Chapman, 17-46.

CURTIS, David R. and Per ANDERSEN. 2001. "Sir John Carew Eccles, A.C." *Biographical Memoirs of Fellows of the Royal Society* 47 (2001): 159-87.

D'ARCY, Martin. 1931. *The Nature of Belief.* London: Sheed and Ward.

1991. *Laughter and the Love of Friends: Reminiscences of the Distinguished Priest and Philosopher Martin Cyril D'Arcy, S.J.* Ed. by William S. Abell. Westminster, MD: Christian Classics.

2017. *The Problem of Evil.* First published 1929. London: Catholic Truth Society.

EATON, Robert. 1908. *Auxilium Infirmorum.* London: Catholic Truth Society.

1925. *The Ministry of Reconciliation: Chapters on Confession.* London: Sands & Co.

1927. *The Divine Refreshment: Chapters on the Blessed Sacrament by Robert Eaton.* Preface by Francis Cardinal Bourne. London: Sands & Co.

1930. *The Apocalypse of St. John, with Expositions of Each Chapter*. Preface by T.E. Bird. London: Sands & Co.

Feeney, Joseph J. 2001. "A Jesuit classmate remembers G.M. Hopkins: An unpublished letter of Joseph Rickaby SJ." *The Month* 34.4: 170.

Ferrández Bru, José Manuel. 2011. "'Wingless fluttering': Some Personal Connections in Tolkien's Formative Years." *Tolkien Studies* 8: 51-65.

2018. *"Uncle Curro": J.R.R. Tolkien's Spanish Connection*. Edinburgh: Luna Press Publishing.

Gardner, Angela, and Neil Holford. 2010. *Wheelbarrows at Dawn: Memories of Hilary Tolkien*. Moreton-in-Marsh, UK: ADC Publications.

Hagerty, James. 2017. *Priests in Uniform: Catholic Chaplains to the British Forces in the First World War*. Leominster, UK: Gracewing.

Jacob, Domnic. 2016. "Blessed John Henry Newman the Musician." In The Oxford Oratory. *The Legacy of St Philip*. Oxford: The Oratory, 87-103.

J.R.R. Tolkien: Life and Legend. An Exhibition to Commemorate the Centenary of the Birth of J.R.R. Tolkien (1892-1973). 1992. Oxford: Bodleian Library.

Martindale, C.C. 1934. *Bernadette of Lourdes*. London: Catholic Truth Society.

1936. "Catholics and Oxford: The Meaning of Campion Hall." *Catholic Herald* 3 July 1936.

1946. *Creative Love: Six Readings Written for Broadcasting in the BBC Home Service During Holy Week 1946*. New York: Sheed and Ward.

McIlwaine, Catherine (ed.). 2018. *Tolkien: Maker of Middle-earth*. Oxford: Bodleian Library.

Newman, John Henry. 1976a. *Letters and Diaries of John Henry Newman*. Volume 29. Oxford: Clarendon.

1976b. *Letters and Diaries of John Henry Newman*. Volume 30. Oxford: Clarendon.

The Oratory School Society. 1999. *O.S. Lives: Obituaries from The Oratory School Magazine, 1962-1992*. Edited by H.A.W. Exeter, UK: The Oratory School Society.

Ordway, Holly. 2023. *Tolkien's Faith: A Spiritual Biography*. Elk Grove Village, IL: Word on Fire Academic.

The Oxford Oratory. 2016. *The Legacy of St Philip*. Oxford: The Oratory.

Oxford University Dante Society. 1965. *Centenary Essays on Dante*. Oxford: Oxford University Press.

PALACE GREEN ARCHIVES. Newman Association. Minutes of the Newman Association, 1949-54. D1/J/1/1/1.

RAFFERTY, Oliver P. 2009. "George Tyrrell and Catholic Modernism." *Thinking Faith* 6 July 2009 <https://www.thinkingfaith.org/articles/20090706_1.htm?>

RICKABY, Joseph. 1899. *Oxford and Cambridge Conferences, 1897-1899*. London: Burns and Oates.

1910. *Newman Memorial Sermons*. London: Longmans, Green and Co.

ROBINSON, Jonathan. 2015. *In No Strange Land: The Embodied Mysticism of Saint Philip Neri*. Kettering, OH: Angelico.

SCULL, Christina, and Wayne G. HAMMOND. 2017. *The J.R.R. Tolkien Companion and Guide: Chronology*. Revised and expanded edition. Boston, MA: Houghton Mifflin.

SIRE, H.J.A. 1997. *Father Martin D'Arcy: Philosopher of Christian Love*. Herefordshire, UK: Gracewing.

TOLKIEN, J.R.R. 1982. *The Old English Exodus*. Edited by Joan Turville-Petre. Oxford: Oxford University Press.

2020. "W.P. Ker Memorial Lecture on Sir Gawain." In *Sir Gawain and the Green Knight, Pearl, and Sir Orfeo*. Edited by Christopher Tolkien. London: HarperCollins, 109-57.

2021. *The Nature of Middle-earth*. Edited by Carl F. Hostetter. Boston, MA: Houghton Mifflin Harcourt.

2023. *The Letters of J.R.R. Tolkien: Revised and Expanded Edition*. Edited by Humphrey Carpenter with the assistance of Christopher Tolkien. London: HarperCollins.

TOLKIEN, Priscilla. 2020. Personal communication to the author. 2 October 2020.

TRISTRAM, Henry. 1934. *Cardinal Newman and the Church of the Birmingham Oratory: A History and a Guide*. Gloucester: The British Publishing Company.

TYRRELL, George. 1905. *Nova et Vetera: Informal Meditations*. London: Longmans, Green, and Co.

TÜRKS, Paul. 1995. *Philip Neri: The Fire of Joy*. Translated by Daniel Utrecht. New York: Alba House.

"University Notes." 1912. *The Tablet*. 8 June 1912.

VAN GOETHEM, Alex. 2019. "Fr Cyril Martindale SJ." *British Jesuit Archives* June 2, 2019. <https://www.jesuitarchives.co.uk/post/fr-cyril-martindale-sj>.

Timothy Padgett

Tolkien and Twentieth Century Ecumenism

Abstract

Tolkien's works have been a treasure for the world since they first appeared decades ago. One of their most amazing qualities is how people from all walks of life and perspectives, people who might well not get along when face to face, all of these may join in a shared joy for these wonderful works. This ability to pull together people of vast differences is not limited to fantasy fans but was demonstrated in Tolkien's life and letters. With the literary friends of Legolas and Gimli and Tolkien's real life friendship, Christians have a veritable how-to for building ecumenical bonds that yet maintain individual integrity.

Faced with the works of J.R.R. Tolkien, the reader sometimes feels as one does when looking into the depths of the sea. The sheer immensity of his imagination and the profundity of his thought are literally awe-inspiring. Even those who are not keen on the types of stories he liked to tell can see he was a master storyteller. It is more than the fact that his works were entertaining. That is true, and decades of book sales and a still-growing cinematic output are ample testimony to this, but it is more than that. While he may have earned a reputation for being squeamish about defining the possibly hidden meanings behind his stories, the realism of his fantasies offers lessons to us about life.

We can think, for example, of the way we learn that it is often the most powerful among us who are most susceptible to certain kinds of temptation. Or, perhaps, it is the reminder that what does not kill us may not make us stronger, that heroic victories can still leave their heroes with wounds that will never fully heal. There are a host of other ways Tolkien's words can add to our wisdom, but one of the most practical, and one made all the more beautiful by its utter mundaneness, is the power and nature of friendship. The friendship we see in Tolkien offers to us more than the sentimental fellowship of the likeminded found in popular culture. Instead, what we see exemplified in the fictional tales of Middle-earth – in the friendship of Frodo and Sam, but particularly that between Legolas and Gimli – was actualized in the life of Tolkien himself.[1] Even as a passionate and, at times, partisan Roman Catholic, he maintained deep and meaningful friendships with those outside his particular communion, most famously with Christopher Wiseman and C.S. Lewis. The combination of these two aspects, the fantastical and the real, offers hope for the rest of us in how to work for a commonality without abandoning our distinctives.

Friendships in Middle-earth

The most obvious picture of friendship in Tolkien's lore is that between two of the most prominent protagonists in *The Lord of the Rings*, Frodo and Sam. Their bond has gained its fame for some very good reasons. Take any Tolkien novice to see the films or to read the books and one of the first things that they will note is how much of the story rests upon the unflappable loyalty of the two hobbits, particularly of Sam toward Frodo. In fact, there are common social media memes noting that nearly all the success of the Fellowship depended upon the determination of Sam to stick with his friend to the end. Who can forget Sam's faithfulness to Frodo, even (or especially) at those dark moments when the latter seemed to have lost is faith in everything else (*LotR* 926)? Or who of us cannot see the gratitude in Frodo's granting to Sam all his worldly possessions (*LotR* 1008)?

Even so, there are some things about their relationship that, while noble and admirable, prevent them from displaying the highest example of friendship from these stories. First, as was hinted above, there is something unbalanced in their dynamic. Frodo is not just Sam's friend; he is also his superior. That is not to say that one cannot be friends with one's employer, but there is a definite element of deference in Sam's fidelity. People today, particularly in the United States, need to bear in mind that these books were neither set nor written in such a hyper-egalitarian culture, but in the remnants of England's class-based society and Middle-earth's clear distinctions of role. There is still something of Sam's batman to Frodo's officer.[2]

1 See the recent study by Casagrande 2022 on friendship in *The Lord of the Rings*.
2 See Hooker 2004.

Second, and perhaps more compelling, is the simple fact that it would have been easy for Frodo and Sam to be friends. Without taking away from the hierarchy issues, they shared a common outlook. They were from the same village, took part in the same customs, enjoyed the same types of activities, and held the same understanding of the world and their place in it. It was a common home they longed for, a common hope they lived for, and a common people they fought for. To be friends and comrades in their great quest would have been as natural as falling.

The same could not be said for another, arguably better, pair of friends in Tolkien's books: Legolas and Gimli. Few of the common traits easing the way to friendship for Frodo and Sam could be said to be true of these two. If they were to become friends, then this commonality would have to be built, not assumed. At the simplest level, they did not grow up in the same place. As anyone can tell who has met a stranger from the same town, there is an immediate camaraderie to be found. The jokes and the assumptions, the priorities and the pet peeves – each of these builds immediate bridges, even between people who have never met.

But obviously, Legolas and Gimli did not come from the same culture. Tertullian may have asked, "What has Athens to do with Jerusalem?" and we might add with greater justification, "What do the forested realms of Mirkwood have to do with the underground halls of the Blue Mountains?" The core assumptions derived from living in such diverse contexts are more than happenstance. They shape the way each views the world, his responsibilities to it, and what it means to succeed in life.

But while people from different places may have trouble seeing the world from the other's perspective, there is nothing inherently conflictual in such a divergence. Had this been the extent of the story, Legolas and Gimli's friendship could well have developed along unremarkable lines. But this was not the whole of their history. They did not merely come from different cultures but from societies that were, if not enemies, then at least disdainful to one another. This tension goes back into the ancient ages of Middle-earth, with a longstanding sense of superiority by the Elves against their Dwarvish neighbors, seeing themselves as elite and enlightened and the others as brutish and servile. This is keenly manifested in Thingol's disdain for these supposedly lesser Dwarves and his death at the hands of the same (*Sil* 280). And that is not even to mention the war that was only just averted at the Battle of the Five Armies. With this as a historical context, it is surprising that the two races ever agreed to any kind of fellowship. Yet, agree they did, and with that begins a remarkable story of a friendship forged in fire.

The first meeting of Legolas and Gimli at the Council of Elrond is not auspicious. Each of our soon-to-be heroes is introduced, not so much by their own virtues but as heirs of earlier names of renown, Thranduil and Gloin (*LotR* 234). The latter of these is quick to note his past grievance with the Elves, something that could well have derailed the Fellowship at the start were it not for Gandalf's quick (and telling) warning, "If all the grievances that stand between Elves and Dwarves are to be brought up here, we may as well abandon this Council" (*LotR* 249).[3] These grievances come up again soon, a little further along in the journey. As they draw near the mines of Moria, Gandalf recalls more prosperous times for that underground land, when trade, not war, was the Dwarves' chief affair, saying: "Those were happier days, when there was still close friendship at times between folks of different race, even between Dwarves and Elves." When Legolas and Gimli each protest that it was not their own kin who had started the breach, Gandalf retorts that he has heard both versions of the story, each with a different party guilty for the parting, and then appeals: "I will not give judgment now. But I beg you two, Legolas and Gimli, at least to be friends and to help me. I need you both" (*LotR* 295).

This need is demonstrated as the Fellowship ventures through Moria and then out the other side. In the darkness of the mines and the overwhelming power of their Orcish enemies, the differences between Elf and Dwarf dwindle to insignificance. It is not that they stop being who and what they are, but, in contrast to what they face together, it is what they have in common that really matters. The importance of this unity is realized as the Fellowship enters Lothlórien. Things almost come to blows when Haldir, the Elf who detains them as they

3 One interesting element here is how different is the portrayal of this scene in Peter Jackson's movies as opposed to Tolkien's own words. Where Jackson has the various races all but come to blows, in Tolkien, Gloin politely drops his complaint after this warning from Gandalf. Whether this was a missed opportunity for drama on behalf of the author or an exaggerated moment on the part of the director is likely a matter of taste.

enter his people's realm, orders only the Dwarf blindfolded, to which affront we read: "Gimli drew his axe from his belt. Haldir and his companions bent their bows. 'A plague on Dwarves and their stiff necks!' said Legolas" (*LotR* 338). The situation is only saved at Aragorn's instigation and Legolas's acquiescence that the entire party be blindfolded. While he is not happy with the way things turn out, Legolas perhaps explains their plight the best, saying: "Alas for the folly of these days [...] Here we all are enemies of the one Enemy, and yet I must walk blind, while the sun is merry in the woodland under leaves of gold!" (*LotR* 339). This griping by the heroic pair may not seem significant, but each is willing to undergo what they see as an injustice for the sake of their mission and the greater cause which they both serve.

There are a great many other places where this growing sense of unity comes to the fore, but few have the delightfully emotive power found in the duo's body-count-contest at Helm's Deep. They had battled Orcs together in the depths of Moria and their lethal combination of axe and arrow had taken their fair share of enemy dead at the breaking of the Fellowship, but with the Battle of Helm's Deep, even their rivalry becomes a point of comradeship. In just a few pages of text, we see their friendship bloom. As they await the onslaught, Legolas admits his discomfort with their stony surroundings, only to note: "But you comfort me, Gimli, and I am glad to have you standing nigh with your stout legs and your hard axe" (*LotR* 520).

Soon thereafter, Gimli comes to Legolas after a bout of fighting to brag about his prowess. "'Two!' said Gimli, patting his axe [...] 'Two?' said Legolas. 'I have done better [...] I make my tale twenty at the least'" (*LotR* 522-23). They draw cheer from one another even as the battle rages around them. When it appears that Gimli is lost behind the lines, Legolas expresses his regret, calling it "evil news," since he "desired to tell Master Gimli that my tale is now thirty-nine" (*LotR* 525-526). By the time the battle is won, it is Gimli who can claim victory over the Elf by a count of forty-two to forty-one. Even so, as Legolas is quick to note, he does not "grudge you the game, so glad am I to see you on your legs!" (*LotR* 530). Their common trial has forged their friendship into what will become an inseparable bond.

Their friendship also comes in a shared affection, not for one another or even for the same object, but for a shared principle: their love for their respective homes. The homelands they loved were not the same, but the love each had for those homelands was the same. They had come to the Council of Elrond in hopes of aiding their native lands and their people, and it was for these that they endured the long road ahead of them. Throughout the story, both of them are afforded the chance to see a long-dreamed-of great site of their respective civilizations. The grandeur of Moria and the litheness of Lórien were each worthy object of admiration for Gimli and Legolas. Each could, in turn, take pride in his own people's accomplishment and grant honor for that of the other.

As they work their way through Moria, Tolkien describes the scene.

> [Gandalf] raised his staff, and for a brief instant there was a blaze like a flash of lightning. Great shadows sprang up and fled, and for a second they saw a vast roof far above their heads upheld by mighty pillars hewn of stone. Before them and on either side stretched a huge empty hall; its black walls, polished and smooth as glass, flashed and glittered (*LotR* 307).

Similarly, upon their entrance into the lands of Lothlórien, the majesty of Elven work was apparent to all, but this time, instead of the austerity of shining rock, it was an arboreal beauty that confronted them.

> At the feet of the trees, and all about the green hillsides the grass was studded with small golden flowers shaped like stars. Among them, nodding on slender stalks, were other flowers, white and palest green: they glimmered as a mist amid the rich hue of the grass. Over all the sky was blue, and the sun of afternoon glowed upon the hill and cast long green shadows beneath the trees" (*LotR* 341).

The wonders which these cultures brought, crafted stone and tended trees, did more than enhance the pride each had for his own kind; it provided an avenue for our heroes to rejoice over what his new friend represented.

This respect finds its culmination at the end of their adventures. With Sauron defeated and the Ring destroyed, the members of the Fellowship departed towards their various responsibilities: scouring the Shire in the case of the Hobbits and reigning and restoring a kingdom in the case of Aragorn. But Legolas and Gimli take the time to make good on a promise they made to one another, to see the potential of what their cultures could bring to the world. First, Legolas returns to Helm's Deep and is so moved by what he sees in the Glittering Caves that he cannot speak, finally allowing that "[n]ever before has a Dwarf claimed a victory over an Elf in a contest of words [...] Now therefore let us go to Fangorn and set the score right!" (*LotR* 956). And so, Legolas longed to return the favor to his friend, saying:

> 'Come Gimli! [...] Now by Fangorn's leave I will visit the deep places of the Entwood and see such trees as are nowhere else to be found in Middle-earth. You shall come with me and keep your word; and thus we will journey on together to our own lands in Mirkwood and beyond.' To this Gimli agreed, though with no great delight, it seemed (*LotR* 959).

This last bit is telling, as even though Gimli is still somewhat fearful to see the forest for himself, he is willing to endure what he would not seek on his own for the sake of one who had become a brother to him through their common quest, common foe, and common appreciation for what is good in the world.

Tolkien's Friendships

These same themes show up in Tolkien's own friendships, specifically his longstanding bond with Christopher Wiseman and his now world-famous friendship with C.S. Lewis. On the surface, the fact that a literature fan would find common cause with other literature fans seems a parallel to a 'Sam and Frodo' style of friendship. There may be something to that, but there is a certain element to Tolkien's relationship with these men that puts them in the Legolas and Gimli camp. While such cross-denominational friendships may not seem like much to people today, the fact that Tolkien was Roman Catholic, Wiseman was Methodist, and Lewis was Anglican entailed tensions which were no small matter to overcome.

Wiseman had been friends with Tolkien for many years. In fact, in what one could call a proto-Inklings group, Wiseman, along with Tolkien and two other friends, Rob Gilson and Geoffrey Smith, created the "Tea Club and Barrovian Society," or TCBS, in 1911. This was a fellowship where the dissimilar became united. After noting their differing emphases, one biographer said: "Common to these three enthusiastic schoolboys was a thorough knowledge of Latin and Greek literature; and from this balance of similar and dissimilar tastes, shared and unshared knowledge, friendship grew" (Carpenter 2014: 70). When Gilson was killed fighting the Germans, Tolkien offered a mournful hope to Smith: "The TCBS was destined to testify for God and Truth in a more direct way even than by laying down its several lives in this war (which is for all the evil of our own side with large view good against evil)" (Carpenter 2014: 9). In the end, only Tolkien and Wiseman emerged from the Great War with their lives intact, even if the memory of their fallen comrades remained with them. Their differences, whether vocational or ecclesial, endured, but their common affections and common foe offered a context for common ground.

Tolkien's bond with C.S. Lewis was not as long-lasting as his friendship with Wiseman, but it is obviously more famous. Whether it is the former's role in the latter's reluctant conversion or the way their shared mix of support and critique for one another's labors left the world a dragon's hoard of treasure from Narnia and the Shire, this friendship has long fascinated their fans. What often escaped the casual reader is that these two titans did not always see eye to eye. There is a lot of fun to be had in noting their differing writing styles, with Tolkien taking decades to craft an all-encompassing and internally consistent world full of, just maybe, too much detail, and Lewis dashing off classics of children's literature in a matter of months, even if at times some of the Pevensie adventures did not quite line up with others.

But such distinctions are superficial, owing more to personality types than to any real dispute. More substantive conflicts may have been born in part by questions of temperament, but they were driven forward under the pressure of belonging to respective religious camps. Specifically, Lewis's marriage to the divorced Joy Davidman likely ruffled some feathers with some of his fellow Anglicans, but it was incomprehensible to the Roman Catholic Tolkien.[4] Yet, nonetheless, their friendship endured. Strained, to be sure, but, as one biographer put it: "With Lewis and Tolkien, a distinct cooling took place in the final

4 "Anyone in any case can see that the enormous extension and facilitation of 'divorce' in our days, since those of (say) Trollopean society, has done great social harm. It is a slippery slope – leading quickly to Reno, and beyond: in fact already to a promiscuity barely restrained by legalities: for a pair can now divorce one another, have an interlude with new partners, and then 're-marry'. A situation is being, has been, produced in which ordinary unphilosophical and irreligious folk are not only not restrained by law from inconstancy, but are actually by law and social custom encouraged to inconstancy" (*Letters* 61).

years, though the similarities that united them were always stronger than the differences that separated them" (Duriez 2003: x).

Some of these differences between Tolkien and his friends may seem small to contemporary minds. After all, Roman Catholics and Protestants cooperate on all sorts of issues regarding the sanctity of life, human sexuality, and church/state relations. Nonetheless, people today must recall that things have not always been this way, and we do not even need to go back to the wars of religion in early modern Europe to see this. Within two weeks of one another in 1951, leading evangelical theologians like Carl F. H. Henry, (Henry 1951: Box 1951), and Francis A. Schaeffer (Schaeffer 1951: Box 57, File 23), wrote letters warning of the dangers in too much cooperation with the Roman Catholic Church, seeing in it not a potential ally but a clear and present danger to their religious and political freedoms.

While he was perhaps not quite so confrontational as they were, at least at that moment, Tolkien was more than a man who just so happened to be a Roman Catholic. Instead, being Roman Catholic was a key part of his self-understanding and of many of the emphases he placed in his writings. Some of this can be put down to the fact that despite hailing from a Protestant family, he followed his only surviving parent into the Roman communion. Then, given the suffering (and in Tolkien's mind, martyrdom) she endured for this choice from her erstwhile co-religionists, their unfairness could easily be seen as opposed to the ostensible justice of Rome (Carpenter 2014: 50). Whatever its source, Tolkien's Roman Catholicism went far deeper than a token attendance at occasional masses at Christmas and Easter. This devotion shows up vividly as the Fellowship makes its way across Middle-earth. As one scholar has noted, the common images of Mary, relics, and the saints appear throughout:

> Tolkien's white Lady also gives out blessed relics such as the phial of Elbereth. Galadriel even appears to Sam in a vision, prompting him to use the star-glass. It gives not only light but hope, responding to Frodo's ebbing and growing will with corresponding power (Freeman 2022: 267).

With these facts in mind, we can now compare Tolkien's own practice of friendship with his emphases in his fictional writings. How did he maintain friendships across denominational lines when his doctrinal stances meant so much? One of the more straightforward reasons he could do this is that neither he nor anyone else can be reduced to a set of positions, even theological ones that are key to an individual's personality. Another reason is that fiction, being fictional, at least if it is done well, will not be a paint-by-numbers piece of propaganda intended to convey only a discrete set of ideals.

As noted above, we see in Tolkien's personal relations an echo of the friendship featured so prominently in *The Lord of the Rings*. Tolkien and Christopher Wiseman seemed, in many ways, a delightful encapsulation of Lewis's now-famous explanation of friendship as that moment when a person can say to another: "What? You too? I thought I was the only one!" (1960: 96). They shared a love of beautiful things, and then shared the common pain of facing down an enemy and losing dear friends in the process. While Lewis, too, had served in the First World War, his connection to Tolkien arose less from this than their shared love for the tried and true and beautiful and their common foe of Modernism's technocratic world. This antipathy was greater than mere atavism. They saw in the priorities of progress a danger not merely to things which they liked but to a world which they loved for its beauty as much as for its truth. Which is to say that, like Legolas and Gimli, Tolkien was able to keep and cultivate his friendships with those with whom he disagreed, not because he ignored their differences but because, in light of what they held in common, there was a context allowing both cobelligerency as well as genuine affection.

Ecumenical Realities

From the fantastical and solely personal we can now move to the concrete and potentially institutional. Many of the same themes expounded for Dwarves and Elves and manifested by Tolkien, Wiseman, and Lewis play out in clarifying the health and wisdom of ecumenical adventures in the twentieth century. For much of the 1900s, and for several years before and after, formal, institutional Christianity was caught up in attempts to forge bonds of peace between the various denominational boundaries of Christendom. While not all of these were for the best, and some of them were downright unhelpful, several aspects of this cooperation reflect the power of Legolas and Gimli.

In a manner of speaking, the most obvious place to begin with any discussion of the twentieth century ecumenical movement would be the series of events which led to the National Council of Churches in the United States and the World Council of Churches globally. There is some merit in this, but there is also reason to pause. For one thing, much of the ecumenical movement among what came to be called Mainline churches in North America too often diluted their distinctives rather than engaging with and genuinely respecting them. Another, and definitely more interesting, reason: as when comparing the friendship of Frodo and Sam with that of Legolas and Gimli, there is great virtue in examining the more unexpected examples of building bridges.

It is admittedly counterintuitive, as there are few terms most unlike in the public imagination than fundamentalism and ecumenism, but the conservative reaction to the theological Modernism of the late nineteenth and early twentieth centuries was, at its core, an attempt to bridge the gap between discrete ecclesial traditions. *The Fundamentals*, which later gave the name to the wider movement, was a document cataloguing the 'fundamental' principles of Christianity, behind which a true unity of purpose and action could be built (Marsden 2006: 119). Whatever their denominational background, bearing in mind that we are now only talking about Protestant groups, the participants in the early fundamentalist movement were motivated by a common love of the truths of Scripture and classical Christian orthodoxy and a common rejection of what they saw as the world-accommodating tenets of theological Modernism. For a brief moment, it seemed as though they could unite against their common foe, assembling elite intellectual voices to offer counsel on the situation, drawing from many denominations of the land, all the while orchestrating mass-appeals out into the pews. But, in the end, they did not succeed, falling before the twinned forces of their rivals' overwhelming institutional power and their own increasingly narrow self-definitions. It is almost as though the Council of Elrond delved into near-unending deliberations over just who could become a member of the Fellowship rather than setting out on their quest.[5]

5 This is a bit of hyperbole. Fundamentalists' reputation for insularity has been exaggerated in the popular and academic imaginations. They continued to be very active in their own channels of social engagement, and were not as dystopian as people today think, but, with their practice of double-separation and inclusion of eschatology into the Fundamentals, they did undermine their own attempts at a united front against Modernism. Madison Trammel engages well with the false reputation of fundamentalism's insular nature (Trammel 2023).

A related group which formed in response to many of the same issues and which faced many of the same problems was the evangelicals. That term has a long history and can be applied in a great many contexts, but here it refers to the postwar, largely American movement led by the likes of Billy Graham and Carl F.H. Henry. They sought to continue the cross-denominational opposition to Modernism without some of what they perceived to be the failings of the fundamentalists who had gone before them. While their theological tenets were largely the same as fundamentalists, evangelicals were far less likely to refuse cooperation with others, so long as those others agreed with them regarding the issue at hand. That is, they did not ignore or diminish the significance of the places they disagreed, but they were content to act as cobelligerents for the sake of a shared goal or common good.

It would be too much to say that the evangelical movement has failed, but it is more than reasonable to say that it has fractured. In fact, in the contemporary world, this internal dissension may be the most prominent feature of evangelicalism, with factions in near constant combat over self-definition.[6] These problems flow significantly from the fact that while people often speak of a singular evangelicalism, and there is just cause for doing so, we must understand that at its core, evangelicalism is not a singular movement, but one born of consensus. It is a cultural and religious force defined not so much by what it is but by what it is not. It is not Modernist nor is it fundamentalist. It is also in many ways a group without a center. There is no Magisterium, no council, no bishop, nor, with the passing of Billy Graham in 2018, any acknowledged figurehead to whom the whole can look for clarification. Looking back again to Middle-earth, it is as though the Fellowship set out from Rivendell with each member choosing his own path forward with little regard to the others' direction.

One of the most successful examples at ecumenical behavior, if only for a time, came in the wake of World War II, as religious and political leaders sought to craft an alliance of sorts among those who differed, perhaps greatly, in theology

6 "Evangelicals are a people who are constantly second-guessing themselves and constantly reimagining their project(s) along those lines. Stated differently, we are an editorial people, or, put more precisely, we are a self-editorializing people. Like most core traits of a collective, this attribute of evangelicalism expresses itself in a bipolar manner" (Thornbury 2013: 17).

but were united in their opposition to Communism's dual dangers of atheism and tyranny. This came in two phases, with the second more productive than the first. With President Truman there came an attempt to bring into fellowship disparate groups through a top-down, homogenizing effort that met with only limited success (Herzog 2011). His successor, President Eisenhower, was able to rally the faithful with greater ease. Partly this was due to the increasingly undeniable nature of the Soviet Union's intentions after 1952 as opposed to what it had seemed in 1945, yet it was also because while Truman sought to have global religious leaders create a common "religious" answer to Communism, Eisenhower merely asked them all to cooperate against a common foe (Inboden 2008). However, as the 1960s wore on, the cultural perception of the Marxist menace became diluted in the midst of the West's own moral travails.

Conclusions

As Christians, we are not as alien to one another as the differing races of Elves and Dwarves. Even when we speak of racial distinctions in our midst, we do not mean anything like the species-level difference we see in *The Lord of the Rings*. But we do differ in terms of our doctrines, articulations, and practices. In the past century or so, many attempts have been made to bridge the gaps between us, and while some have had greater success than others, none has done so to widespread satisfaction. Those which have seen success beyond the superficial level of mere organizational unity have been those which could find a place for their constituent parts without compromising their overall common affections, foes, and goals, if only for a time.[7]

When it comes to disagreements within the faith, we need to keep in mind that these are arguments over the interpretation of a commonly agreed upon understanding of reality. They are disputes over a known quantity of theological, historical, and philosophical information, not "cleverly devised myths" where everyone's view is as true as another's. As the X-Files used to say, the truth is out there. It is not determined or corrupted by debates over its nature. And furthermore, despite their reputation, Christians actually have a very high degree of

7 See my *Swords and Plowshares: American Evangelical Views on War, 1937-1973.*

doctrinal agreement. Yes, there are ten thousand denominations cluttering the photo album of Christ's family. And, yes, for the entire history of Christianity, theological discussions have carried on with clear marks of disunity. But, for all those ten thousand denominations and all those years of debate, the core tenets of the Christian Faith have been settled and agreed to by nearly all who claim the name Christian.

Yes, Methodists and Eastern Orthodox and whoever else have some very real points of tension, but the central affirmations of their respective traditions are rooted in the same basic truths. The vast majority of Christian groups have agreed upon the vast majority of Christian doctrine from the time of the apostles to the present. Certainly, there were ancient heretical groups where the word of an ersatz prophet trumped the Word of God, and contemporary revisionists for whom God still speaks in the inner voice of the community. Yet, Christian believers in the ancient world and those of our own day can all recite the same statements of faith.

We all confess that the Supreme Being of the universe spoke through the prophets and Apostles. We declare that Jesus has come in the flesh, and that, even now, the Holy Spirit abides in us, sustaining us, and holding us safe until Christ returns. We all can say together the words of the Apostle's, Nicene, and Chalcedonian Creeds. This is not to suggest that the disputes are immaterial. Some of the distinctions between traditions have far-reaching consequences. A thousand years ago, the Eastern and Western branches of Christendom split in two, seemingly on account of a single Latin word – *filioque* – added to one of the core creeds.

Yet, the Church not without hope, and that hope is highlighted by an old friend, not only of Tolkien but of us all. In his famous book, *Mere Christianity*, C.S. Lewis hits on something quite profound. He compares his work describing the core ideas of the faith as akin to the hallway in a house. He recognized the importance of the various traditions and their respective understandings and disputes, declaring that they are the rooms where life happens.

> When you have reached your own room, be kind to those who have chosen different doors and to those who are still in the hall. If they are wrong they need your prayers all the more; and if they are your enemies, then you are

> under orders to pray for them. That is one of the rules common to the whole house (Lewis 2000: 8).

The core truths of Christianity are simple enough to be grasped by a child and yet expansive enough to embrace ecclesial 'rooms' all around the world. If all we can grasp at a given time is the 'hallway' of creeds common to all Christians, then we may take heart that we are in a good place, even as we test and approve the doors to the rooms where particular traditions reside. What Lewis described so well with his hallway and rooms, his own ecumenical compatriot did in even greater detail in his portrayal of the cross-cultural friendship of Legolas and Gimli. Like Legolas and Gimli, we too are united by our common goal, common foe, and common love for what is beautiful and true. Their unity was not rooted in uniformity, nor were their compromises a matter of wholly subsuming their distinctives for the common good. Instead, it was a question recognizing in one another not an exact echo of their own thoughts but a common reflection of a higher good. This higher good does not eliminate our differences or solve our disputes, but it does offer solid ground upon which we may have a greater perspective for deeper connections.

About the Author

Timothy Padgett is the Resident Theologian at the Colson Center in Colorado. He is the author of *Swords and Plowshares*, a study of evangelical views on war, and the volume editor of *Dual Citizens*, a survey of political ideas in *Christianity Today*. His main areas of study are church and state, war and peace, and the ways the ideas of Christianity have played out across history. He lives in Colorado Springs with his wife and four children.

Bibliography

Carpenter, Humphrey. 2014. *J.R.R. Tolkien: A Biography.* Boston, MA: Mariner Books.

Casagrande, Cristina. 2022. *Friendship in The Lord of the Rings.* Translated by Eduardo Boheme. Edinburgh: Luna Press Publishing.

Duriez, Colin. 2003. *Tolkien and Lewis: The Gift of a Friendship.* Santa Monica, CA: Hidden Spring Press.

Freeman, Austin. 2022. *Tolkien Dogmatics: Theology Through Mythology with the Maker of Middle-earth.* Bellingham, WA: Lexham Press.

Henry, Carl F.H. Letter to the Editor of *Pasadena Star-News*, November 7, 1951, Carl F.H. Henry Papers, Box 1951 1, File Protestants and other Americans for the Separation of Church and State, Rolfing Library Archives, Trinity Evangelical Divinity School, Deerfield, IL.

Herzog, Jonathan P. 2011. *The Spiritual Industrial Complex: America's Religious Battle against Communism in the Early Cold War.* New York: Oxford University Press.

Hooker, Mark T. 2004. "Frodo's Batman." *Tolkien Studies* 1: 125-36.

Inboden, William. 2008. *Religion and American Foreign Policy, 1945-1960: The Soul of Containment.* New York: Cambridge University Press.

Lewis, C.S. 1960. *The Four Loves.* New York: HarperCollins.

2000. *Mere Christianity.* In *The Complete C.S. Lewis Signature Classics.* San Francisco, CA: HarperSanFrancisco.

Marsden, George. 2006. *Fundamentalism and American Culture.* New York: Oxford University Press.

Padgett, Timothy. 2018. *Swords and Plowshares: American Evangelical Views on War, 1937-1973.* Bellingham, WA: Lexham Press.

Schaeffer, Francis, A. Letter to President Harry S. Truman. November 19, 1951, Francis A. Schaeffer Collection, Box 57, File 23, The Library, Southeastern Baptist Theological Seminary, Wake Forest, North Carolina.

Thornbury, Gregory Alan. 2013. *Recovering Classic Evangelicalism.* Wheaton, IL: Crossway.

Trammel, Madison. 2023. *Fundamentalists in the Public Square: Evolution, Alcohol, and Culture Wars after the Scopes Trial.* Bellingham, WA: Lexham Press.

Walking Tree Publishers

Zurich and Jena

Walking Tree Publishers was founded in 1997 as a forum for publication of material related to Tolkien and Middle-earth studies.

www.walking-tree.org

Cormarë Series

The *Cormarë Series* collects papers and studies dedicated exclusively to the exploration of Tolkien's work. It comprises monographs, thematic collections of essays, conference volumes, and reprints of important yet no longer (easily) accessible papers by leading scholars in the field. Manuscripts and project proposals are evaluated by members of an independent board of advisors who support the series editors in their endeavour to provide the readers with qualitatively superior yet accessible studies on Tolkien and his work.

News from the Shire and Beyond. Studies on Tolkien
Peter Buchs & Thomas Honegger (eds.), Zurich and Berne 2004, Reprint, First edition 1997 (Cormarë Series 1), ISBN 978-3-9521424-5-5

Root and Branch. Approaches Towards Understanding Tolkien
Thomas Honegger (ed.), Zurich and Berne 2005, Reprint, First edition 1999 (Cormarë Series 2), ISBN 978-3-905703-01-6

Richard Sturch, *Four Christian Fantasists. A Study of the Fantastic Writings of George MacDonald, Charles Williams, C.S. Lewis and J.R.R. Tolkien*
Zurich and Berne 2007, Reprint, First edition 2001 (Cormarë Series 3), ISBN 978-3-905703-04-7

Tolkien in Translation
Thomas Honegger (ed.), Zurich and Jena 2011, Reprint, First edition 2003 (Cormarë Series 4), ISBN 978-3-905703-15-3

Mark T. Hooker, *Tolkien Through Russian Eyes*
Zurich and Berne 2003 (Cormarë Series 5), ISBN 978-3-9521424-7-9

Translating Tolkien: Text and Film
Thomas Honegger (ed.), Zurich and Jena 2011, Reprint, First edition 2004 (Cormarë Series 6), ISBN 978-3-905703-16-0

Christopher Garbowski, *Recovery and Transcendence for the Contemporary Mythmaker. The Spiritual Dimension in the Works of J.R.R. Tolkien*
Zurich and Berne 2004, Reprint, First Edition by Marie Curie Sklodowska, University Press, Lublin 2000, (Cormarë Series 7), ISBN 978-3-9521424-8-6

Reconsidering Tolkien
Thomas Honegger (ed.), Zurich and Berne 2005 (Cormarë Series 8), ISBN 978-3-905703-00-9

Tolkien and Modernity 1
Frank Weinreich & Thomas Honegger (eds.), Zurich and Berne 2006 (Cormarë Series 9), ISBN 978-3-905703-02-3

Tolkien and Modernity 2
Thomas Honegger & Frank Weinreich (eds.), Zurich and Berne 2006 (Cormarë Series 10), ISBN 978-3-905703-03-0

Tom Shippey, *Roots and Branches. Selected Papers on Tolkien by Tom Shippey*
Zurich and Berne 2007 (Cormarë Series 11), ISBN 978-3-905703-05-4

Ross Smith, *Inside Language. Linguistic and Aesthetic Theory in Tolkien*
Zurich and Jena 2011, Reprint, First edition 2007 (Cormarë Series 12), ISBN 978-3-905703-20-7

How We Became Middle-earth. A Collection of Essays on The Lord of the Rings
Adam Lam & Nataliya Oryshchuk (eds.), Zurich and Berne 2007 (Cormarë Series 13), ISBN 978-3-905703-07-8

Myth and Magic. Art According to the Inklings
Eduardo Segura & Thomas Honegger (eds.), Zurich and Berne 2007 (Cormarë Series 14), ISBN 978-3-905703-08-5

The Silmarillion – Thirty Years On
Allan Turner (ed.), Zurich and Berne 2007 (Cormarë Series 15), ISBN 978-3-905703-10-8

Martin Simonson, *The Lord of the Rings and the Western Narrative Tradition*
Zurich and Jena 2008 (Cormarë Series 16), ISBN 978-3-905703-09-2

Tolkien's Shorter Works. Proceedings of the 4th Seminar of the Deutsche Tolkien Gesellschaft & Walking Tree Publishers Decennial Conference
Margaret Hiley & Frank Weinreich (eds.), Zurich and Jena 2008 (Cormarë Series 17), ISBN 978-3-905703-11-5

Tolkien's The Lord of the Rings: Sources of Inspiration
Stratford Caldecott & Thomas Honegger (eds.), Zurich and Jena 2008 (Cormarë Series 18), ISBN 978-3-905703-12-2

J.S. Ryan, *Tolkien's View: Windows into his World*
Zurich and Jena 2009 (Cormarë Series 19), ISBN 978-3-905703-13-9

Music in Middle-earth
Heidi Steimel & Friedhelm Schneidewind (eds.), Zurich and Jena 2010 (Cormarë Series 20), ISBN 978-3-905703-14-6

Liam Campbell, *The Ecological Augury in the Works of JRR Tolkien*
Zurich and Jena 2011 (Cormarë Series 21), ISBN 978-3-905703-18-4

Margaret Hiley, *The Loss and the Silence. Aspects of Modernism in the Works of C.S. Lewis, J.R.R. Tolkien and Charles Williams*
Zurich and Jena 2011 (Cormarë Series 22), ISBN 978-3-905703-19-1

Rainer Nagel, *Hobbit Place-names. A Linguistic Excursion through the Shire*
Zurich and Jena 2012 (Cormarë Series 23), ISBN 978-3-905703-22-1

Christopher MacLachlan, *Tolkien and Wagner: The Ring and Der Ring*
Zurich and Jena 2012 (Cormarë Series 24), ISBN 978-3-905703-21-4

Renée Vink, *Wagner and Tolkien: Mythmakers*
Zurich and Jena 2012 (Cormarë Series 25), ISBN 978-3-905703-25-2

The Broken Scythe. Death and Immortality in the Works of J.R.R. Tolkien
Roberto Arduini & Claudio Antonio Testi (eds.), Zurich and Jena 2012 (Cormarë Series 26), ISBN 978-3-905703-26-9

Sub-creating Middle-earth: Constructions of Authorship and the Works of J.R.R. Tolkien
Judith Klinger (ed.), Zurich and Jena 2012 (Cormarë Series 27), ISBN 978-3-905703-27-6

Tolkien's Poetry
Julian Eilmann & Allan Turner (eds.), Zurich and Jena 2013 (Cormarë Series 28), ISBN 978-3-905703-28-3

O, What a Tangled Web. Tolkien and Medieval Literature. A View from Poland
Barbara Kowalik (ed.), Zurich and Jena 2013 (Cormarë Series 29), ISBN 978-3-905703-29-0

J.S. Ryan, *In the Nameless Wood*
Zurich and Jena 2013 (Cormarë Series 30), ISBN 978-3-905703-30-6

From Peterborough to Faëry; The Poetics and Mechanics of Secondary Worlds
Thomas Honegger & Dirk Vanderbeke (eds.), Zurich and Jena 2014 (Cormarë Series 31), ISBN 978-3-905703-31-3

Tolkien and Philosophy
Roberto Arduini & Claudio R. Testi (eds.), Zurich and Jena 2014 (Cormarë Series 32), ISBN 978-3-905703-32-0

Patrick Curry, *Deep Roots in a Time of Frost. Essays on Tolkien*
Zurich and Jena 2014 (Cormarë Series 33), ISBN 978-3-905703-33-7

Representations of Nature in Middle-earth
Martin Simonson (ed.), Zurich and Jena 2015, (Cormarë Series 34), ISBN 978-3-905703-34-4

Laughter in Middle-earth
Thomas Honegger & Maureen F. Mann (eds.), Zurich and Jena 2016 (Cormarë Series 35), ISBN 978-3-905703-35-1

Julian Eilmann, *J.R.R. Tolkien – Romanticist and Poet*
Zurich and Jena 2017 (Cormarë Series 36), ISBN 978-3-905703-36-8

Binding Them All. Interdisciplinary Perspectives on J.R.R. Tolkien and His Works
Monika Kirner-Ludwig, Stephan Köser, Sebastian Streitberger (eds.), Zurich and Jena 2017 (Cormarë Series 37), ISBN 978-3-905703-37-5

Claudio Testi, *Pagan Saints in Middle-earth*
Zurich and Jena 2017 (Cormarë Series 38), ISBN 978-3-905703-38-2

Music in Tolkien's Work and Beyond
Julian Eilmann & Friedhelm Schneidewind (eds.), Zurich and Jena 2019 (Cormarë Series 39), ISBN 978-3-905703-39-9

Sub-creating Arda: World-building in J.R.R. Tolkien's Works, its Precursors, and Legacies
Dimitra Fimi & Thomas Honegger (eds.), Zurich and Jena 2019 (Cormarë Series 40), ISBN 978-3-905703-40-5

"Something Has Gone Crack": New Perspectives on J.R.R. Tolkien and the Great War
Janet Brennan Croft and Annika Röttinger (eds.), Zurich and Jena 2019 (Cormarë Series 41), ISBN 978-3-905703-41-2

Tolkien and the Classics
Roberto Arduini, Giampaolo Canzonieri & Claudio A. Testi (eds.), Zurich and Jena 2019 (Cormarë Series 42), ISBN 978-3-905703-42-9

José María Miranda Boto, *Law, Government, and Society in J.R.R. Tolkien's Works*
Zurich and Jena 2022 (Cormarë Series 43), ISBN 978-3-905703-43-6

Middle-earth, or There and Back Again
Łukasz Neubauer (ed.), Zurich and Jena 2020 (Cormarë Series 44), ISBN 978-3-905703-44-3

Tolkien and the Classical World
Hamish Williams (ed.), Zurich and Jena 2021 (Cormarë Series 45), ISBN 978-3-905703-45-0

Nancy Bunting and Seamus Hamill-Keays, *The Gallant Edith Bratt. J.R.R. Tolkien's Inspiration*. Zurich and Jena 2021 (Cormarë Series 46), ISBN 978-3-905703-46-7

Nólë Hyarmenillo: An Anthology of Iberian Scholarship on Tolkien
Nuno Simões Rodrigues, Martin Simonson, and Angélica Varandas (eds.), Zurich and Jena 2022 (Cormarë Series 47), ISBN 978-3-905703-47-4

The Songs of the Spheres: Lewis, Tolkien and the Overlapping Realms of their Imaginations
Łukasz Neubauer and Guglielmo Spirito (eds.), Zurich and Jena 2024 (Cormarë Series 48), ISBN 978-3-905703-48-1

Richard Z. Gallant, *Germanic Heroes, Courage, and Fate: Northern Narratives of J.R.R. Tolkien's Legendarium*. Zurich and Jena 2024 (Cormarë Series 49), ISBN 978-3-905703-49-8

Thomas Honegger, *Tweaking Things a Little. Essays on the Epic Fantasy of J.R.R. Tolkien and G.R.R. Martin.* Zurich and Jena 2023 (Cormarë Series 50), ISBN 978-3-905703-50-4

The Romantic Spirit in the Works of J.R.R. Tolkien
Will Sherwood and Julian Eilmann (eds.), Zurich and Jena 2024 (Cormarë Series 51), ISBN 978-3-905703-51-1

Nancy Bunting, Seamus Hamill-Keays, and Toby Widdicombe,
Celebrating Tolkien's Legacy. Essays by Nancy Bunting, Seamus Hamill-Keays, and Toby Widdicombe. Zurich and Jena 2024 (Cormarë Series 52),
ISBN 978-3-905703-52-8

Tolkien among the Theologians
Austin M. Freeman (ed.), Zurich and Jena 2025 (Cormarë Series 53),
ISBN 978-3-905703-53-5

Verlyn Flieger, *A Real Taste for Fairy Stories. Essays.* Zurich and Jena 2025 (Cormarë Series 54), forthcoming

Arda Notebooks. The Best of "I Quaderni di Arda"
Roberto Arduini, Claudio A. Testi, and Wu Ming 4 (eds.), Zurich and Jena 2025 (Cormarë Series 55), forthcoming

Beowulf and the Dragon

The original Old English text of the 'Dragon Episode' of Beowulf is set in an authentic font and bound in hardback as a high quality art book. Illustrated by Anke Eissmann and accompanied by John Porter's translation. Introduction by Tom Shippey. Limited first edition of 500 copies. 84 pages. Selected pages can be previewed on: www.walking-tree.org/beowulf

Beowulf and the Dragon, Zurich and Jena 2009 , ISBN 978-3-905703-17-7

Tales of Yore Series

The *Tales of Yore Series* provides a platform for qualitatively superior fiction that will appeal to readers familiar with Tolkien's world:

The Monster Specialist

Sir Severus le Brewse, among the least known of King Arthur's Round Table knights, is preferred by nature, disposition, and training to fight against monsters rather than other knights. After youthful adventures of errantry with dragons, trolls, vampires, and assorted beasts, Severus joins the brilliant sorceress Lilava to face the Chimaera in The Greatest Monster Battle of All Time to free her folk from an age-old curse. But their adventures don't end there; together they meet elves and magicians, friends and foes; they join in the fight to save Camelot and even walk the Grey Paths of the Dead. With a mix of Malory, a touch of Tolkien, and a hint of humor, The Monster Specialist chronicles a tale of courage, tenacity, honor, and love.

The Monster Specialist is illustrated by Anke Eissmann.

Edward S. Louis, *The Monster Specialist*
Zurich and Jena 2014 (Tales of Yore Series No. 3), ISBN 978-3-905703-23-8

Tales of Yore Series (earlier books, presently unavailable)

Kay Woollard, *The Terror of Tatty Walk. A Frightener*
CD and Booklet, Zurich and Berne 2000 (Tales of Yore Series No. 1), ISBN 978-3-9521424-2-4

Kay Woollard, *Wilmot's Very Strange Stone or What came of building "snobbits"*
CD and booklet, Zurich and Berne 2001 (Tales of Yore Series No. 2), ISBN 978-3-9521424-4-8

Information for authors

Authors interested in contributing to our publications can learn more about the services we offer on the "services for authors" section of our web pages.

www.walking-tree.org/authors

Manuscripts and project proposals can be submitted to the board of editors:

Walking Tree Publishers
e-mail: info@walking-tree.org

www.ingramcontent.com/pod-product-compliance
Ingram Content Group UK Ltd.
Pitfield, Milton Keynes, MK11 3LW, UK
UKHW021828190726
13853UKWH00003B/1250

9 783905 703535